# Vocabulary Workout for the SSAT/ISEE

## Complete Edition

Editorial:
Justin Grosslight, head author and editor.

First Edition, 2017

ISBN: 978-0-9984841-5-0

10 9 8 7 6 5 4 3 2 1

# Vocabulary Workout for the SSAT/ISEE

## Complete Edition

**Justin Grosslight**

**Published by Manda Education, LLC**

# Preface

Becoming an expert in any language is hard work. Regardless of whether English is your mother tongue, more advanced reading and vocabulary skills often accrue slowly and only with a sustained commitment to reading intricate material. Because of this, transitioning from communicating in popular English to becoming a consumer of scholarly and intellectual prose can be arduous work. While there is no supplement for reading erudite materials, building a vocabulary and an understanding of intellectual concepts is critical for language mastery.

In writing this edition of *Vocabulary Workout*, I had in mind the myriad individuals who are fluent in conversational English but who want to take their writing and vocabulary skills to the next level, especially those prepping for their SSAT and ISEE exams. Many of today's students and professionals seek to develop these skills, but find the task extraneous to their immediate needs, overly pedantic, or simply time consuming. *Vocabulary Workout* is meant to ease that process. Unlike other vocabulary books, many of which are merely extended lists, this book is replete with exercises; there are also lessons to help you understand roots of words and intellectual terms. And the words are useful: they have been gleaned from statistical examination of SSAT and ISEE college exams, which, in turn, excerpt their readings from a wide array of sophisticated prose materials.

These words are suitable for either classroom study or independent preparation. Do note, however, that the words in this book do not constitute an exhaustive vocabulary list necessary for success. This book is the first of two volumes used to help students prepare for their SSAT and ISEE exams. One can also purchase a complete edition of *Vocabulary Workout* that combines the contents of both volumes in one text.

Writing this book has been an evolving process, and I have enjoyed receiving feedback as it develops. In particular, I would like to thank Robert Fouldes, Nicoleta Marinescu, Tracy Nguyen, and Sonya Petkova for their contributions, sustained support, proofreading, and constructive criticism. Several students – Jack Le, Tram Huynh, Thanh Doan, Quoc Huynh, Tan Khoa, Trong Phan – have gladly provided input, corrected errors, and given frank suggestions as they used drafts of this book to prepare for their SSAT examinations.

I hope that this book will be as immensely useful to you as it has been for the students who have used it in its gestation period. With that said, good luck on your vocabulary endeavors!

Justin Grosslight

# How to Use This Book

This book is intended to help build your vocabulary; it is a strategically organized catalogue of words that appear in intellectual and scholarly English, especially on secondary school entrance examinations. It is not, however, intended to be your sole source of learning words. Ideally, this book should be used in tandem with reading other scholarly and intellectual materials to help nurture your vocabulary growth.

Often to fully understand a word and its meaning(s), it is helpful to see a word in context many times. To reinforce this idea, the exercises contained in this book often require dictionary use. By looking up words in a dictionary, you can read samples of their uses in various settings and then apply what you have learned to the exercises in this text. Doing so will provide an active approach to building a vocabulary. This book's exercises also use a consistent intellectual vocabulary to complement the focal words of each lesson. Learning these words should further enhance your verbal skills.

At a stable pace, one should be able to absorb approximately fifty words, or ten lessons, per week. We have provided review quizzes after every ten lessons to help facilitate your study. One can study more words, of course, but diminishing returns may occur if more than twenty lessons are absorbed each week. Ideally this book should be studied at a moderate pace consistently over a long duration, allowing for time to let words sink in slowly. There are many more reasons why someone should use this book: whether you want to build a more solid vocabulary, you want to prepare for an examination, or you simply hope to sound erudite, all are good reasons for using this text. Whatever your purpose of study, however, it is imperative that you not give up on learning words.

Possessing a solid vocabulary can help you get in a good academic program, can make you more attractive for a corporate job, and can make you sound more articulate and knowledgeable. We hope you enjoy your endeavor to broaden your vocabulary with *Vocabulary Workout*!

# TABLE OF CONTENTS

# The Origins of English

English belongs to the family of Indo-European languages, which today comprise many languages spoken on the Earth. Most directly, the roots of English lay with Latin, the language of the Roman Empire that was spoken in the Mediterranean region two thousand years ago. From Latin emerged two families of European languages, Romance Languages and Germanic Languages. English is a Germanic language by structure and heritage, but also has borrowed much in style and vocabulary from French over the centuries (hence its proximity to French on the chart below). Many of the origins of English words stem from Latin, and still more come from Greek. The dashed line connecting Greek and Latin indicates that the languages had a cultural overlap, but that the former did not directly spawn the latter.

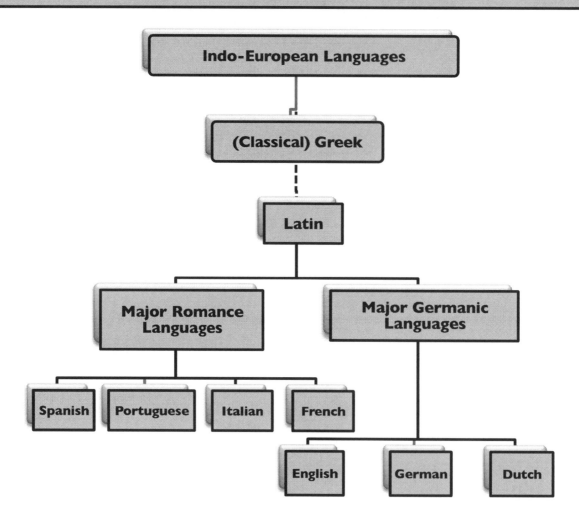

In future sections we will explore techniques on how to decipher words you do not know. Often the best way to do this is to have an understanding of the roots of a word. Nearly all of the roots for English words come from Greek and Latin. As English became more globalized from the early modern era to today, it spread beyond its original confines of England thus borrowing and assimilating words from other languages. According to the Global Language Monitor, the English language contains over one million words and that number is growing. Though many such words are outmoded, over 170,000 are in current use. Luckily, to sound intellectual or scholarly, you only need to know a subset of these words.

# Lesson I

## THE LOUSY BOSS

## NEW WORDS

**elusive**
iˈloosiv

**impress**
imˈpres

**occupy**
ˈäkyəˌpī

**mettle**
ˈmetl

**derelict**
ˈderəˌlikt

Most people thought Jordan was a terrible boss because he was so **elusive**. Not only was he **derelict** of his management duties at work, but he also would send memos filled with typos that failed to **impress** his employees. Because of these complications, workers at the company would **occupy** their time trying to figure out Jordan's whereabouts and the veracity of his credentials. For in the eyes of many, Jordan lacked the **mettle** to be a competent and effective superior.

**Definitions:**       Try matching the words in the list with the appropriate definitions. If you are stuck, check the glossary in the back of the book or the passage at the top of the page.

1. elusive _____ b _____ a. 1. to make one feel admiration and respect; 2. to make a mark upon an object by using a stamp or seal; 3. to fix an idea in someone's mind

2. impress _____ A _____ b. hard to find, catch, or achieve

3. occupy _____ C _____ c. 1. to reside or have one's business in; to be situated in; to fill or take up; to hold (a job); 2. (military) to enter, take control of, and remain in a place

4. mettle _____ d _____ d. one's ability to manage a difficult situation in an enthusiastic and spirited way

5. derelict _____ e _____ e. (adj.) in poor condition due to neglect and/or disuse; (n.) 1. a person lacking a job, home, or property; 2. a person negligent in doing his or her duty

**Sentences:**       Try to use the words above in a sentence below. Remember that a word ending may be changed or its figure of speech slightly altered.

6. I would like to move in and _____ occupy _____ the home on the beach.

7. It is very hard to _____ impress _____ a brilliant professor: one's work needs to be truly amazing to stand out.

8. Jeremy was a(n) _____ elusive _____ person: it was difficult for people to locate him or for them to know his business plans and intentions.

9. The new boss fired all the _____ derelict _____ in the company to keep costs down and increase efficiency.

10. Yogya's _____ mettle _____ was tested when he had to prepare and pass his final exams as his poor father was dying.

3

# Lesson 2

## THE WOES OF A BUSINESSMAN

Despite his notable **generosity** to his family members, David would **urge** them to become more self-sufficient and not rely on his lucrative business for support. With his characteristic sharp and **pithy** remarks, David made it clear to them that they needed to stop complaining and to take financial action. David's sense of familial duty would often **compel** him to help his less entrepreneurial relatives; however, sometimes one could see the frustration in his eyes, even sadness and a certain **melancholy**: perhaps he just wished to be left alone.

---

### NEW WORDS

**urge**
ərj

**pithy**
ˈpiTHē

**generosity**
ˌjenəˈräsitē

**melancholy**
ˈmelənˌkälē

**compel**
kəmˈpel

---

**Definitions:** Try matching the words in the list with the appropriate definitions. If you are stuck, check the glossary in the back of the book or the passage at the top of the page.

1. urge _____ a _____
2. pithy _____ e _____
3. generosity _____ d _____
4. melancholy _____ c _____
5. compel _____ b _____

a. (n.) a strong desire or impulse; (v.) to try to persuade; to recommend strongly; to encourage (an animal or person) to move rapidly or in a certain direction

b. to force or oblige someone or something; to bring about something by the use of pressure or force

c. (adj.) having or feeling sad and pensive; (n.) a feeling of sadness, typically with no apparent cause

d. the quality of being kind, giving, and helpful

e. brief and forceful in expression

**Sentences:** Try to use the words above in a sentence below. Remember that a word ending may be changed or its figure of speech slightly altered.

6. Janet had a(n) _____melancholy_____ feeling for a few weeks after her boyfriend of four years terminated the relationship.

7. Often it is hard to _____compel_____ a lazy person to work hard and to achieve results.

8. Barbara _____urge_____ her little cousin to study Spanish because she knew it would be an important global language in the future.

9. In business, it is best to respond to emails in a(n) _____pithy_____ manner rather than a longwinded one.

10. Seth thanked all of his constituents for their _____generosity_____ in supporting him in his bid to run for city mayor.

## NEW WORDS

**commodious**
kə'mōdēəs

**obdurate**
'äbd(y)ərit

**paragon**
'parə,gän, -gən

**languid**
'laNGgwid

**flinch**
flinCH

## THE MAGNIFICENT MANSION

Many people believe that the mansion for sale on the hill is the **paragon** of elite living. Its rooms are **commodious**, providing plenty of room to sprawl out after a hard day's work. Its couches are large and soft – perfect for a **languid** person to doze throughout a relaxing afternoon. But when a rich stranger arrived from abroad and offered to buy the estate, its owner was **obdurate** and refused to negotiate. Rumors have it that the current owner did not even **flinch** when an offer was made for ten times the asking price.

**Definitions:** Try matching the words in the list with the appropriate definitions. If you are stuck, check the glossary in the back of the book or the passage at the top of the page.

1. commodious ___A___    a. roomy and comfortable

2. obdurate ___e___    b. 1. concerning a person, manner, or gesture showing a lack of exertion or effort; lacking energy; 2. a time period that's peaceful or pleasantly lazy

3. paragon ___e___    c. very stubbornly refusing to change one's opinion or course of action

4. languid ___b___    d. (n.) a fast, nervous movement of the body as an instinctive response to pain, surprise, or fear; (v.) to make a fast, nervous movement of the body as an instinctive response to pain, surprise, or fear

5. flinch ___d___    e. a person or thing regarded as the perfect example of something

**Sentences:** Try to use the words above in a sentence below. Remember that a word ending may be changed or its figure of speech slightly altered.

6. Nathan's little sister scolded him for being so ___languid___: he refused to get off the couch and cook her lunch all afternoon.

7. If someone waves his or her hand very near my eyes, I am likely to ___flinch___.

8. Many people see Americans as a ___paragon___ of democracy and open-mindedness; nevertheless, America is still rife with problems.

9. The rooms in this house are so ___commodious___ that I feel I could stretch out almost anywhere.

10. Shareen was ___obdurate___ and refused to compromise with her fiancé in choosing an appropriate wedding venue.

# Lesson 4

## FAMILY SECRETS

After the death of his parents, Patrick had to **assume** full responsibility for paying their **mortgage** and personal debts. Patrick's father had never been a financially successful man. During his last visit to the house, Patrick was surprised to come upon his father's diary, which was full of **elaborate** information about an overseas business venture. The discovery was enough to **whet** his curiosity and Patrick phoned his father's business partner. It turned out that Patrick's father had led a double life which neither Patrick nor his mother ever suspected. The old man was an **enigma** that Patrick was just beginning to uncover.

## NEW WORDS

**elaborate**
iˈlab(ə)rit (adj.); iˈlabəˌrāt (v.)

**mortgage**
ˈmôrgij

**assume**
əˈsoom

**whet**
(h)wet

**enigma**
iˈnigmə

**Definitions:**    Try matching the words in the list with the appropriate definitions. If you are stuck, check the glossary in the back of the book or the passage at the top of the page.

1. elaborate ___*e*___
2. mortgage ___*d*___
3. assume ___*a*___
4. whet ___*c*___
5. enigma ___*b*___

a. 1. to suppose to be the case without proof; 2. to take or begin to have power or responsibility; 3. to seize power or control over something; 4. to take on a characteristic or quality for a role

b. a mystery

c. 1. to acutely arouse someone's interest in something; 2. to sharpen the blade of an object (usually a knife)

d. (n.) the charging of property (usually a home) by a debtor to a creditor as security for a debt; (v.) to convey property to a creditor as security on a loan

e. (adj.) 1. having many carefully arranged or designed details; detailed in plan or design; 2. lengthy and exaggerated; (v.) to add more detail concerning something already said

**Sentences:**    Try to use the words above in a sentence below. Remember that a word ending may be changed or its figure of speech slightly altered.

6.    Unlike June's writing, which is very ___*elaborate*___, mine is concise and direct.

7.    It is easy to ___*assume*___ that Daysha hates pets since she has never owned one; in reality, however, she is allergic to animal fur.

8.    Exactly how or why the British colony in Roanoke disappeared in around 1587 remains a(n) ___*enigma*___ to most historians.

9.    An inspiring teacher can surely ___*whet*___ one's interest in learning.

10.   Most Americans take a(n) ___*mortgage*___ to help them finance their home(s).

6

## NEW WORDS

**immaculate**
iˈmakyəlit

**obvious**
ˈäbvēəs

**invincible**
inˈvinsəbəl

**typical**
ˈtipikəl

**lavish**
ˈlaviSH

### WEDDING PLANNING

It is **obvious** that weddings are important events in many peoples' lives. Because this is so, it is **typical** for an American bride and groom and their respective families to spend months planning the blessed event. Some families opt for very **lavish** weddings to be held at opulent estates or resort hotels, while others prefer a cozier, intimate event. But in either scenario, everyone hopes for an event that is **immaculate**. For at this time in a couple's lives, they often feel like they are **invincible** and that nothing in the world could tear them apart.

**Definitions:** Try matching the words in the list with the appropriate definitions. If you are stuck, check the glossary in the back of the book or the passage at the top of the page.

1. immaculate _____ a. characteristic of a particular person, thing, group, era, or genre

2. obvious _____ b. easily perceived or understood; easily apparent; self-evident; blatant

3. invincible _____ c. too powerful to be overcome or defeated

4. typical _____ d. 1. perfectly neat or clean; 2. free of mistakes

5. lavish _____ e. (adj.) extremely rich, luxurious, or elaborate; characterizing a person who is very generous or extravagant; given to profusion; (v.) to heap generous quantities upon

**Sentences:** Try to use the words above in a sentence below. Remember that a word ending may be changed or its figure of speech slightly altered.

6. Most parents _____ excessive praise upon their children because they are proud of their offspring.

7. Jamie is such an amazing basketball player that he seems _____: nobody can stand in his way or prevent him from scoring.

8. It is _____ to me that the reason Jason's grades have not improved is because he never completes his homework assignments.

9. It is _____ for a boy to ask a girl to dinner and a movie on a first date.

10. After a long day of cleaning, one could say that our kitchen and living room looked _____.

# Lesson 6

## AN UNEXPECTED ENCOUNTER

The noise in the crowd rose to a **clamor**. He put his hands over his ears and closed his eyes. He was so tired of the same old speeches. Every new face seemed to be making the same obvious and **trite** remarks. Suddenly he felt as though someone was watching him. As if **telepathic**, he opened his eyes and sharply moved his body, causing him to **reel** backwards. He almost hit the person behind him. To his **delight**, the mysterious girl he had noticed before was standing there, smiling at him with a knowing glance, as if sharing his emotions.

## NEW WORDS

**clamor**
ˈklamər

**reel**
rēl

**telepathic**
ˌteləˈpaTHik

**delight**
diˈlīt

**trite**
trīt

**Definitions:** Try matching the words in the list with the appropriate definitions. If you are stuck, check the glossary in the back of the book or the passage at the top of the page.

1.  clamor _____
2.  reel _____
3.  telepathic _____
4.  delight _____
5.  trite _____

a.  (n.) a cylinder upon which thread, film, wire, or other materials can be wound; (v.) to feel disoriented, bewildered, or off-kilter from a setback

b.  capable of transmitting thoughts to people without knowing their thoughts; psychic

c.  (n.) a loud and confused noise, perhaps protest; (v.) to shout loudly and insistently as a group, often to protest or demand

d.  concerning a remark, opinion, or idea that has lost its import and freshness due to overuse

e.  (n.) a great pleasure; (v.) to please (someone) greatly; to take great pleasure in something

**Sentences:** Try to use the words above in a sentence below. Remember that a word ending may be changed or its figure of speech slightly altered.

6.  Troy could not immediately understand what the _____ outside his apartment was about: why were people protesting and what for?

7.  Many clairvoyants claim to be _____ and to have direct communication with spirits or individuals of a higher power.

8.  Often people make _____ remarks because they seem conventional rather than because they have any real import.

9.  Ricardo was _____ when he received all "A"s on his report card.

10. Adriana was _____ after she heard that her cousin died in an automobile accident.

8

## NEW WORDS

**savor**
ˈsāvər

**premonition**
ˌprēmə'niSHən, ˌprem-

**token**
ˈtōkən

**lewd**
lood

**repose**
ri'pōz

## GETTING ONE'S COMEUPPANCE

The dirty old man had made a fortune on closing real estate deals and secretly cheating others in the process. Now, at the age of seventy, he thought he could **savor** his retirement. He called his **token** psychic to ask about his future, and she said she had a **premonition** that his life was about to fall apart. The following day, a woman filed a lawsuit against the man for making **lewd** comments about her at a videotaped gala earlier in the season. And one of the man's chief business rivals went to the media claiming that this old man led a life of **repose** rather than one of hard work. Suddenly the old man felt that enjoying his golden years was out of his grasp.

**Definitions:** Try matching the words in the list with the appropriate definitions. If you are stuck, check the glossary in the back of the book or the passage at the top of the page.

1. savor _____ c a. an object serving as a visible or tangible representation of a fact; a characteristic or distinctive sign or mark of something

2. premonition _____ e b. offensive and crude in a sexual way

3. token _____ a c. to taste, drink, or enjoy something thoroughly and completely

4. lewd _____ b d. (n.) a state of rest, sleep, or tranquility, composure; (v.) to be lying, sitting, or at rest in a particular place

5. repose _____ d e. a strong feeling that something (typically unpleasant) is about to happen

**Sentences:** Try to use the words above in a sentence below. Remember that a word ending may be changed or its figure of speech slightly altered.

6. Maureen purchased a snow globe with the Manhattan skyline as a(n) _____token_____ of her trip to New York.

7. Donald's _____lewd_____ comments about women made his girlfriend feel uncomfortable.

8. Tram likes to _____savor_____ her favorite meals, so she eats very slowly and relishes the flavor of the great food.

9. Most people need some time for _____repose_____ after a long day's work.

10. I had a _____premonition_____ that our business venture was going to fail when I noticed that my business partner quit coming to work every day.

# Lesson 8

## AN ANONYMOUS ACT OF KINDNESS

Jemma was a **precocious** child who could speak ten languages by the age of nine. Her language learning abilities were **unprecedented**. Naturally, Jemma wanted to enroll in college early; however, she was not able to afford it financially. But after Jemma showcased her abilities on a local television show, a **confidential** donor made a **pledge** of paying for half of for her higher education tuition. Jemma was deeply touched, and she knew she would always **cherish** the stranger's generous gesture.

---

### NEW WORDS

**cherish**
ˈCHeriSH

**confidential**
ˌkänfəˈdenCHəl

**pledge**
plej

**precocious**
priˈkōSHəs

**unprecedented**
ˌənˈpresəˌdentid

---

**Definitions:** Try matching the words in the list with the appropriate definitions. If you are stuck, check the glossary in the back of the book or the passage at the top of the page.

1. cherish _____ a. intended to be kept secret
2. confidential _____ b. never done or known before
3. pledge _____ c. (n.) 1. a solemn promise or understanding; 2. a promise of a donation to a charity; (v.) 1. to commit by solemn promise; 2. to formally declare or promise that something will be the case
4. precocious _____ d. to protect and care for something or someone lovingly; to hold dear
5. unprecedented _____ e. (of a child) having developed certain skills or abilities at an earlier age than usual; indicative of early development

**Sentences:** Try to use the words above in a sentence below. Remember that a word ending may be changed or its figure of speech slightly altered.

6. Vu ___pledged___ to be a responsible and faithful husband in his wedding vows.
7. The password to my safe box is _____ information not to be disclosed to strangers.
8. When Richard Nixon (1913-94) resigned as present on August 9, 1974, the event was _____: he became the first American leader to voluntarily depart office.
9. Alex is a (mathematically) _____ child: at the age of thirteen she is already learning twelfth grade math!
10. I _____ the time I spend with my cousins, as I rarely get to see them and my experiences with them are packed with meaning and memories.

10

## NEW WORDS

**conversation**
ˌkänvərˈsāSHən

**lax**
laks

**intriguing**
inˈtrēgiNG

**ruminate**
ˈrooməˌnāt

**calamity**
kəˈlamitē

# Lesson 9

## SPOILING CHILDREN

Often spoiling her son Jack with expensive gifts and seldom reprehending him for his mischief, Emily unknowingly turned Jack into a selfish and demanding bully. It was not until Jack seriously injured a friend when fighting over a toy that he found **intriguing** did Emily realize that he had gone too far. As she began to **ruminate** upon this **calamity**, and had a candid **conversation** with his teachers about Jack's misbehaviors, Emily realized that her **lax** parenting did more harm than good.

**Definitions:** Try matching the words in the list with the appropriate definitions. If you are stuck, check the glossary in the back of the book or the passage at the top of the page.

| | | | | | |
|---|---|---|---|---|---|
| 1. | conversation | b | a. | not strict, severe, or careful; loose; relaxed |
| 2. | lax | a | b. | an informal exchange of ideas by spoken words |
| 3. | intriguing | c | c. | arousing curiosity or interest; fascinating |
| 4. | ruminate | d | d. | to think deeply about something |
| 5. | calamity | e | e. | a disaster |

**Sentences:** Try to use the words above in a sentence below. Remember that a word ending may be changed or its figure of speech slightly altered.

6. Even though she is very famous today, I once had many _____Conversations_____ with Meghan and enjoyed our chats immensely.

7. These seemingly _____intriguing_____ yet trivial matters can build up to become a major threat one day.

8. I witnessed a _____calamity_____ when two golf carts collided head on outside my kitchen window.

9. Often teachers who are _____lax_____ cannot effectively compel their students to study when it is necessary.

10. Often a course of action is more effective than spending time _____ruminate_____ on a matter.

# Lesson 10

## REVIVING THE ECONOMY

The new mayor gazed upon the **expanse** of the vineyards in front of him, hoping to **renovate** the economy of this fertile but nearly inaccessible region. Knowing that this region had a rich **heritage** of wine production, he wanted to extend its interregional **commerce** to the rest of the country. However, transporting the wine on the bad rural roads was a **tedious** and sometimes dangerous process. The mayor resolved to repair some of the main roads in order to facilitate the transportation process.

<table>
<tr><td colspan="2">NEW WORDS</td></tr>
<tr><td>expanse<br>ikˈspans</td></tr>
<tr><td>tedious<br>ˈtēdēəs</td></tr>
<tr><td>heritage<br>ˈheritij</td></tr>
<tr><td>renovate<br>ˈrenəˌvāt</td></tr>
<tr><td>commerce<br>kəˈmens</td></tr>
</table>

**Definitions:** Try matching the words in the list with the appropriate definitions. If you are stuck, check the glossary in the back of the book or the passage at the top of the page.

| | | | | |
|---|---|---|---|---|
| 1. | expanse | _e_ | a. | 1. the act of buying and selling, trade; 2. social dealings between people |
| 2. | tedious | _d_ | b. | to restore something old into a good state |
| 3. | heritage | _c_ | c. | valued objects and qualities like cultural traditions, unsullied countryside, and historic buildings that have been passed down over generations current |
| 4. | renovate | _b_ | d. | extremely long, slow, or dull; tiresome; monotonous |
| 5. | commerce | _A_ | e. | an area of something that contains a wide and continuous surface; the distance to which something can stretch |

**Sentences:** Try to use the words above in a sentence below. Remember that a word ending may be changed or its figure of speech slightly altered.

6. Next week the restaurant will close to _____*renovate*_____ its kitchen and seating areas; when it reopens, I imagine it will be more modern and in vogue.

7. Allan found the task of writing an index for his book to be ___*tedious*___: associating words with page numbers for hours on end was extremely draining.

8. If a nation places a trade embargo on another, _____*commerce*_____ will cease to exist between the two countries.

9. It is part of American _____*heritage*_____ to eat turkey on Thanksgiving.

10. The Sahara Desert covers a wide _____*expansion*_____ of land in Northern Africa.

12

# Word Search

## Lessons 1-10

```
M N G T Y P I C A L B N Y M
E L E P M O C G T G O R N D
L E T A R U D B O I R L T M
A P R E M O N I T I O N C Z
N E E D G Z D A A S G I M G
C G L H R N S I S S H T H Y
H A B G S R I E U T S E R E
O G I P E I R U A G R U C R
L T C V L P R P G I N R M Y
Y R N R M E E E T I E A P E
L O I I O L D A H M R U L R
C M V J E V G G M C C T E L
Z R N T K E A O E C Q E N N
R T I M K G C S O Z L B R I
```

1 (v.) 1. to make one feel admiration and respect; 2. to make a mark upon an object by using a stamp or seal; 3. to fix an idea in someone's mind
2 (v.) 1. to reside or have one's business in; to be situated in; to fill or take up; to hold (a job); 2. (military) to enter, take control of, and remain in a place
3 (adj.) having or feeling sad and pensive; (n.) a feeling of sadness, typically with no apparent cause
4 (v.) to force or oblige someone or something; to bring about something by the use of pressure or force
5 (adj.) stubbornly refusing to change one's opinion or course of action
6 (adj.) 1. concerning a person, manner, or gesture showing a lack of exertion
7 (n.) the charging of property (usually a home) by a debtor to a creditor as security for a debt; (v.) to convey property to a creditor as security on a loan
8 (v.) 1. to suppose to be the case without proof; 2. to take or begin to have power or responsibility; 3. to seize power or control over something; 4. to take on a characteristic or quality for a role
9 (adj.) too powerful to be overcome or defeated

10 (adj.) characteristic of a particular person, thing, group, era, or genre
11 (n.) a cylinder upon which thread, film, wire, or other materials can be wound; (v.) to feel disoriented, bewildered, or off-kilter from a setback
12 (adj.) capable of transmitting thoughts to people without knowing their thoughts; psychic
13 (v.) to taste, drink, or enjoy something thoroughly and completely
14 (n.) a strong feeling that something (typically unpleasant) is about to happen
15 (v.) to protect and care for something or someone lovingly; to hold dear
16 (n.) 1. a solemn promise or understanding; 2. a promise of a donation to a charity; (v.) 1. to commit by solemn promise; 2. to formally declare or promise that something will be the case
17 (n.) an informal exchange of ideas by spoken words
18 (adj.) arousing curiosity or interest; fascinating
19 (n.) valued objects and qualities like cultural traditions, unsullied countryside, and historic buildings that have been passed down over generations
20 (v.) 1. the act of buying and selling, trade; 2. social dealings between people

# Vocabulary Review
## Lessons 1-10

**Directions:** Match each word with its best approximate definition. Note that definitions are not necessarily repeated verbatim from the lesson exercises.

| | | | | |
|---|---|---|---|---|
| 1. | elusive | _____ | a. | never done or known before |
| 2. | mettle | _____ | b. | concise and forcefully expressive |
| 3. | pithy | _____ | c. | to restore (usually a building) to be in a good state or tasteful |
| 4. | generosity | _____ | d. | spotless; flawless |
| 5. | commodious | _____ | e. | a state of rest, sleep, or tranquility |
| 6. | paragon | _____ | f. | a mystery |
| 7. | whet | _____ | g. | a person or thing regarded as the perfect example of something |
| 8. | enigma | _____ | h. | easily perceived or understood; clear; blatant |
| 9. | immaculate | _____ | i. | to think deeply about something |
| 10. | obvious | _____ | j. | intended to be kept either private or secret |
| 11. | delight | _____ | k. | to please someone greatly |
| 12. | trite | _____ | l. | concerning a remark, opinion, or Idea that is overused and thus of ~~very little import~~ |
| 13. | lewd | _____ | m. | not sufficiently strict, severe, or careful |
| 14. | repose | _____ | n. | to excite or stimulate; to sharpen |
| 15. | confidential | _____ | o. | the quality of being kind and willing to give |
| 16. | unprecedented | _____ | p. | crude and offensive in a sexual way |
| 17. | lax | _____ | q. | hard to catch or grasp |
| 18. | ruminate | _____ | r. | a person's ability to cope well with difficulties |
| 19. | tedious | _____ | s. | too long, dull, or slow; monotonous |
| 20. | renovate | _____ | t. | roomy and spacious |

# Introduction to Word Roots

As we have seen, many of the origins of English come from (Classical) Greek and Latin.  Though these languages are defunct today, English contains a number of words with roots whose derivatives stem from these languages.

Consider, for example the (Classical) Greek word φόβος, or phobos. Translated into English as "phobia" or "phobe," this word means "fear." While (Classical) Greek is no longer an active language, the root "phobia" persists in English language to describe an extreme irrational fear of something.  Consider the following examples:

| | |
|---|---|
| **agoraphobia (n.):** | extreme irrational fear of large crowded places |
| **arachnophobia (n.):** | extreme irrational fear of spiders |
| **technophobe (n.):** | a person who is afraid of or who dislikes technology |
| **xenophobia (n.):** | extreme irrational fear of people from other countries |

Just as was so with (Classical) Greek, English has words whose root derive from Latin.  Consider, for example, the Latin word *placere*, meaning to please.  Certain English words containing "plac" are related to the concept of pleasing someone or something:

| | |
|---|---|
| **placate (v.):** | to make less angry or hostile |
| **implacable (adj.):** | unable to be pleased or appeased (note that the root "im" means "not" and is taught in our first word root lesson) |

Roots, therefore, can help us decipher potential meanings of words without knowing exactly what a word means.  Note, however, that not every word has roots, nor does a word that contains letters that look like a root imply that the word is related to its root meaning.  The word "placard" refers to a poster or sign used in public display, which has nothing to do with pleasing anyone.  In this book, we provide you with a number of units to help you identify and practice identifying word roots.

# Word Roots: Unit I

## ROOTS AND THEIR MEANINGS

| | | | |
|---|---|---|---|
| In/il/im/ir: | not | chron: | time |
| ex/ej: | out | a: | without |
| re: | again | morph: | shape |

**Here are a few examples of some words that use the above roots:**

intolerable:     not tolerable
illegal:     not legal
improper:     not proper
incapable:     not capable
irrational:     not rational
exit:     (place) to go out
eject:     to force or throw out
chronology:     telling a story where events are arranged in order of their occurrence
amorphous:     having no definite shape

**Now try to fill in the table below by finding the appropriate root(s) and interpreting the meaning of each word:**

| Word | Root(s) | Guessed Meaning | Actual Meaning |
|---|---|---|---|
| inaccurate | | | |
| incapable | | | |
| illegitimate | | | |
| impolite | | | |
| inactive | | | |
| excrete | | | |
| chronicle | | | |
| morphology | | | |
| asexual | | | |
| atypical | | | |
| anachronism | | | |

16

| | | | |
|---|---|---|---|
| irreverent | | | |
| apolitical | | | |
| inexplicable | | | |

**Remember that not every group of letters forming a root implies that there is a root for a given word. Consider, for example, the word "apple." One may think that the "a" in apple means not, but the "a" is merely a letter. Also the word "real" has "re" in the beginning, but it has nothing to do with doing something again. Roots, therefore, are only tools to help *possibly* identify the meaning of a word if you are completely stuck.**

# Occupations and Careers I

As you learn more advanced English, you will be exposed to many papers that discuss what different scholars, intellectuals, or professionals do in their careers. Knowing what people in different careers do is helpful for understanding the gist of many pieces of writing. Furthermore, people in these careers are discussed frequently on school entrance examinations. The list of occupational roles below and in the next section is not exhaustive, but rather is an attempt to help define a number of specific and sophisticated occupations to which you may be exposed to or read about as an intellectual.

## SCIENTIFIC JOBS

anatomist:     one who practices anatomy, e.g. the body structures of humans and other living creatures, often through dissection to examine their innards

astronomer:    one who practices astronomy, e.g. celestial objects, space, and the physical universe as a whole

biologist:     one who practices biology, e.g. living organisms, their morphology, physiology, anatomy, behavior, and distribution

botanist:      one who practices botany, e.g. plants, their physiology, structure, genetics, ecology, distribution, classification, and economic importance

chemist:       one who practices chemistry, e.g. chemicals and their reactions

| | |
|---|---|
| **geneticist:** | one who practices genetics, e.g. heredity and the variation of inherited characteristics through genes |
| **geologist:** | one who practices geology, e.g. Earth's physical structure and composition, its history, and forces that affect it |
| **meteorologist:** | one who practices meteorology, e.g. the study of the atmosphere and the weather |
| **oceanographer:** | one who practices oceanography, e.g. the physical and biological processes of the seas |
| **paleontologist:** | one who practices paleontology, e.g. the fossil elements of animals and plants |
| **physicist:** | one who practices physics, e.g. the study of the nature and properties of matter and energy |
| **seismologist:** | one who practices seismology, e.g., the science of earthquakes and related incidents |
| **zoologist:** | one who practices zoology, e.g. the behavior, structure, distribution, and classification of animals |

## MEDICAL OR MEDICALLY RELATED JOBS

| | |
|---|---|
| **anesthesiologist:** | one who practices anesthesia, e.g. administering gases or drugs to make patients insensitive to pain before surgical operations |
| **coroner:** | an official who investigates deaths, especially violent or suspicious deaths |

| | |
|---|---|
| **hygienist:** | specialist who promotes sanitary conditions to maintain good health |
| **pharmacist:** | specialist who is professionally qualified to prepare and dispense drugs |
| **surgeon:** | one who practices surgery, e.g. the treatment of the body through incision and manipulation |
| **veterinarian:** | a doctor and surgeon for animals |

# NEW WORDS

**din**
din

**zany**
'zānē

**clairvoyant**
kle(ə)r'voiənt

**ethical**
'eTHikəl

**withstand**
wiTH'stand, wiTH-

## FROM CONSTRUCTION TO CORRUPT PROGNOSTICATION

Noah could no longer **withstand** going to work and operating a crane every day. He detested the monotony of the job and especially loathed the **din** made by bulldozers and cement trucks at the construction site. So he chose to quit his job in pursuit of a rather **zany** adventure: he wanted to be a seer. Not knowing how to commence with this task, he sought out a local **clairvoyant** and solicited her advice. In confidence, she urged him not to be **ethical** and to do everything he could to prey on his clients' weaknesses in order to take as much money as possible from them. Thus began Noah's corrupt career in prognostication.

**Definitions:** Try matching the words in the list with the appropriate definitions. If you are stuck, check the glossary in the back of the book or the passage at the top of the page.

1. din _____ *e*
2. zany _____ *c*
3. clairvoyant _____ *a*
4. ethical _____ *b*
5. withstand _____ *d*

a. (adj.) having the ability to see or predict events in the future beyond normal sense; (n.) a person who claims to have the supernatural ability to see events in the future beyond normal sense

b. of or relating to moral principles; morally correct

c. amusingly unconventional and idiosyncratic

d. to remain undisturbed or unaffected by something, to resist; to offer strong resistance or opposition to

e. a loud, unpleasant, and prolonged noise

**Sentences:** Try to use the words above in a sentence below. Remember that a word ending may be changed or its figure of speech slightly altered.

6. Simon is a strong person; he is able to _____*withstand*_____ intense criticism about his work habits and still can succeed in his career.

7. Elizabeth has the _____*zany*_____ notion of planting plastic flowers instead of real ones on her property because they would require less upkeep.

8. Most fortunetellers claim to possess _____*ethical*_____ powers.

9. It is not _____*ethical*_____ to cheat in an exam.

10. The machines paving the road outside my home created a protracted _____*din*_____, thus making it difficult to concentrate.

# Lesson 12

## MANAGEMENT TRANSITION FEARS

As vice president of the company, Rynna worried that the business may not **flourish** when the CEO resigns in December. After all, it was the CEO's dedication and charisma that gave the company a rich and effective **texture**. Rynna, along with other top executives, worried that the employees would begin to work at a **sedate** pace in the absence of the CEO, thus hindering productivity and profits. Executive discussions also transpired about whether to **poach** a top executive from a competitor company. Because the ultimate decision was not to steal an executive competitor, Rynna told herself that she must metaphorically **fasten** her seat belt and prepare for a very turbulent corporate ride during its transition state.

**NEW WORDS**

**sedate**
si'dāt

**texture**
'teksCHər

**fasten**
'fasən

**poach**
pōCH

**flourish**
'fləriSH

**Definitions:** Try matching the words in the list with the appropriate definitions. If you are stuck, check the glossary in the back of the book or the passage at the top of the page.

1. sedate _____ a.____ a. calm, dignified, and unhurried; quiet and dull

2. texture _____ b.____ b. the feel, quality, or appearance of a substance or surface; the quality created by a combination of elements in a musical or literary work

3. fasten _____ d.____ c. 1. to illegally hunt or catch; 2. to acquire in a secretive way

4. poach _____ c.____ d. to close or join securely; to fix in place; to fix one's attention on something

5. flourish _____ e.____ e. (n.) an elaborate literary or rhetorical expression; (v.) for a person or other living organism to grow in a healthy or vigorous way, usually as the result of a favorable environment

**Sentences:** Try to use the words above in a sentence below. Remember that a word ending may be changed or its figure of speech slightly altered.

6. It is important to __fasten__ your seatbelt when you drive a car.

7. Adding hot pepper sauce sauce to ice cream not only seems unpalatable, but it also changes the __texture__ of the food, making it taste grainy rather than smooth.

8. In order for a child to __flourish__, it is necessary to provide that child with a strong and stable environment.

9. Medicine was used to __sedate__ Long, who is typically energetic and hyper, before the surgery.

10. Often teams __poach__ athletes from competing teams in order to enhance their status and competitiveness.

## NEW WORDS

**judge**
jəj

**tome**
tōm

**procure**
prəˈkyoor, prō-

**invariable**
inˈve(ə)rēəbəl

**subsist**
səbˈsist

## THE MATH PROFESSOR

The math professor had never seen an argument like this before, so he told his doctoral student that he was unfit to **judge** whether the research was sound until he conducted further research. In doing so, the professor aimed to **procure** a **tome** of algebraic research that discussed theories similar to the one that his student had presented. But the book the professor sought was hard to acquire, and the professor had to **subsist** on his intellect alone until the text arrived. After doing further research, the professor concluded that his student's argument was valid and brilliant. From that point on, he had **invariable** support for the student who presented this work.

**Definitions:** Try matching the words in the list with the appropriate definitions. If you are stuck, check the glossary in the back of the book or the passage at the top of the page.

1. judge _____ *d*
2. tome _____ *d*
3. procure _____ *e*
4. invariable _____ *b*
5. subsist _____ *c*

a. (n.) an individual with the authority to decide cases in courts of law; an individual who decides the results of competition or infractions of rules; (v.) 1. to form an opinion or conclusion about; 2. to decide a case in court; 3. to decide the results of a competition

b. unchanging

c. to maintain or support oneself, generally at a minimal level

d. a book, particularly one that is large, heavy, and scholarly

e. to obtain something, usually with effort

**Sentences:** Try to use the words above in a sentence below. Remember that a word ending may be changed or its figure of speech slightly altered.

6. I am not a good _____ *judge* of whether this wine is of high quality because I rarely drink.

7. Stranded in the woods on a camping trip, the boys were forced to _____ *subs* on only water and crackers for three days.

8. Paula's dissertation was a _____: she wrote over five hundred pages about plant collecting in early modern Italy.

9. A good spouse will be _____ committed to his or her partner.

10. It is difficult for Americans to _____ durians because not many grocers wish to stock the smelly and exotic Southeast Asian fruit.

# Lesson 14

## THE MEDICAL INTERVIEW

While waiting in the **antechamber** to the interview room, Alex felt his courage **wane**. The traditional medical (Aesculapian) **symbol** on the wall of a staff and snakes suddenly scared him. Alex had always been sure that he wanted to become a medical doctor. His father was a famous physician who had invested an **abundant** amount of money and effort into Alex' education. Destiny seemed to be determined for Alex from a young age; all he had to do was **cooperate**. All of a sudden, for the first time in his life, Alex felt overwhelmed by an uncomfortable feeling of doubt.

**Definitions:**    Try matching the words in the list with the appropriate definitions. If you are stuck, check the glossary in the back of the book or the passage at the top of the page.

1.  symbol _____ *b*
2.  antechamber _____ *e*

3.  abundant _____ *a*
4.  cooperate _____ *d*

5.  wane _____ *c*

a.  existing or available in great quantities
b.  a thing that represents or stands for something else, especially a material object that stands for something else
c.  to decrease in vigor or power; to recede; to ebb
d.  to act jointly and work toward the same end; to assist someone (or an organization) and comply with his or her (its) requests
e.  a small room leading to a big one

**Sentences:**    Try to use the words above in a sentence below. Remember that a word ending may be changed or its figure of speech slightly altered.

6.  Uriah waited in the __antechamber__ for his host to lead him into the conference room.
7.  Bananas are generally _____ in tropical forests, as trees which grow them are numerous.
8.  I am waiting to swim until the tide ___wane___.
9.  Even though they are siblings, Sherry and Meryl have difficulty trying to ___cooperate___ on team projects.
10. A heart is a(n) ___symbol___ that is used to stand for love.

## THE TRIAL

## NEW WORDS

**tempt**
tem(p)t

**lament**
lə'ment

**rotund**
rō'tənd, 'rō͵tənd

**elocution**
͵elə'kyooSHən

**extrapolate**
ik'strapə͵lāt

A master of **elocution**, James vividly described the scene to the jury who seemed to be mesmerized by his charismatic voice and **rotund** physique. They seemed to be moved by his **lament** for the lack of love and attention that his late wife had expressed towards him. James knew he could **tempt** them to see him as the emotional victim of a dysfunctional, abusive relationship. From his heartfelt story and soft manner of speaking, it was very difficult to **extrapolate** any proof that he might have been an aggressor.

**Definitions:**     Try matching the words in the list with the appropriate definitions.  If you are stuck, check the glossary in the back of the book or the passage at the top of the page.

1.   tempt         _____      a.   the skill of articulate and expressive speech
2.   lament        _____      b.   to entice; to allure; to try to entice one to do
                                         something that he or she finds attractive but that he or
                                         she also knows is wrong
3.   rotund        _____      c.   to extend the application of a method or a conclusion
                                         to an unknown trend by assuming that existing trends
                                         will continue or that similar methods will be applicable
4.   elocution     _____      d.   plump; round or spherical
5.   extrapolate   _____      e.   (n.) 1. a passionate expression of grief or sorrow; 2. a
                                         song or poem expressing sorrow; 3. an expression of
                                         disappointment; (v.) to mourn a person's death

**Sentences:**     Try to use the words above in a sentence below.  Remember that a word ending may be changed or its figure of speech slightly altered.

6.      Howard looked positively _____ after putting on fifty pounds last year.
7.      A good speaker delivers a speech with excellent _____ and thus moves his or her audience.
8.      Sara _____ the fact that she chose not to finish college and worried that it was too late to return for her degree.
9.      Jake _____ me to visit his new restaurant by offering me a free meal.
10.     Physicists often must _____ upon their data to come up with sound hypotheses.

# Lesson 10

## THE RIGHT FIT

While never being on the skinny side, Jeffrey had always managed to maintain a good figure. In spite of his efforts, however, Jeffrey felt himself becoming quite **corpulent** at the end of the holiday season. His chest was **heaving** with increasingly more difficult breaths and his **sturdy** stomach was bulging out grotesquely. "It is **essential** that I **rescind** the contract I made with my weight loss agency," Jeffrey thought to himself. "Being under a contractual obligation to lose weight seems to have had the exact opposite effect for me," he concluded.

---

## NEW WORDS

**corpulent**
ˈkôrpyələnt

**rescind**
riˈsind

**essential**
iˈsenCHəl

**sturdy**
ˈstərdē

**heave**
hēv

---

**Definitions:**     Try matching the words in the list with the appropriate definitions. If you are stuck, check the glossary in the back of the book or the passage at the top of the page.

1.     corpulent  _____     a.     (n.) a push, haul, or throw requiring great effort; (v.) 1. to push, haul, or throw with great effort; 2. to produce a sigh

2.     rescind  _____     b.     strong and solidly built; showing resistance and determination

3.     essential  _____     c.     to revoke, cancel, or appeal (a law, order, or judgment)

4.     sturdy  _____     d.     absolutely necessary; extremely important

5.     heave  _____     e.     fat (describing a person)

**Sentences:**     Try to use the words above in a sentence below. Remember that a word ending may be changed or its figure of speech slightly altered.

6.     It is _____ to get eight hours of sleep each day if you want to function properly.

7.     Nancy tried to _____ Mark's marriage proposal after she discovered that Mark had been lying to her during their courtship.

8.     One final _____ should push the piano up the ramp and into our foyer.

9.     Unlike the wobbly old table, this one appears to be much more _____.

10.     Helga was so _____ that she needed two airplane seats instead of one to support her body.

# Lesson 17

## TO CAPTIVATE AN AUDIENCE

The journalist knew that the new debate show was just another **gimmick** to **generate** interest among ordinary citizens. Television producers claimed that they would **astound** the audience with a **captivating** show that supposedly presented new and unusual perspectives. However, the journalist could immediately see that the same old political views were hidden behind the new glossy cover. He was aware that the hype would wear off very quickly and that viewers would experience **eventual** disappointment with the new show.

**Definitions:**     Try matching the words in the list with the appropriate definitions. If you are stuck, check the glossary in the back of the book or the passage at the top of the page.

| | | | | | |
|---|---|---|---|---|---|
| 1. | generate | _____ | a. | to produce; to cause a particular situation or emotion to come about |
| 2. | astound | _____ | b. | occurring at the end or as a result of a sequence of events; ultimate; final |
| 3. | gimmick | _____ | c. | a device or trick aimed at attracting attention, publicity, or business |
| 4. | captivating | _____ | d. | to shock or greatly surprise |
| 5. | eventual | _____ | e. | capable of attracting and holding interest |

**Sentences:**     Try to use the words above in a sentence below. Remember that a word ending may be changed or its figure of speech slightly altered.

6.   The physics professor's lecture this morning was so _____ that I suddenly felt inspired to pursue a doctorate after I graduate.

7.   I was _____ when I heard that my cousin Trevor possessed a winning lottery ticket.

8.   Smoking and drinking led to Isidor's _____ and tragic demise.

9.   It can be hard to _____ innovative ideas because there are myriad people and conceptions already in existence.

10.  Many businesses use advertising _____ to try and procure clientele.

# Lesson 18

## THE SADISTIC HUSBAND

The wife repeatedly reminded her husband of his household responsibilities, but the old **sluggard** refused to move from the couch. In his view, his wife was supposed to be **submissive** to him and follow his orders – not the other way around. He could not **relinquish** his control over her or his love for spending endless hours in front of the television. In fact, her pleas would **entice** him to act in an even more **tyrannical** manner. He derived pleasure from deriding her and making her feel powerless.

---

### NEW WORDS

**sluggard**
ˈsləgərd

**submissive**
səbˈmisiv

**entice**
enˈtīs

**relinquish**
riˈliNGkwiSH

**tyrannical**
təˈranikəl

---

**Definitions:**  Try matching the words in the list with the appropriate definitions. If you are stuck, check the glossary in the back of the book or the passage at the top of the page.

| | | | | |
|---|---|---|---|---|
| 1. | sluggard | _____ | a. | to voluntarily give up |
| 2. | submissive | _____ | b. | a lazy person |
| 3. | entice | _____ | c. | to attract or tempt by offering pleasure or advantage |
| 4. | relinquish | _____ | d. | exercising power in an arbitrary or cruel way |
| 5. | tyrannical | _____ | e. | ready to conform to the commands or will of others |

**Sentences:**  Try to use the words above in a sentence below. Remember that a word ending may be changed or its figure of speech slightly altered.

6.  Ellie's uncharacteristic _____ behavior terrified her childhood friends, who remembered her as a cooperative and sensitive person.

7.  The dictator refused to _____ his power; only with a coup was he deposed and peace reinstated in our homeland.

8.  Parents often try to _____ their children to study in school by rewarding them with money or presents for obtaining good grades.

9.  Quinn is a(n) _____ when it comes to work: rarely is she on time and it takes much effort to get her off of her couch and engaged with customers.

10.  Too often people are _____ to their superiors and avoid expressing themselves in a candid, creative manner.

## NEW WORDS

**focus**
ˈfōkəs

**detail**
diˈtāl, ˈdētāl

**potent**
ˈpōtnt

**tolerate**
ˈtäləˌrāt

**ridicule**
ˈridiˌkyool

# Lesson 19

## THE BAD PORTRAIT PAINTER

Even though he was middle aged, Vincent hoped that he would one day become a famous portrait painter. Unfortunately, he was subject to **potent ridicule** by his coworkers for articulating this dream. Looking at his work, they laughed at his inability to **focus** on any **detail** of a person's face. His painting was so terrible, they said, that one could hardly distinguish between a nose and an ear. Vincent would often endure spells of depression after receiving such criticism. But he eventually learned to **tolerate** their criticism. While he never became famous, Vincent continued to create many mediocre works before he retired from pursuing art.

**Definitions:**     Try matching the words in the list with the appropriate definitions. If you are stuck, check the glossary in the back of the book or the passage at the top of the page.

1.  focus  _____  a.  (n.) the subjection of someone or something to contemptuous or dismissive language or behavior; (v.) to subject someone or something to contemptuous and dismissive language or behavior

2.  detail  _____  b.  having great power, influence, or effect

3.  potent  _____  c.  to allow the existence, practice, or occurrence of something; to be able to withstand something, to endure or accept

4.  tolerate  _____  d.  (n.) 1. the center of interest or activity; 2. the state or quality of having or producing clear visual definition; (v.) 1. to adapt to the prevailing level of light so as to see clearly; 2. to pay attention to (focus on)

5.  ridicule  _____  e.  (n.) an individual feature, fact, or item; (v.) to give particulars of, describe item by item

**Sentences:**     Try to use the words above in a sentence below. Remember that a word ending may be changed or its figure of speech slightly altered.

6.  Art hated being _____ by the class bully and got his principal involved.

7.  It is important to _____ on achieving goals; otherwise, one can be distracted and not accomplish as much or as quickly.

8.  A surgeon must pay great attention to _____, for if he or she is only slightly off in an operation, a patient's life may be jeopardized.

9.  Indian restaurants often possess a(n) _____, distinctive smell of curry.

10.  Learning to _____ differences in other people helps individuals get along better with their peers.

29

# Lesson 20

## UNCOMFORTABLE MEMORIES

The **reminiscence** of his turbulent early days would often come to him unexpectedly, in a **stealthy** manner like a thief. The violent and erratic behavior of his gang had caused **mayhem** in his childhood neighborhood. He had become notorious for his cruelty and anger even among his friends. He was older now and understood that his previous actions were nothing to **commend**. He wished that he could undo all the madness that he had caused; however, there was no way to fix the past.

---

**NEW WORDS**

**reminiscence**
ˌreməˈnisəns

**stealthy**
ˈstelTHē

**mayhem**
ˈmāˌhem

**commend**
kəˈmend

**notorious**
nəˈtôrēəs, nō-

---

**Definitions:**    Try matching the words in the list with the appropriate definitions. If you are stuck, check the glossary in the back of the book or the passage at the top of the page.

| | | | | |
|---|---|---|---|---|
| 1. | reminiscence _____ | a. | famous or well-known, especially for a bad deed or quality |
| 2. | stealthy _____ | b. | a story or recollection of past events |
| 3. | mayhem _____ | c. | to praise formally or officially; to present as suitable for approval or acceptance; recommend |
| 4. | commend _____ | d. | behavior done in a surreptitious manner so as to not be seen or heard |
| 5. | notorious _____ | e. | damaging or violent disorder; chaos |

**Sentences:**    Try to use the words above in a sentence below. Remember that a word ending may be changed or its figure of speech slightly altered.

6.    Most thieves need to be _____ in their operation so that they are not caught.

7.    Great _____ ensued after a great earthquake demolished large swaths of greater Kathmandu.

8.    The _____ German politician Adolf Hitler (1889-1945) exterminated over six million Jews in German concentration camps during World War II.

9.    Astrid _____ her little sister for her hard work and efforts in the school talent show.

10.    Marco's latest book contained many _____ from his early childhood in Catalonia.

# Crossword Puzzle
## Lessons 11-20

ACROSS

7   (v.) to praise formally or officially; to present as suitable for approval or acceptance; recommend
12  (v.) 1. to illegally hunt or catch; 2. to acquire in a secretive way
13  (adj.) absolutely necessary; extremely important
14  (adj.) behavior done in a surreptitious manner so as to not be seen or heard
15  (n.) a loud, unpleasant, and prolonged noise
16  (v.) to maintain or support oneself, generally at a minimal level
18  (n.) a small room leading to a big one
19  (n.) a thing that represents or stands for something else, especially a material object that stands for something else

DOWN

1   (n.) the feel, quality, or appearance of a substance or surface; the quality created by a combination of elements in a musical or literary work
2   (v.) to allow the existence, practice, or occurrence of something; to be able to withstand something, to endure or accept
3   (n.) a book, particularly one that is large, heavy, and scholarly
4   (adj.) ready to conform to the commands or will of others
5   (v.) to produce; to cause a particular situation or emotion to come about
6   (adj.) exercising power in an arbitrary or cruel way
7   (adj.) having the ability to see or predict events in the future beyond normal sense; (n.) a person who claims to have the supernatural ability to see events in the future beyond normal sense
8   (n.) 1. the center of interest or activity; 2. the state or quality of having or producing clear visual definition; (v). 1. to adapt to the prevailing level of light so as to see clearly; 2. to pay attention to (focus on)
9   (n.) 1. a passionate expression of grief or sorrow; 2. a song or poem expressing sorrow; 3. an expression of disappointment; (v.) to mourn a person's death
10  (adj.) fat (describing a person)
11  (n.) a device or trick aimed at attracting attention, publicity, or business
17  (v.) to entice; to allure; to try to entice one to do something that he or she finds attractive but that he or she also knows is wrong

# Vocabulary Review
## Lessons 11-20

**Directions: Match each word with its best approximate definition. Note that definitions are not necessarily repeated verbatim from the lesson exercises.**

| | | | | | |
|---|---|---|---|---|---|
| 1. | zany | _____ | a. | strong and solidly built | |
| 2. | ethical | _____ | b. | existing or available in large quantities; plentiful | |
| 3. | sedate | _____ | c. | a lazy or torpid person | |
| 4. | fasten | _____ | d. | the recollection of past events | |
| 5. | procure | _____ | e. | to close or join securely; to fix or hold in place | |
| 6. | invariable | _____ | f. | round or spherical (of a person) | |
| 7. | abundant | _____ | g. | to tempt or attract by offering pleasure or advantage | |
| 8. | wane | _____ | h. | amusingly unconventional and idiosyncratic | |
| 9. | rotund | _____ | i. | having great power, influence, or effect | |
| 10. | elocution | _____ | j. | morally good or correct | |
| 11. | rescind | _____ | k. | to calm someone, typically by administering a drug | |
| 12. | sturdy | _____ | l. | an individual feature, fact, or item | |
| 13. | astound | _____ | m. | to obtain | |
| 14. | captivating | _____ | n. | capable of attracting and holding interest | |
| 15. | sluggard | _____ | o. | to revoke, cancel, or appeal (a law or agreement) | |
| 16. | entice | _____ | p. | to shock or greatly surprise | |
| 17. | detail | _____ | q. | to decrease in vigor, power, or extent | |
| 18. | potent | _____ | r. | chaos; violent or damaging disorder | |
| 19. | reminiscence | _____ | s. | never changing | |
| 20. | mayhem | _____ | t. | the skill of articulate and expressive speech | |

# Word Roots: Unit 2

## ROOTS AND THEIR MEANINGS

| | | | |
|---|---|---|---|
| ante: | before | pre: | before |
| loc/loq/log: | to speak | bi/di: | two |
| sci: | to know | bene: | good |
| sub: | under, less than | inter: | between, among |

## Here are a few examples of some words that use the above roots:

antedate: to date before something; to come before something else in time
loquacious: talkative
science the study of how the world works (biologically, chemically, physically or otherwise); knowing about the world through these properties
predecease: to die before someone or something
subordinate: lower in rank or position; to work under someone
benefit: an advantage
bicycle: a pedal-powered vehicle with two wheels
interstate: existing or carried between states

## Now try to fill in the table below by finding the appropriate root(s) and interpreting the meaning of each word:

| Word | Root(s) | Guessed Meaning | Actual Meaning |
|---|---|---|---|
| antecedent | | | |
| subservient | | | |
| eloquent | | | |
| prescient | | | |
| beneficial | | | |
| predecessor | | | |
| dialogue | | | |
| interlocutor | | | |
| biweekly | | | |

| | | | |
|---|---|---|---|
| subway | | | |
| internecine | | | |
| benediction | | | |
| dichotomy | | | |
| submissive | | | |
| conscience | | | |
| predetermined | | | |

# Occupations and Careers II

This section continues the list of occupations and careers from the previous section. As before, we have broken them up by field.

## SOCIAL SCIENCE RELATED JOBS

**anthropologist:** one who practices anthropology, e.g. the study of humankind, its culture, its development, or its evolution and ecology

**cartographer:** one who practices cartography, e.g. the practice of drawing maps

**demographer:** one who practices demography, e.g. the study of births, deaths, income, and other structural elements of human populations

**psychiatrist:** one who practices psychiatry, e.g. one with whom one can discuss personal, mental, and social problems; unlike a psychologist a psychiatrist can prescribe medication to help a patient

**psychologist:** one who practices psychology, e.g. the study of the mind and emotions that govern behavior in specific contexts; a therapist with whom one can discuss personal, mental, and social problems

**sociologist:** one who practices sociology, e.g. the study of social problems relative to the structure, development, and functioning of human society

## JOBS IN THE LEGAL FIELD

**bailiff:** an official of the court who keeps order, looks after prisoners, executes writs, and carries out arrests

**criminologist:** one who practices criminology, e.g. the study of crime and criminals

**magistrate:** a civil officer or lay judge who administers the law for minor offenses or for screening of larger offenses

## POLITICAL JOBS

**governor:** the elected head of a state in the United States; the title of the head of a colony in British colonies

**mayor:** someone elected head of a town, city, or other designated municipality

**representative:** (1) someone who serves in the United States House of Representatives; (2) a person (often legally) elected to speak on behalf of a group and imbued with legislative power

**senator:** someone who serves on the United States Senate

## NEW WORDS

**divulge**
di'vəlj, dī-

**gouge**
gouj

**barren**
'barən

**liberty**
'libərtē

**repulse**
ri'pəls

# Lesson 21

## THE PRIVILEGED STUDENT

Two boys got into a fight last week: Martin tried to **gouge** out the eye of his rival, Baron. He was angry that Baron would not **divulge** the name of the boy who scratched his car. Martin could not believe that anyone would take the **liberty** to do such a thing. He knew he could not **repulse** all the hatred towards him for being the richest boy in the school. At the same time, Martin was also convinced that all the boys' attempts to destabilize him were **barren**: his father owned the school and the teachers would do whatever he wanted of them.

**Definitions:**   Try matching the word in the box with the appropriate definition. If you are stuck, check the glossary in the back of the book or the passage at the top of the page.

| | | | | |
|---|---|---|---|---|
| 1. | divulge | _____ | a. | to make private or sensitive information known |
| 2. | gouge | _____ | b. | to scoop; to make a groove, hole, or indentation; to cut or force something out roughly or brutally |
| 3. | barren | _____ | c. | empty, bleak, and lifeless; (of land) too poor to produce substantial vegetation |
| 4. | liberty | _____ | d. | 1. to drive back an attack or an enemy by force; 2. to cause someone to feel intense distaste and aversion |
| 5. | repulse | _____ | e. | 1. the state of being free within society; the state of not being incarcerated or enslaved; 2. the power to act as one pleases |

**Sentences:**   Try to use the words above in a sentence below. Remember that a word ending may be changed or its figure of speech slightly altered.

6.   Lilly was _____ when her boyfriend threw up all over her new dress.

7.   Many Americans cherish the fact that they have the _____ of free speech and can thus voice themselves without concern.

8.   I hope the lady behind the counter _____ out a huge scoop of chocolate ice cream for me when I order.

9.   Polly couldn't help herself and thus _____ to the media that her sister was dating a prince.

10.   Much to the contrary of stereotypes, not all deserts are _____: some are sprawling with vegetation and animal life.

# Lesson 22

## PROHIBITION CULTURE

In the **era** known as Prohibition (1920-33), it was easy for a wealthy criminal to make money. Because the manufacture, transportation, and sale of alcohol was forbidden in the United States during this time, a crime boss could pay a **henchman** to smuggle liquor across the border from Canada. Activities of this sort had a **profound** effect on cities near the American border, thus creating a culture of illegal bootlegging. Yet the era quickly drew to a close as Americans strengthened their **stance** against prohibition. Though promoting drinking was hardly **exemplary**, the American government concluded that it was better to allow the sale of alcohol than to contend with an increase in gang fighting and illegal drinking joints (called *speakeasies*) than to try and enforce a complete nationwide ban on alcohol.

### NEW WORDS

**stance**
stans

**profound**
prə'found, prō-

**henchman**
'henCHmən

**exemplary**
ig'zemplərē

**era**
'i(ə)rə, 'erə

**Definitions:** Try matching the words in the list with the appropriate definitions. If you are stuck, check the glossary in the back of the book or the passage at the top of the page.

| | | | | |
|---|---|---|---|---|
| 1. | stance | _____ | a. | 1. serving as a desirable model; representing the best of its kind; 2. (in terms of punishment) serving as a warning or deterrent |
| 2. | profound | _____ | b. | 1. (of a state, quality, or emotion) very great or intense; 2. (concerning a statement or person) having or showing great knowledge or insight |
| 3. | henchman | _____ | c. | a faithful supporter, especially one inclined to engage in unethical behavior by way of practice |
| 4. | exemplary | _____ | d. | 1. the attitude of a person or organization toward something; 2. the way in which someone stands; posture |
| 5. | era | _____ | e. | a long and distinct period of history with a particular feature or characteristic |

**Sentences:** Try to use the words above in a sentence below. Remember that a word ending may be changed or its figure of speech slightly altered.

6. We no longer live in a(n) _____ where people need to deliver mail on horseback.

7. One of Guido's _____ helped the criminals rob the bank.

8. Rather than being noncommittal, it is best to take a _____ in politics and fight for causes one believes in.

9. The Internet has had a(n) _____ impact on the way citizens communicate, learn, and transact their business.

10. Malik is a(n) _____ student: he always has his homework completed and receives excellent grades.

38

## NEW WORDS

**hygiene**
ˈhī jēn

**specter**
ˈspektər

**official**
əˈfiSHəl

**revelation**
ˌrevəˈlāSHən

**veto**
ˈvētō

## THE CORRUPTED POLITICIAN

The **hygiene** levels observed in the neighborhood were despicable, and the **specter** of disease and famine hung over the dilapidated streets. A need for urgent measures was apparent, especially after the **revelation** that a number of children had died from malnutrition and sickness in the past month. The **official** record showed that some policies had been proposed to improve the conditions of the neighborhood; however, it became clear that the new mayor had used his power of **veto** to reject the proposed bills.

**Definitions:**     Try matching the words in the list with the appropriate definitions. If you are stuck, check the glossary in the back of the book or the passage at the top of the page.

| 1. | hygiene | _____ | a. | a constitutional right to reject a decision or a proposal made by a law-making body |
| 2. | specter | _____ | b. | a ghost |
| 3. | official | _____ | c. | conditions or practices conducive to maintaining health and preventing disease, especially through cleanliness |
| 4. | revelation | _____ | d. | a surprising and previously unknown fact, typically made or revealed in a dramatic way |
| 5. | veto | _____ | e. | (adj.) relating to an authority or body and its duties, actions, or responsibilities; (n.) a person holding public office and having official duties |

**Sentences:**     Try to use the words above in a sentence below. Remember that a word ending may be changed or its figure of speech slightly altered.

6. Countries on the United Nations Security Council can _____ certain legislative acts.

7. Yolanda broke up with her boyfriend because of his bad _____: she could no longer tolerate being near him for another minute without him showering.

8. Walking through the spooky house, I was convinced that there was a(n) _____ haunting the corridor.

9. Even though it looks like the Republican Party has won the election, television networks have yet to make a(n) _____ announcement of a party victory.

10. It was a(n) _____ to Winona that she was adopted, for she thought that the individuals she had grown up with were her biological family.

# Lesson 24

## A TROUBLESOME TENANT

Aaqil regretted renting his friend Alex the upstairs floor of his house. Unemployed and irresponsible, Alex was not **willing** to pay the rent on time, and had put off doing so for four months. By **decree**, Aaqil had the right to **evict** Alex from his house. However, he still hesitated to take action. Knowing that Aaqil was softhearted, Alex often made empty promises that he would pay up soon, bribed Aaqil with **delectable** meals, and made **melodramatic** claims about true friendship.

## NEW WORDS

**evict**
i ˈvikt

**melodramatic**
ˌmelədrəˈmatik

**delectable**
diˈlektəbəl

**decree**
diˈkrē

**willing**
ˈwiliNG

**Definitions:** Try matching the words in the list with the appropriate definitions. If you are stuck, check the glossary in the back of the book or the passage at the top of the page.

1. evict _____ a. to expel someone from a property with the assistance of the law
2. melodramatic _____ b. delicious; tasty
3. delectable _____ c. ready, eager, or prepared to do something
4. decree _____ d. overly emotional or dramatic
5. willing _____ e. an official order issued by a ruler or legal authority

**Sentences:** Try to use the words above in a sentence below. Remember that a word ending may be changed or its figure of speech slightly altered.

6. The korma dishes at the new Indian restaurant are _____.
7. Having a friend who is _____ can be very emotionally taxing: dealing with myriad ups and downs can be very draining.
8. The king issued a _____ that all subjects must wear pink floppy hats on Thursdays.
9. Victor finally took action to _____ his tenant after the latter did not pay rent for three months.
10. Unfortunately my parents are not _____ to pay for me to take a trip to Japan and learn about Kyoto's history.

# Lesson 25

## THE BEGINNING OF THE END

## NEW WORDS

**chronic**
ˈkränik

**tangible**
ˈtanjəbəl

**contemporary**
kənˈtempəˌrerē

**retaliation**
riˌtalēˈāSHən

**medley**
ˈmedlē

As he began complaining of **chronic** fatigue due to work stress, his lack of interest in family matters became more and more **tangible**. He often would spend the evenings by himself listening to some weird jazz musician who sounded like a drunken **contemporary** of the swing musician Glenn Miller (1904-44). In **retaliation**, his wife stopped speaking to him almost entirely. She felt a **medley** of contradictory emotions: she still loved him, yet a certain hostility towards him began to creep into her heart.

**Definitions:**  Try matching the words in the list with the appropriate definitions.  If you are stuck, check the glossary in the back of the book or the passage at the top of the page.

| | | | | |
|---|---|---|---|---|
| 1. | chronic | _____ | a. | the action of returning an attack; a counterattack |
| 2. | tangible | _____ | b. | a varied mixture of people or things; a mixture |
| 3. | contemporary | _____ | c. | 1. perceptible by touch; 2. clear and definite, real |
| 4. | retaliation | _____ | d. | (adj.) 1. living or occurring at the same time; 2. belonging or occurring in the present; (n.) 1. a person or living thing existing at the same time as another; 2. a person of roughly the same age as another |
| 5. | medley | _____ | e. | persisting for a long time or constantly recurring |

**Sentences:**  Try to use the words above in a sentence below.  Remember that a word ending may be changed or its figure of speech slightly altered.

6.  Tonight's symphony will contain a _____ of music from various early modern European maestros.

7.  Johnny destroyed his brother's computer as _____ for the latter destroying the former's cell phone.

8.  Ideas and concepts alone are not _____: only when they are developed or used for a practical end can one touch or hold the results.

9.  The German mathematician Johannes Kepler (1571-1630) was a(n) _____ of the Danish astronomer Tycho Brahe (1546-1601); in fact, both men knew each other and briefly worked together in Prague.

10.  Gambling has been a(n) _____ problem for Jerry, who has squandered his life savings playing poker over the years.

41

# Lesson 26

## THE MOMENT OF TRUTH

When the **soothsayer** predicted that Jack's wife would die from her heart disease, Jack simply could not react in a **rational** manner. He began to scream, to stomp his feet, and to **vent** his frustration. It became clear that the calm appearance that he possessed was a **camouflage** that hid his insecurities. To always seem happy and in control had been a major **objective** in Jack's life; however, on hearing the dismal predictions about his ill wife, he simply broke down.

**Definitions:**    Try matching the words in the list with the appropriate definitions. If you are stuck, check the glossary in the back of the book or the passage at the top of the page.

1.    vent    _____    a.    (adj.) not influenced by personal feelings; (n.) a thing aimed at or sought; a goal

2.    soothsayer _____    b.    based on accordance with reason or logic

3.    rational    _____    c.    (n.) the disguising of people (especially military personnel), equipment, and installations by covering them to make them blend in with natural surroundings; material used for such disguise; an animal's covering that lets it blend in with natural surroundings; (v.) to hide or disguise the presence of a person, animal, or object; to conceal the existence of something undesirable

4.    camouflage _____    d.    a person supposedly able to see the future

5.    objective    _____    e.    to give free expression to a strong emotion

**Sentences:**    Try to use the words above in a sentence below. Remember that a word ending may be changed or its figure of speech slightly altered.

6.    It is _____ to logically consider all of the successes and drawbacks before making a major life decision.

7.    Chameleons are able to change color and thus _____ themselves in local surroundings to avoid being preyed upon.

8.    Marion _____ her anger at Jake when she realized that he had lost his wedding ring.

9.    The _____ of soccer is to score as many goals as possible while preventing the opposing team from doing so.

10.    In many Asian cultures, it is customary to visit a(n) _____ to seek advice before embarking on a business venture.

## NEW WORDS

**plight**
plīt

**opulent**
ˈäpyələnt

**wound**
woond

**wreak**
rēk

**imply**
imˈplī

## THE LOSS OF FAMILY PROPERTY

A businessman found himself in a sorry **plight**. The unstable market had begun to **wreak** havoc in his industry and he was losing his money and assets fast. Potential bankruptcy would **imply** that he could lose his **opulent** seaside villa. The subject of the villa became an open **wound** for the businessman: he could not bear the thought of losing the luxurious property, which had belonged to his family for nearly three centuries.

**Definitions:**     Try matching the words in the list with the appropriate definitions. If you are stuck, check the glossary in the back of the book or the passage at the top of the page.

| | | | | |
|---|---|---|---|---|
| 1. | plight | _____ | a. | to inflict a large amount of harm or damage |
| 2. | opulent | _____ | b. | a difficult, dangerous, or unfortunate situation |
| 3. | wound | _____ | c. | to strongly suggest the truth, existence, or logical consequence of something |
| 4. | wreak | _____ | d. | ostentatiously rich and luxurious; extremely lavish |
| 5. | imply | _____ | e. | (n.) an injury to living tissue caused by a cut, blow, or other impact; (v.) to inflict an injury on someone |

**Sentences:**     Try to use the words above in a sentence below. Remember that a word ending may be changed or its figure of speech slightly altered.

6.     Timothy was _____ when his brother accidentally shot him with a BB gun.

7.     Though Katharine did not announce her departure, she _____ that such a decision was imminent when she delegated most of her responsibilities to coworkers.

8.     Many people are awed by the _____ décor in the palace of the Sultan of Brunei.

9.     The _____ of the coal workers was illuminated by the magazine, which published graphic pictures of their poor working conditions.

10.     Flooding near the coastline has _____ havoc on the local inhabitants.

# Lesson 28

## LIKE FATHER, LIKE DAUGHTER

The old man, who was now dying, had been a passionate **advocate** of human rights. Prior to his death, his daughter hired someone to **engrave** some of her father's most famous statements on his tombstone. She deeply respected her father and tried to imitate his stage presence whenever she spoke in front of an audience. She would even **mimic** his facial expressions and **swivel** her eyes in various directions the way her father had done before audiences. Losing him was an **ordeal** for her and she tried to be reminded of him in as many ways as possible.

**Definitions:** Try matching the words in the list with the appropriate definitions. If you are stuck, check the glossary in the back of the book or the passage at the top of the page.

1. engrave _____ a. to imitate someone's actions or words, typically with an attempt to ridicule

2. advocate _____ b. a painful or horrific experience, often one that is protracted

3. swivel _____ c. to cut or carve a text or design on the surface of a hard object

4. mimic _____ d. (n.) a person who publicly supports or recommends a particular cause or policy; 2. a person who pleads on someone else's behalf; (v.) to publicly recommend or support

5. ordeal _____ e. (n.) a coupling between two parts that enables one to revolve about the other; (v.) to turn about a point or axis on a coupling between two parts that enables one to revolve about the other

**Sentences:** Try to use the words above in a sentence below. Remember that a word ending may be changed or its figure of speech slightly altered.

6. Sally had the name of her favorite pet _____ on a locket, which contained a picture of her and her dog.

7. Most attorneys are hired to act as a(n) _____ on behalf of their clients.

8. Often apes _____ the behavior of their peers to learn social norms.

9. It was quite a(n) _____ to drive fifty miles in a blizzard.

10. Office chairs that _____ are much more relaxing to work in than simple stationary ones.

## NEW WORDS

**neophyte**
ˈnēəˌfīt

**daft**
daft

**divergent**
diˈvərjənt, dī-

**exonerate**
igˈzänəˌrāt

**empathy**
ˈempəTHē

## TO ERR IS HUMAN

The two executive directors – one male and one female – of the multinational company have **divergent** policies regarding **neophyte** mishaps on the job. Generally it is always considered unfortunate when new, inexperienced employees miss the mark on specific tasks. However, the way that management addresses these mistakes differs along gender lines. While the male director shows great **empathy** and feels inclined to **exonerate** junior employees who make random mistakes, the female director shows only impatience before **daft** performance that embarrasses the company before its clients.

**Definitions:** Try matching the word in the box with the appropriate definition. If you are stuck, check the glossary in the back of the book or the passage at the top of the page.

| | | | | |
|---|---|---|---|---|
| 1. | neophyte | _____ | a. | to absolve someone from blame for a wrongdoing |
| 2. | daft | _____ | b. | a person who is new to a subject, skill, or belief |
| 3. | divergent | _____ | c. | silly; foolish |
| 4. | exonerate | _____ | d. | tending to be different or to develop in different directions |
| 5. | empathy | _____ | e. | the ability to understand and share the feelings of another |

**Sentences:** Try to use the words above in a sentence below. Remember that a word ending may be changed or its figure of speech slightly altered.

6. Robert is a(n) _____ at golf: he has neither advanced skill nor expertise to beat a pro at a round of the game.

7. Abbot was so _____ as to ask an obese, non-pregnant woman when her baby was due.

8. New evidence presented to the police will help _____ Connie from being charged with murder.

9. People who lack _____ for others are often construed as callous and narcissistic.

10. Jodi and Molly may be twins, but they took _____ life paths: one is a successful entrepreneur and the other is a waif.

# Lesson 30

## A MATTER OF CHARACTER

His **judicious** use of money even in more affluent times was one of the qualities she found attractive in her husband. They would order cheap Chinese food on big holidays. Going to **matinee** shows to save some money was another **idiosyncrasy** in his character. Most women would not see much **charisma** in a man who was so tight when it came to finances; however, she had always preferred **durable** and stable things, and she found Stephen's ways appealing.

**Definitions:** Try matching the words in the list with the appropriate definitions. If you are stuck, check the glossary in the back of the book or the passage at the top of the page.

| | | | | |
|---|---|---|---|---|
| 1. | judicious _____ | a. | having done or showing good judgment or sense |
| 2. | idiosyncrasy_____ | b. | a mode of behavior or way of thought peculiar to an individual; a distinctive characteristic peculiar to a person or thing |
| 3. | matinee _____ | c. | a daytime theater performance or movie showing |
| 4. | charisma _____ | d. | compelling attractiveness or charm that can inspire others |
| 5. | durable _____ | e. | able to withstand wear, pressure, or damage |

**Sentences:** Try to use the words above in a sentence below. Remember that a word ending may be changed or its figure of speech slightly altered.

6. New watches are more _____ than ones from a century ago: they can withstand getting wet or being dropped and stillb operate.

7. Pundits believe that part of the reason Hillary was not elected is because she lacked the _____ to excite voters.

8. It is _____ to consider all of the ramifications and minutiae of a business contract before signing it.

9. One of Mai-Linh's _____ is that she talked to her stuffed animal raccoons every day.

10. I prefer going to a _____ because evening cinema tickets are more expensive.

# Word Search

## Lessons 21-30

```
R I E G A L F U O M A C L
E I D T A N G I B L E Y L
V E M I L A N O I T A R Q
E B T P O B E N G D A F T
L V T A L S Y L V O D T H
A D A K R Y Y O B S U E N
T E V R E E C N T A N G H
I C S L G A N A C C R Y E
O R D L T N N O H R G U E
N E N E U C E M X I A V D
M E U Q E P A R E E I S B
Z T O Y N N E N Y C Y Y Y
R B W K Y B E R T K D T N
```

1  (v.) to scoop; to make a groove, hole, or indentation; to cut or force something out roughly or brutally
2  (v.) 1. to drive back an attack or an enemy by force; 2. to cause someone to feel intense distaste and aversion
3  (n.) 1. the attitude of a person or organization toward something; 2. the way in which someone stands; posture
4  (n.) a faithful supporter, especially one inclined to engage in unethical behavior by way of practice
5  (n.) conditions or practices conducive to maintaining health and preventing disease, especially through cleanliness
6  (n.) a surprising and previously unknown fact, typically made or revealed in a dramatic way
7  (v.) to expel someone from a property with the assistance of the law
8  (n.) an official order issued by a ruler or legal authority
9  (adj.) 1. perceptible by touch; 2. clear and definite, real
10 (n.) a varied mixture of people or things; a mixture
11 (adj.) based on accordance with reason or logic

12 (n.) the disguising of people (especially military personnel), equipment, and installations by covering them to make them blend in with natural surroundings; material used for such disguise; an animal's covering that lets it blend in with natural surroundings; (v.) to hide or disguise the presence of
13 (n.) an injury to living tissue caused by a cut, blow, or other impact; (v.) to inflict an injury on someone
14 (v.) to strongly suggest the truth, existence, or logical consequence of something
15 (v.) to cut or carve a text or design on the surface of a hard object
16 (n.) a person who publicly supports or recommends a particular cause or policy; 2. a person who pleads on someone else's behalf; (v.) to publicly recommend or support
17 (adj.) silly; foolish
18 (v.) to absolve someone from blame for a wrongdoing
19 (n.) a mode of behavior or way of thought peculiar to an individual; a distinctive characteristic peculiar to a person or thing
20 (adj.) able to withstand wear, pressure, or damage

# Vocabulary Review
## Lessons 21-30

**Directions:** Match each word with its best approximate definition. Note that definitions are not necessarily repeated verbatim from the lesson exercises.

| | | | | | |
|---|---|---|---|---|---|
| 1. | divulge | _____ | a. | a beginner; a novice | |
| 2. | barren | _____ | b. | to make known private or sensitive information | |
| 3. | profound | _____ | c. | a dangerous, unfortunate, or difficult situation | |
| 4. | era | _____ | d. | a daytime movie showing or theater performance | |
| 5. | specter | _____ | e. | to reject; a constitutional right to reject a proposal or decision made by a legally authorized body | |
| 6. | veto | _____ | f. | having, showing, or done with good judgment or sense | |
| 7. | melodramatic | _____ | g. | desolate; empty; lacking signs of life | |
| 8. | delectable | _____ | h. | tasty | |
| 9. | chronic | _____ | i. | the action of harming someone in response to being harmed | |
| 10. | retaliation | _____ | j. | to imitate another, typically with the intention to ridicule | |
| 11. | vent | _____ | k. | a long, distinct period of history with a distinct feature or characteristic | |
| 12. | soothsayer | _____ | l. | to cause or inflict a large amount of harm or damage | |
| 13. | plight | _____ | m. | a ghost | |
| 14. | wreak | _____ | n. | the ability to understand and share the feelings of another | |
| 15. | mimic | _____ | o. | concerning a state, quality, or emotion that is very great or intense | |
| 16. | ordeal | _____ | p. | to give free expression to a strong emotion | |
| 17. | neophyte | _____ | q. | persisting for a long time or constantly recurring | |
| 18. | empathy | _____ | r. | a painful, difficult, or horrific experience | |
| 19. | judicious | _____ | s. | a person presumably able to see the future | |
| 20. | matinee | _____ | t. | emotionally or sensationally exaggerated | |

# Word Roots: Unit 3

## ROOTS AND THEIR MEANINGS

| | | | |
|---|---|---|---|
| phil: | love of | intra: | within, inside |
| pot: | power, ability | culp: | blame |
| omni: | all, every | anthr/andr: | man, mankind |

## Here are a few examples of some words that use the above roots:

| | |
|---|---|
| philosophy: | the study of the nature of knowledge, reality, or existence |
| potent: | having great power, influence, or effect |
| intramural: | situated or taking place within the walls of a building or within a single educational institution or community |
| omniscient: | knowing everything |
| culprit: | a person who is responsible for a crime |
| anthropology: | the study of humankind, its existence, its evolution, and its development |

## Now try to fill in the table below by finding the appropriate root(s) and interpreting the meaning of each word:

| Word | Root(s) | Guessed Meaning | Actual Meaning |
|---|---|---|---|
| philanthropy | | | |
| omnipotent | | | |
| philology | | | |
| culpable | | | |
| anthropomorphic | | | |
| excrete | | | |
| android | | | |
| intravenous | | | |
| exculpate | | | |
| potentate | | | |

# Lesson 31

## RIGHTING THE WRONGS OF THE PAST

James suddenly felt a **qualm** about the success of his business deal. He knew that his clients' interests were bound to **intersect** with his; however, he was also aware that the previous company owner had treated the same clients poorly. James became worried that the clients may not want to leave the past without any **redress**. Nevertheless, the business deal was very important to James and he decided to use his skills of **perseverance** and negotiation to see it through. He was going to **uphold** his initial position, regardless of what happened.

**Definitions:**      Try matching the words in the list with the appropriate definitions. If you are stuck, check the glossary in the back of the book or the passage at the top of the page.

1.    perseverance _____    a.    (n.) a remedy or compensation for a wrong or grievance; (v.) to remedy or set right an undesirable situation

2.    intersect _____    b.    to divide something by passing or lying across it

3.    uphold _____    c.    steadfastness in doing something despite difficulty or delay in achieving success

4.    redress _____    d.    to confirm or support something that has happened; to maintain a custom or practice

5.    qualm _____    e.    an uneasy feeling of doubt, worry, or fear, especially about one's own conduct; a misgiving

**Sentences:**      Try to use the words above in a sentence below. Remember that a word ending may be changed or its figure of speech slightly altered.

6.    Doug did not know how to _____ the wrong that had happened when he ignored his wife, who begged him for help in an emergency.

7.    Two parallel lines never _____.

8.    I am impressed by Melinda's _____: in spite of losing her job and family, she has created a new career and vast support network.

9.    It is hard for even the most self-assured people not to have _____ about some of their past behaviors.

10.    The purpose of a sheriff is to _____ the law in any cases where it is challenged or obstructed.

50

**BUSINESS ETIQUETTE**

## NEW WORDS

**limber**
ˈlimbər

**inadvertent**
ˌinədˈvərtnt

**gape**
gāp

**peculiar**
pəˈkyoolyər

**negotiation**
nəˌgōSHēˈāSHən

Harry's **negotiation** with the obese Chinese businessmen went sour after he made several **inadvertent** remarks about how corpulent people were lazy. As Harry denigrated overweight individuals, onlookers watched the **gape** in the Chinese businessman's mouth grow. Harry seemed to believe that only under **peculiar** circumstances could a heavy person be successful at a job. Furthermore, Harry equated career flexibility with physical flexibility: in his mind, only **limber** individuals were versatile enough to smoothly transition between careers. Unfortunately, only after the Chinese businessman abruptly got up and walked away did Harry realize that he was insulting and tactless in his remarks.

**Definitions:** Try matching the words in the list with the appropriate definitions. If you are stuck, check the glossary in the back of the book or the passage at the top of the page.

1. limber _____ a. discussion aimed at reaching an agreement
2. inadvertent _____ b. to stare with one's mouth open wide, typically in amazement or wonder; to become wide or open
3. gape _____ c. not resulting from or achieved through deliberate planning
4. peculiar _____ d. 1. strange or odd; unusual; 2. belonging exclusively to
5. negotiation _____ e. lithe; supple

**Sentences:** Try to use the words above in a sentence below. Remember that a word ending may be changed or its figure of speech slightly altered.

6. One of Myrna's _____ habits is that she always eats dessert before she eats a meal.
7. Kel sat with his mouth _____ open after hearing that his parents had decided to get a divorce.
8. Two countries often enter _____ to discuss terms of a bilateral trade agreement.
9. Ian _____ tripped and stumbled down the steps, thus injuring his leg.
10. Most gymnasts must have _____ bodies in order to be competitive.

# Lesson 33

## THE GAMING GENERATION

Martin was **hesitant** to allow his son to play video games because he was convinced that gaming had a **pernicious** effect on young children. He wanted his son to experience **gratification** from doing chores at home rather than only from pleasurable activities. However, the young boy could not escape the **fate** of his generation. He began to play video games at his friends' houses and became addicted to them: they provided such sheer **bliss** that he completely forgot his father's words.

---

### NEW WORDS

**bliss**
blis

**pernicious**
pər'niSHəs

**fate**
fāt

**gratification**
ˌgratəfiˈkāSHən

**hesitant**
ˈhezitənt

---

**Definitions:**     Try matching the words in the list with the appropriate definitions. If you are stuck, check the glossary in the back of the book or the passage at the top of the page.

| | | | | | |
|---|---|---|---|---|---|
| 1. | bliss | _____ | a. | perfect happiness; great joy | |
| 2. | pernicious | _____ | b. | tentative, unsure, or slow in acting or speaking | |
| 3. | fate | _____ | c. | pleasure, typically when attained from the satisfaction of a desire | |
| 4. | gratification | _____ | d. | the development of events beyond a person's control, regarded as determined by a supernatural power | |
| 5. | hesitant | _____ | e. | having a harmful effect, especially in a harmful or subtle way | |

**Sentences:**     Try to use the words above in a sentence below. Remember that a word ending may be changed or its figure of speech slightly altered.

6.     Jonah was in a state of _____ when he found the long lost teddy bear from his childhood years after having supposed it had been indefinitely lost.

7.     Often two people who are enemies will say _____ things about each other.

8.     There is not much _____ in helping people who do not reciprocate or express their thanks for your efforts.

9.     The _____ of the passengers on the airliner was sealed as the plane's engines malfunctioned and it crashed into the ocean.

10.     Michael was _____ to take a job offer in Hong Kong because he was not sure if he could trust his potential new supervisor.

## NEW WORDS

**stature**
ˈstaCHər

**maneuver**
məˈnoovər

**dexterity**
dekˈsteritē

**lethargic**
ləˈTHärjik

**accommodate**
əˈkäməˌdāt

# Lesson 34

## LIFE AFTER WORK

Back in the day, Adam had been a man of international **stature** in the business world. Selling the biggest company in his country to foreign investors was an extremely risky yet successful **maneuver**. Adam was known for his verbal **dexterity** and ability to persuade others. He always found a way to **accommodate** even the most demanding clients. After retirement, however, Adam became a shadow of himself. He remained in bed all day, **lethargic** and apathetic, as if nothing in the world interested him any longer.

**Definitions:**     Try matching the words in the list with the appropriate definitions.  If you are stuck, check the glossary in the back of the book or the passage at the top of the page.

1.    stature    _____    a.    sluggish, apathetic

2.    maneuver    _____    b.    (n.) a movement or series of moves that requires skill and care; 2. a carefully planned scheme or action; (v.) 1. to move skillfully or carefully; 2. to carefully guide or manipulate something or someone to achieve an end

3.    dexterity    _____    c.    1. to provide lodging or sufficient space for; 2.to fit in with the wishes or needs of

4.    lethargic    _____    d.    1. a person's natural height; 2.importance or reputation gained by ability or achievement

5.    accommodate _____    e.    skill at performing tasks, especially with the hands

**Sentences:**     Try to use the words above in a sentence below.  Remember that a word ending may be changed or its figure of speech slightly altered.

6.    Bill epitomized a(n) _____ person: he sat on the couch all day eating potato chips instead of doing something energizing and productive.

7.    In general, dwarves are beings that have a very short or small _____.

8.    It is difficult to _____ one's car through traffic during rush hour in Oakland.

9.    Most airlines can _____ special dietary needs of travelers who notify them in advance of their requirements and/or restrictions.

10.    In order to be an effective magician, one must possess great _____, especially with his or her hands.

# Lesson 35

## THE IMPORTANCE OF BEING FRIENDLY

The prisoner was able to **construe** from his inmates' facial expressions that he was not welcome at their table. His peers often would **expel** him from communal activities, hoping that their actions would **goad** him into becoming more socially aggressive. However, the prisoner found that his natural shyness was a powerful **barrier** to generating any closer contact. Even the guards found him passive. The warden, however, was more **lenient** with the prisoner in his words: perhaps the warden just felt sorry for him.

**Definitions:**    Try matching the words in the list with the appropriate definitions.  If you are stuck, check the glossary in the back of the book or the passage at the top of the page.

1.    construe    _____    a.    (of punishment or a person in authority) tending to be permissive, merciful or tolerant

2.    goad    _____    b.    to interpret a word or action in a particular way

3.    expel    _____    c.    to provoke or annoy someone so as to stimulate some action or reaction

4.    barrier    _____    d.    an object that prevents movement or access

5.    lenient    _____    e.    to deprive someone membership or involvement in a school or organization; to force someone to leave a place

**Sentences:**    Try to use the words above in a sentence below.  Remember that a word ending may be changed or its figure of speech slightly altered.

6.    Frida's mom _____ her daughter's excitement about going to the theme park with friends as a sign of her love for rollercoasters, not a sign of thrill to escape the family.

7.    During the years 1961-1989, the Berlin Wall served as a(n) _____ that divided East and West Germany into respective capitalist and communist parts.

8.    Sanford was _____ from school after he tried to punch his principal in the face.

9.    If parents are too _____ with rules for their children, such children may not learn how to discipline themselves in order to be successful.

10.    Ariel's friends tried to _____ her into making fun of the old man, but Ariel obstinately refused.

## NEW WORDS

**apathy**
'apəTHē

**realize**
'rē(ə)ˌlīz

**diverse**
di'vərs, dī-

**vehement**
'vēəmənt

**virtuous**
'vərCHəwəs

## AGAINST RACISM

Lindsey had been leading a quiet and **virtuous** life, with a clear **apathy** for social engagement. However, when her best friend Jim was lynched for his outspoken stance on Jim Crow laws, Lindsey began to **realize** that she needed to take action and became a strong advocate of civil rights. She gathered a **diverse** group of people who shared the same sentiments and led a **vehement** protest against racial segregation and abuse. Lindsey also founded an organization that offered assistance to African Americans who struggled financially.

**Definitions:** Try matching the words in the list with the appropriate definitions. If you are stuck, check the glossary in the back of the book or the passage at the top of the page.

| | | | | |
|---|---|---|---|---|
| 1. | apathy | _____ | a. | lack of interest, enthusiasm, or concern |
| 2. | realize | _____ | b. | showing a great deal of variety; very different |
| 3. | diverse | _____ | c. | showing strong feeling, especially forceful, passionate, or intense |
| 4. | vehement | _____ | d. | 1. to become fully aware of something as fact; 2. to cause something desired or anticipated to happen; 3. to give actual or physical form to an idea or plan; 4. to make money or a profit from a transaction |
| 5. | virtuous | _____ | e. | exhibiting high moral standards |

**Sentences:** Try to use the words above in a sentence below. Remember that a word ending may be changed or its figure of speech slightly altered.

6. Sandra's mother was _____ about forbidding her daughter to go out late at night because it was unsafe.

7. It is not always easy to _____ when someone is covertly trying to manipulate you in a business deal.

8. Unlike many other countries, America contains a(n) _____ set of cultures and races within its borders.

9. Generally, honest and hard working people are seen to be _____ and to possess good character.

10. Lindsay was _____ about going to lunch with her girlfriends: she did not seem to care one way or another whether she saw them in the afternoon for a meal.

# Lesson 37

## TO SELL A VIDEO GAME

There was a **glut** of video games on the market. To make his game stand out, James sought to find an item that would **accompany** it, thus making the game more visible in stores. James also hoped to **reduce** the price of his video game by using less expensive packaging. A successful new video game, he thought, would **quell** the fears in his company that it could go bankrupt, and James's usually **garrulous** employees had become very reserved under such circumstances. James believed that launching his product would raise their spirits, and he was determined to have his colleagues help him find a way to sell his newest product.

**Definitions:** Try matching the words in the list with the appropriate definitions. If you are stuck, check the glossary in the back of the book or the passage at the top of the page.

1.  glut _____ a. excessively talkative in a roundabout way, especially on trivial matters
2.  garrulous _____ b. an excessively abundant supply of something
3.  reduce _____ c. to put an end to rebellion or disorder, usually by force
4.  accompany _____ d. to make or become smaller in size, amount, or degree
5.  quell _____ e. to go somewhere with someone as a companion or escort; to be present or occur at the same time as something else; to provide something as a complement or addition to something else

**Sentences:** Try to use the words above in a sentence below. Remember that a word ending may be changed or its figure of speech slightly altered.

6.  There is a(n) _____ of golf balls in the country club pro shop; the store is almost completely filled with them!
7.  The police did little to _____ the raging protests downtown: people kept demonstrating throughout the night.
8.  This cake is too sweet! Next time you make it you should _____ the amount of sugar you use in the batter.
9.  It is standard for American presidents to be _____ by secret service members when they go out of the White House.
10. Unlike Todd, who is by nature reticent, Doris is rather _____.

## NEW WORDS

**settle**
ˈsetl

**foundation**
founˈdāSHən

**void**
void

**inscribe**
inˈskrīb

**terminate**
ˈtərməˌnāt

# Lesson 38

## MEMORIES AND NEW BEGINNINGS

After a three-week voyage, the couple decided to **terminate** their journey and **settle** in a small mountainous village. They wanted to build a new **foundation** for their lives there, unencumbered by the past. The death of their child had left a huge **void** in their lives, but they knew they had to start their lives over. The man asked a local stone mason to **inscribe** the name of the child over a mantelpiece for them. They hoped that seeing the child's name everyday would bring them some comfort and the necessary strength to move on.

**Definitions:**    Try matching the words in the list with the appropriate definitions. If you are stuck, check the glossary in the back of the book or the passage at the top of the page.

1.    settle    _____    a.    1. to resolve or reach an agreement an argument or problem; 2. to adopt a more steady and secure lifestyle, usually with a job and a home; 3. to sit or come to rest in a comfortable position

2.    foundation    _____    b.    to bring to an end

3.    void    _____    c.    to write or carve words or symbols on something, especially as a permanent record

4.    inscribe    _____    d.    1. the lowest load-bearing part of a building, typically underground; 2. the underlying basis or principle for something; 3. an institution or organization with an endowment

5.    terminate    _____    e.    (adj.) 1. not valid or legally binding; 2. completely empty; (n.) a completely empty space; (v.) to declare that something is not valid or legally binding

**Sentences:**    Try to use the words above in a sentence below. Remember that a word ending may be changed or its figure of speech slightly altered.

6.    By the age of forty, most people have decided to _____ with a spouse and have a home and children.

7.    The _____ of a healthy relationship is clear, honest communication.

8.    Companies unable to pay their full workforce must _____ employees.

9.    After my cat Chairman Meow died, I felt a(n) _____ in my life: there was no purring buddy to lift my spirits when I was lonely or down.

10.    Brandon _____ the name of his girlfriend on a bracelet and gave it to her as a birthday gift.

# Lesson 39

## EMERGENCY IN THE HOTEL

As John walked down the corridor, he saw an **obese** man lying on the floor. The man looked at him and whispered that John needed to go into the his room and get his medicine immediately. He was panting heavily and sweating profusely. John approached the stranger's room with **trepidation**. He felt that going through someone's personal things was a **breach** of privacy. In addition, he only had a **rudimentary** knowledge of the man's condition. At the same time, he knew that he needed to **lull** the man's anxiety until the paramedics came.

**Definitions:**    Try matching the words in the list with the appropriate definitions.  If you are stuck, check the glossary in the back of the book or the passage at the top of the page.

1.    breach    _____    a.    a feeling of fear or agitation about something that may happen

2.    lull    _____    b.    involving or limited to basic principles

3.    obese    _____    c.    (n.) a temporary interval of quiet or lack of activity; (v.) to calm or send to sleep typically with soothing sounds or movements

4.    rudimentary    _____    d.    grossly fat or overweight

5.    trepidation    _____    e.    (n.) 1. an act of breaking a law, agreement, or code of conduct; 2. a gap in a wall, barrier, or defense made by an army; (v.) to break a law, agreement, or code of conduct; 2. to make a gap in and break through a wall, barrier, or defense

**Sentences:**    Try to use the words above in a sentence below.  Remember that a word ending may be changed or its figure of speech slightly altered.

6.    When someone _____ another person's trust, the relationship between both people can be seriously jeopardized.

7.    Usually there is a _____ in tempestuous weather when one is in the eye of a hurricane.

8.    With much _____, the princess watched in fear as the knight tried to slay the dragon attacking her palace.

9.    Tommy is still struggling with _____ math skills: each week I try to ensure that he knows his multiplication tables.

10.    A person who weighs 500 pounds is certainly _____.

## NEW WORDS

**dilapidated**
di'lapi,dātid

**ratify**
'ratə,fī

**manufacture**
,manyə'fakCHər

**presage**
'presij, pri'sāj

**truce**
troos

# Lesson 40

## PICKING UP THE PIECES

The battle left remains of buildings and **dilapidated** houses everywhere. Following a **truce** between the two warring sides, representatives of both parties decided to **ratify** laws to reopen local factories. After much destruction, the factories needed to **manufacture** many new products so that life in the region could resume. It was clear that a spirit of economic resurgence had to **presage** decisions about the political future of the region.

**Definitions:** Try matching the words in the list with the appropriate definitions. If you are stuck, check the glossary in the back of the book or the passage at the top of the page.

1. dilapidated _____    a.    to sign or give formal consent to a law, agreement, or treaty to render it valid

2. ratify _____    b.    (n.) a sign or warning that something (typically bad) will happen; an omen or portent; (v.) (of an event) to be a sign that something (typically bad) will happen

3. manufacture _____    c.    (n.) the making of articles on a large scale using machinery; (v.) 1. to make something on a large scale using machinery; 2. to invent or fabricate evidence or story

4. presage _____    d.    a building or object in a state of disrepair or ruin as a result of age or neglect

5. truce _____    e.    an agreement between enemies or opponents to stop fighting

**Sentences:** Try to use the words above in a sentence below. Remember that a word ending may be changed or its figure of speech slightly altered.

6. Jane's untimely death was _____ by a high fever and a loss of appetite.

7. If you do not take care of your home it will become _____ over time, thus requiring substantial renovation to maintain it.

8. Congress must _____ the bill before new rules can be put into action.

9. In the twentieth century, Detroit had many automotive plants where cars were
_____.

10. After fighting for twenty years, the two countries called a _____ and ceased fighting.

# Crossword Puzzle
## Lessons 31-40

ACROSS

2  (v.) to confirm or support something that has happened; to maintain a custom or practice
4  (n.) 1. a person's natural height; 2.importance or reputation gained by ability or achievement
7  (v.) to make or become smaller in size, amount, or degree
8  (adj.) having a harmful effect, especially in a harmful or subtle way
15 (adj.) showing strong feeling, especially forceful, passionate, or intense
17 (n.) a temporary interval of quiet or lack of activity; (v.) to calm or send to sleep typically with soothing sounds or movements
18 (adj.) not resulting from or achieved through deliberate planning
19 (adj.) (of punishment or a person in authority) tending to be permissive, merciful or tolerant
20 (n.) pleasure, typically when attained from the satisfaction of a desire

DOWN

1  (v.) to interpret a word or action in a particular way
3  (n.) a movement or series of moves that requires skill and care; 2. a carefully planned scheme or action; (v.) 1. to move skillfully or carefully; 2. to carefully guide or manipulate something or someone to achieve an end
5  (v.) to go somewhere with someone as a companion or escort; to be present or occur at the same time as something else; to provide something as a complement or addition to something else
6  (adj.) showing a great deal of variety; very different
9  (adj.) involving or limited to basic principles
10 (n.) the making of articles on a large scale using machinery; (v.) 1. to make something on a large scale using machinery; 2. to invent or fabricate evidence or a story
11 (n.) steadfastness in doing something despite difficulty or delay in achieving success
12 (v.) 1. to resolve or reach an agreement an argument or problem; 2. to adopt a more steady and secure lifestyle, usually with a job and a home; 3. to sit or come to rest in a comfortable position
13 (adj.) a building or object in a state of disrepair or ruin as a result of age or neglect
14 (n.) discussion aimed at reaching an agreement
16 (n.) 1. the lowest load-bearing part of a building, typically underground; 2. the underlying basis or principle for something; 3. an institution or organization with an endowment

# Vocabulary Review
## Lessons 31-40

**Directions: Match each word with its best approximate definition. Note that definitions are not necessarily repeated verbatim from the lesson exercises.**

| | | | | | |
|---|---|---|---|---|---|
| 1. | intersect | _____ | a. | strange, odd, or unusual |
| 2. | qualm | _____ | b. | exhibiting high moral standards |
| 3. | limber | _____ | c. | an excessively abundant supply of something |
| 4. | peculiar | _____ | d. | an uneasy feeling of doubt |
| 5. | bliss | _____ | e. | an agreement between enemies or opponents to stop fighting for a time |
| 6. | hesitant | _____ | f. | excessively talkative in a roundabout way |
| 7. | dexterity | _____ | g. | to write or carve words into something |
| 8. | lethargic | _____ | h. | unsure or tentative in acting or speaking |
| 9. | goad | _____ | i. | skill in performing tasks, especially with the hands |
| 10. | barrier | _____ | j. | great joy or perfect happiness |
| 11. | apathy | _____ | k. | an obstacle – literal or intangible – that prevents access or progress |
| 12. | virtuous | _____ | l. | feeling of fear that something bad may happen |
| 13. | glut | _____ | m. | concerning a body part that is lithe; supple |
| 14. | garrulous | _____ | n. | lack of interest, enthusiasm, or concern |
| 15. | void | _____ | o. | to divide something by passing or lying across it |
| 16. | inscribe | _____ | p. | to provoke or annoy someone with the hope that a reaction will be solicited |
| 17. | obese | _____ | q. | to give formal consent to a treaty, thus making it valid |
| 18. | trepidation | _____ | r. | grossly overweight |
| 19. | ratify | _____ | s. | sluggish and apathetic |
| 20. | truce | _____ | t. | an emptiness; not valid or legally binding |

# Word Roots: Unit 4

## ROOTS AND THEIR MEANINGS

| | | | |
|---|---|---|---|
| **super:** | over, beyond | **post:** | after |
| **terr:** | earth | **bel(l):** | war |
| **amb:** | walk | **trans:** | across |
| **mis/mit:** | to send | **fid:** | trust, faith |

## Here are a few examples of some words that use the above roots:

superhero: a fictional icon who does good deeds and who possesses powers greater than what humans are capable of possessing

terracentric: a model or system of the universe in which the Earth is at the center rather than the sun.

amble: to walk in a casual, relaxed, slow pace

postdate: to assign a later date than the actual one to a document or event

bellicose: exhibiting aggression and willingness to fight

transcend: to go beyond the range or limits of something

remit: to send money in payment as form of a gift (one of many definitions of remit)

fidelity: faithfulness to a person, belief, or cause by showing signs of support and/or loyalty

## Now try to fill in the table below by finding the appropriate root(s) and interpreting the meaning of each word:

| Word | Root(s) | Guessed Meaning | Actual Meaning |
|---|---|---|---|
| intermittent | | | |
| amble | | | |
| transnational | | | |
| belligerent | | | |
| fiduciary | | | |

| | | | |
|---|---|---|---|
| transmit | | | |
| subterranean | | | |
| posterior | | | |
| rebellion | | | |
| supercede | | | |
| terrain | | | |
| superconductor | | | |
| infidelity | | | |
| terrarium | | | |
| ambulatory | | | |
| missive | | | |
| transit | | | |

# Lesson 41

## DISORDER IN THE CLASSROOM

The atmosphere in the classroom became **turbulent** when a few boys began fighting and screaming. It was an **uncanny** sight for the new teacher who gave them a **stern** look. The boys did not seem intimidated by the new teacher, who tried to **upbraid** the students for the classroom fight. Upon seeing that he could not solve the problem with his voice alone, the teacher realized that **superficial** measurements would not suffice; he needed to take the boys to the headmaster to solve the matter.

**Definitions:**      Try matching the words in the list with the appropriate definitions. If you are stuck, check the glossary in the back of the book or the passage at the top of the page.

| | | | | |
|---|---|---|---|---|
| 1. | turbulent | _____ | a. | strange or mysterious in an unsettling way |
| 2. | uncanny | _____ | b. | (adj.) describing a person who is serious and unrelenting, especially in matters of assertion of authority and exertion of discipline; strict and severe; (n.) the rearmost part of a ship or boat |
| 3. | stern | _____ | c. | existing or occurring on the surface; not thorough, deep, or complete; shallow |
| 4. | upbraid | _____ | d. | characterized by conflict, disorder, or confusion; liquid that moves violently and unsteadily |
| 5. | superficial | _____ | e. | to scold; to find fault with someone |

**Sentences:**      Try to use the words above in a sentence below. Remember that a word ending may be changed or its figure of speech slightly altered.

6. A flight can experience great _____ when an airplane flies through an air pocket.

7. Akisha _____ her sister when the latter forgot to attend the former's birthday party.

8. That woman on the train station bench bears a(n) _____ resemblance to the American actress, Emma Stone.

9. Luckily, Rodney's wound was only _____: beneath the surface of his skin, there was no deep damage to underlying muscles or tissue.

10. Unlike Max, who is lax, Vern is rather _____ in his dealings.

# Lesson 42

## THE AFTERMATH

The recent bombing incident left the embassy buried in **debris** and killed many innocent civilians. The culprit, claiming to be fed up with the **hypocrisy** of the government in dealing with its foreign affairs, had devised an **intricate** bombing plan to take matters into his own hands. Since the damage of such a terrorist act was severe, this **insurgent** was sentenced to death. Worried that the current **meager** protection of governmental buildings could not withstand future attacks, the local government also tightened its security.

**Definitions:**     Try matching the words in the list with the appropriate definitions. If you are stuck, check the glossary in the back of the book or the passage at the top of the page.

| | | | | |
|---|---|---|---|---|
| 1. | debris | _____ | a. | (adj.) rising in active revolt; (n.) a rebel or revolutionary |
| 2. | intricate | _____ | b. | lacking in quantity or quality |
| 3. | meager | _____ | c. | scattered fragments of something wrecked or destroyed |
| 4. | hypocrisy | _____ | d. | the practice of claiming to have certain moral standards or beliefs to which one's behavior does not conform |
| 5. | insurgent | _____ | e. | very complicated or detailed |

**Sentences:**     Try to use the words above in a sentence below. Remember that a word ending may be changed or its figure of speech slightly altered.

6.    After San Francisco's giant 1906 earthquake, _____ from crumbled buildings was found all across town.

7.    I was expecting a giant platter at Devon's dinner party, but instead was served only a(n) _____ three grains of rice!

8.    The design on the Persian carpet was _____ and contained images of many shapes in many colors.

9.    The _____ populace held a coup and deposed the king.

10.    Louisa sensed _____ when her parents demand she have a lucrative career after college; when she was young they had told her to follow her dreams regardless of income.

# Lesson 43

## BROTHERLY RELATIONS

Two brothers bought a copper tank as a **souvenir** from the history museum. The older brother, Tom, commanded his younger sibling to **burnish** the tank every day. The younger child, Tin, was **meek** and gentle and accepted the order – likely because he feared Tom's **pugnacious** nature. Moreover, Tom often would hurl hurtful **barbed** comments at his little brother, thus helping to motivate Tin's willing compliance.

<table>
<tr><td colspan="2">NEW WORDS</td></tr>
<tr><td>pugnacious</td><td>pəgˈnāSHəs</td></tr>
<tr><td>souvenir</td><td>ˌsoovəˈni(ə)r</td></tr>
<tr><td>barbed</td><td>bärbd</td></tr>
<tr><td>burnish</td><td>ˈbərniSH</td></tr>
<tr><td>meek</td><td>mēk</td></tr>
</table>

**Definitions:** Try matching the words in the list with the appropriate definitions. If you are stuck, check the glossary in the back of the book or the passage at the top of the page.

| | | | | |
|---|---|---|---|---|
| 1. | pugnacious | _____ | a. | quiet, gentle, submissive; easily imposed upon |
| 2. | souvenir | _____ | b. | to polish |
| 3. | barbed | _____ | c. | eager to argue, quarrel, or fight |
| 4. | burnish | _____ | d. | a thing kept as a reminder of a person, place, or event |
| 5. | meek | _____ | e. | having sharp projections on an object so as to make extraction difficult; deliberately hurtful |

**Sentences:** Try to use the words above in a sentence below. Remember that a word ending may be changed or its figure of speech slightly altered.

6. Robin is often _____ and enjoys picking fights with her coworkers.

7. Magnets, spoons, and figurines are among my favorite _____ to purchase when I travel to an exotic place.

8. Unlike Sean, who is tactful, Daryl's _____ comments have often offended other people.

9. Being a socialite is not a lifestyle for the _____: one is perpetually in the limelight and media in this role.

10. Eileen spent hours trying to _____ her resume so that it looked attractive to potential employers.

**DOG DAYS**

## NEW WORDS

**feral**
ˈfi(ə)rəl, ˈferəl

**quarantine**
ˈkwôrənˌtēn

**atrophy**
ˈatrəfē

**robust**
rōˈbəst, ˈrōˌbəst

**pliable**
ˈplīəbəl

Mr. Ford's pet dog was put temporarily into **quarantine** after it had arrived in the new country. Such a policy was standard practice, as the nation needed to ensure that all pets entering its borders were **robust** and not **feral**. Luckily for Mr. Ford, his dog was healthy. Despite the long voyage, none of the dog's muscles had begun to **atrophy** and the dog was excited to jump about and fetch balls. It even enjoyed gnawing on a **pliable** rubber toy that stretched when pulled. The dog appeared to have completed its overseas voyage in good spirits, and Mr. Ford was happy to begin a new chapter of his life with his canine buddy.

**Definitions:** Try matching the words in the list with the appropriate definitions. If you are stuck, check the glossary in the back of the book or the passage at the top of the page.

1. feral _____ a. (n.) a state, period, or place of isolation in which people or animals that have arrived from elsewhere or been exposed to infectious or contagious diseases have been placed; (v.) to impose isolation on a person or animal (typically one carrying a disease)

2. quarantine _____ b. strong and healthy; vigorous

3. atrophy _____ c. 1. for a body tissue to waste away, typically due to the degeneration of cells; 2. to gradually decline in effectiveness or vigor due to underuse or neglect

4. robust _____ d. 1. easily bent; flexible; 2. easily influenced

5. pliable _____ e. (usually of an animal) in a wild state, especially after escaping domesticity or captivity

**Sentences:** Try to use the words above in a sentence below. Remember that a word ending may be changed or its figure of speech slightly altered.

6. Residents in my town having contracted the deadly plague were _____ so that others would not be infected.

7. If one does not keep up with weight lifting, his or her muscles will _____ in time.

8. Unlike dogs, coyotes are _____ animals unsuited to dwell with humans.

9. The town's annual celebration was quite _____; it included a number of festivities ranging from fireworks to street art to two live concerts.

10. Unlike wood, which snaps and breaks under pressure, rubber is more _____ when outside forces act on it.

# Lesson 45

## THE SECRET SUPPORTER

After receiving no government funding for his research, Martin did not even have a **modicum** of hope to see his project materialize. However, by some strange **cosmic** circumstance, on the last day before the funding deadline, an **anonymous** donor decided to **contribute** a large amount of money to support Martin's project. It was nothing short of a miracle. Martin did not know whether it was a **random** coincidence that someone had seen his project at the last minute or whether some affluent person had been observing his work for a long time and finally decided to help.

## NEW WORDS

**modicum**
ˈmädikəm, ˈmōd-

**anonymous**
əˈnänəməs

**cosmic**
ˈkäzmik

**random**
ˈrandəm

**contribute**
kənˈtribyoot, -byət

**Definitions:** Try matching the words in the list with the appropriate definitions. If you are stuck, check the glossary in the back of the book or the passage at the top of the page.

1.  modicum _____   a.   of or relating to the universe or things beyond Earth

2.  anonymous _____   b.   to give (something, often money) in order to help achieve or provide something

3.  cosmic _____   c.   a small quantity of a particular thing, especially one that is valuable

4.  random _____   d.   (of a person) not identified by name, or of unknown name

5.  contribute _____   e.   made, done, or chosen without method or conscious thought

**Sentences:** Try to use the words above in a sentence below. Remember that a word ending may be changed or its figure of speech slightly altered.

6.  If scientists unearthed a new planet in our solar system, such a finding would challenge our notion of the _____ order.

7.  Drawing names out of a hat to win a prize is a very _____ way to select winners.

8.  Some people believe it is best to give _____ feedback rather than to furnish one's name next to criticism.

9.  Daniel was so selfish that he didn't even have a(n) _____ of concern about how his actions could impact others.

10. Smoking, alcoholism, and lack of exercise all _____ to one appearing physically aged.

## NEW WORDS

**deter**
di'tər

**bounty**
'bountē

**drawback**
'drô͵bak

**request**
ri'kwest

**predate**
prē'dāt

# Lesson 46

## A CHANGE IN POLICY

The computer programming camp was well known for its quality, as its graduates typically received a **bounty** of job offers within one year of completing the program. Yet a major **drawback** of the camp that might **deter** some people from signing up was its exorbitant cost. To attract a more diverse pool of participants, the head of the camp decided to lower the price and offer scholarships for students from low-income backgrounds. Any student already registered for the upcoming camp whose payment might **predate** the adoption of this policy could still **request** a partial refund.

**Definitions:**     Try matching the words in the list with the appropriate definitions.  If you are stuck, check the glossary in the back of the book or the passage at the top of the page.

| | | | | |
|---|---|---|---|---|
| 1. | deter | _____ | a. | a feature that renders something less acceptable; a disadvantage or problem |
| 2. | bounty | _____ | b. | (n.) an act of asking politely or formally for something; (v.) to ask politely or formally for something |
| 3. | drawback | _____ | c. | to discourage someone from doing something, typically by instilling doubt or fear |
| 4. | request | _____ | d. | to exist or occur at a date earlier than something |
| 5. | predate | _____ | e. | 1. generosity, liberality; abundance; 2. a monetary gift or reward given by a government, usually for killing or capturing a criminal |

**Sentences:**     Try to use the words above in a sentence below.  Remember that a word ending may be changed or its figure of speech slightly altered.

6.   There is a(n) _____ of ten thousand dollars for anyone who can bring the outlaw to the sheriff, who will deliver justice.

7.   Little could _____ Tiffany's strong interest in quitting her job and moving to Barbados.

8.   Barbara made a(n) _____ to her boss for a week off so that she could attend her sister's wedding in Almaty.

9.   One of the _____ of living in Boston is that the winter climate can be unbearable for many people.

10.   Alphabetic language seems to _____ the birth of Christianity in world history.

# Lesson 47

## THE REVIVAL

The company business had fallen into a boring **routine** after feelings of complacency had managed to **invade** its leadership.  Perhaps it was a sign of **mercy** to the CEO that a new and exciting client appeared out of nowhere and boosted the morale of the corporate management.  Little by little, the company began to operate at full **blast** again after many months of stagnation.  Within a year, there was a **stampede** of new applicants who were applying for jobs at the company and the business began to grow.

### NEW WORDS

**routine**
roo'tēn

**mercy**
'mərsē

**blast**
blast

**stampede**
stam'pēd

**invade**
in'vād

**Definitions:**   Try matching the words in the list with the appropriate definitions.  If you are stuck, check the glossary in the back of the book or the passage at the top of the page.

1.   routine   _____   a.   (n.) a sudden panicked rush of a number of horses, cattle, or other animals; (v.) (of horses, cattle, or other animals) to rush wildly in a sudden mass

2.   mercy   _____   b.   for an armed forces to enter a region and occupy it; to enter an area in large numbers; for a disease to spread into an organism or body part; to encroach or intrude on

3.   blast   _____   c.   compassion or forgiveness shown toward someone whom it is within one's power to punish or harm

4.   stampede   _____   d.   (adj.) performed as part of regular procedure; (n.) a sequence of actions regularly followed

5.   invade   _____   e.   (n.) 1. a destructive wave of compressed air spreading outward from an explosion; 2. a strong gust of wind or air; 3. a single loud noise emanating from a horn or other musical instrument; (v.) 1. to blow up or break apart something with explosives; 2. to make or cause to make a loud continuous musical or other noise

**Sentences:**   Try to use the words above in a sentence below.  Remember that a word ending may be changed or its figure of speech slightly altered.

6.   Lizzie ran to the curb as a(n) _____ of horses ran down the highway.

7.   Dave likes having a(n) _____ that he can follow to keep him on task.

8.   The despotic pharaoh showed no _____ for his subjects and forced many of them to travail in the punishing weather to build his pyramids.

9.   When I exited the casino, a(n) _____ of air flew in my face.

10.   The horror film is about aliens that _____ Earth and destroy humans.

70

## NEW WORDS

**taciturn**
ˈtasiˌtərn

**glint**
glint

**manifold**
ˈmanəˌfōld

**communicate**
kəˈmyoonəˌkāt

**salutation**
ˌsalyəˈtāSHən

### THE MYSTERIOUS NEIGHBOR

The little boy greeted the old neighbor every morning but the man would only respond with a **taciturn** look at his **salutation**. It was obvious that the old man did not want to **communicate** with anyone, least of all with a little child. The boy had **manifold** interests every day so he would forget about the old man quickly. However, every time that he saw the old neighbor through the window, there was a **glint** of recognition and curiosity in his eyes.

**Definitions:** Try matching the words in the list with the appropriate definitions. If you are stuck, check the glossary in the back of the book or the passage at the top of the page.

| | | | |
|---|---|---|---|
| 1. | taciturn _____ | a. | to share or exchange information, news, or ideas |
| 2. | glint _____ | b. | a gesture or utterance made as a greeting or acknowledgement of another's arrival or departure |
| 3. | manifold _____ | c. | (n.) a small flash of light; (of one's eyes) a shine with a particular emotion; (v.) to give out or reflect small flashes of light |
| 4. | communicate _____ | d. | a person who is reserved and uncommunicative in speech; saying little |
| 5. | salutation _____ | e. | many and various |

**Sentences:** Try to use the words above in a sentence below. Remember that a word ending may be changed or its figure of speech slightly altered.

6. The reasons for my moving from Cleveland to Miami are _____: I prefer warm weather, there are more job opportunities in the latter location, and I have relatives there.

7. Waving hello when one arrives is a common _____ in America and much of Europe.

8. Even though Jay was depressed, I could still sense a(n) _____ of hope in his eyes that he could create a successful and profound future.

9. It can be difficult for two people from different cultures to _____ effectively, as each person has different values and mores.

10. The _____ librarian sat at her desk reading books and rarely spoke unless she was addressed.

71

# Lesson 49

**A SWEET REVENGE**

The teenagers decided to **vandalize** the car of the richest boy in class. They were **deft** with their instruments and were able to open the car within seconds. The rich boy's **blatant** superiority had made them very angry. He would **jeer** at them and humiliate them in front of others because they were the poorest kids in school. This served as a strong **incentive** for the boys to damage the expensive car.

**Definitions:**     Try matching the words in the list with the appropriate definitions. If you are stuck, check the glossary in the back of the book or the passage at the top of the page.

| | | | | |
|---|---|---|---|---|
| 1. | blatant | _____ | a. | a thing that motivates or encourages one to do something |
| 2. | jeer | _____ | b. | typically bad behavior done openly and unashamedly |
| 3. | incentive | _____ | c. | neatly skillful and quick in one's movements |
| 4. | vandalize | _____ | d. | (n.) a rude, mocking remark; (v.) to make rude and mocking comments, typically in a rude manner |
| 5. | deft | _____ | e. | to deliberately destroy or damage public or private property |

**Sentences:**     Try to use the words above in a sentence below. Remember that a word ending may be changed or its figure of speech slightly altered.

6. There is little _____ for someone to work a job without either salary or the ability to develop specific career skills.

7. Marianne is a(n) _____ musician and is able to play several brass and woodwind instruments with ease.

8. The spectators _____ at Ryan after he missed his final field goal and lost the football game.

9. After mooring their ships in the harbor, pirates _____ the city of St. Augustine.

10. That Brian had had an accident at lunch was _____ obvious: he returned in the afternoon with a big spaghetti sauce stain on his otherwise immaculate white shirt.

## NEW WORDS

**mature**
məˈCHoor, -ˈt(y)oor

**malign**
məˈlīn

**fortify**
ˈfôrtəˌfī

**murky**
ˈmərkē

**caprice**
kəˈprēs

## A WILL OF ONE'S OWN

Growing up, Lucy and Emily's aunt Euridice regularly lectured them in a disparaging tone about the necessity of securing a wealthy, educated husband. Now at **mature** ages, Lucy and Emily no longer allow their aunt to **malign** them with **murky** rhetoric about the prospect of marriage. Preferring to remain single and enjoy a young adulthood of **caprice**, the girls do not even think of dating. In their opinion, no man can **fortify** their lives: only by following their passions can they find true happiness and inner meaning.

**Definitions:** Try matching the words in the list with the appropriate definitions. If you are stuck, check the glossary in the back of the book or the passage at the top of the page.

1. mature _____ a. (adj.) fully developed physically; full-grown; (v.) to become physically or emotionally developed

2. malign _____ b. to strengthen a place with defensive works so as to protect it from attack; to strengthen or invigorate someone mentally or physically

3. fortify _____ c. (adj.) evil in nature or effect, malevolent; (v.) to speak about another in a spitefully cruel manner

4. murky _____ d. dark and gloomy, usually because of thick mist

5. caprice _____ e. a sudden and unaccountable change of mood or behavior

**Sentences:** Try to use the words above in a sentence below. Remember that a word ending may be changed or its figure of speech slightly altered.

6. Taylor, who is very steadfast, has very little patience for people who are _____ and thus change their mind erratically.

7. It takes a(n) _____ person to be able to take responsibility for his or her actions.

8. Extra beams were added to the building's frame in order to _____ it.

9. Often in a political campaign, candidates attempt to _____ their opponents in an attempt to gain support.

10. Haunted places often are situated in a(n) _____ ambiance at night.

# Word Search

## Lessons 41-50

```
L S U O M Y N O N A M E A G E R D
T D M Z Q T R N P Y P R Y R M R Q
U R R R C K T Y P J Y C U L G G R
R A Q I N O E P N R R T V D T M V
B W T T N E N E R E A N Y M Z N B
U B Y Z N E V T M M Y Y T J T D B
L A G L F E V I R N R U T I C A T
E C J E Y X G U T I R G B P M P M
N K R B R T Y R O N B E L P N M Y
T A W W L H N N U S E U T I K J V
L Y K Q P A E U G S T C T S N L N
M N K O Y D T Q O I N Q N E D T Z
Q J R W A J N A T B L I N I D B Q
T T T V J J Y D N V R A X B Y L Q
A J N D G B L Z M T D Y M Y T T N
Y I X K X X M G N K L D T N G Z W
```

1 (adj.) characterized by conflict, disorder, or confusion; liquid that moves violently and unsteadily

2 (adj.) describing a person who is serious and unrelenting, especially in matters of assertion of authority and exertion of discipline; strict and severe; (n.) the rearmost part of a ship or boat

3 (adj.) lacking in quantity or quality

4 (adj.) rising in active revolt; (n.) a rebel or revolutionary

5 (adj.) a thing kept as a reminder of a person, place, or event

6 (adj.) quiet, gentle, submissive; easily imposed upon

7 (adj.) (usually of an animal) in a wild state, especially after escaping domesticity or captivity

8 (v.) 1. for a body tissue to waste away, typically due to the degeneration of cells; 2. to gradually decline in effectiveness or vigor due to underuse or neglect

9 (adj.) (of a person) not identified by name, or of unknown name

10 (v.) to give (something, often money) in order to help achieve or provide something

11 (n.) 1. generosity, liberality; abundance; 2. a monetary gift or reward given by a government, usually for killing or capturing a criminal

12 (n.) a feature that renders something less acceptable; a disadvantage or problem

13 (n.) compassion or forgiveness shown toward someone whom it is within one's power to punish or harm

14 (v.) for an armed forces to enter a region and occupy it; to enter an area in large numbers; for a disease to spread into an organism or body part; to encroach or intrude on

15 (adj.) a person who is reserved and uncommunicative in speech; saying little

16 (n.) a small flash of light; (of one's eyes) a shine with a particular emotion; (v.) to give out or reflect small flashes of light

17 (adj.) typically bad behavior done openly and unashamedly

18 (n.) a thing that motivates or encourages one to do something

19 (adj.) fully developed physically; full-grown; (v.) to become physically or emotionally developed

20 (adj.) evil in nature or effect, malevolent; (v.) to speak about another in a spitefully cruel manner

# Vocabulary Review
## Lessons 41-50

**Directions:** Match each word with its best approximate definition.  Note
that definitions are not necessarily repeated verbatim from the
lesson exercises.

| | | | | | |
|---|---|---|---|---|---|
| 1. | uncanny | _____ | a. | quarrelsome; combative |
| 2. | upbraid | _____ | b. | easily bent or influenced; flexible |
| 3. | debris | _____ | c. | extremely complex or detailed |
| 4. | intricate | _____ | d. | dark and gloomy, often due to thick mist |
| 5. | pugnacious | _____ | e. | many and various |
| 6. | burnish | _____ | f. | to make rude, often loud, mocking remarks |
| 7. | robust | _____ | g. | to exist at an earlier point in time than something |
| 8. | pliable | _____ | h. | to deliberately destroy or damage something (usually public property) |
| 9. | modicum | _____ | i. | scattered fragments remaining after something has been wrecked or destroyed |
| 10. | cosmic | _____ | j. | a panicked rush of horses (or cattle or other animals) |
| 11. | deter | _____ | k. | relating to the universe, especially as distinct from Earth |
| 12. | predate | _____ | l. | a sequence of actions regularly followed; a fixed program |
| 13. | routine | _____ | m. | strong and healthy; vigorous |
| 14. | stampede | _____ | n. | strange or mysterious, especially in an unsettling way |
| 15. | manifold | _____ | o. | to scold or find fault with someone |
| 16. | communicate | _____ | p. | to strengthen or invigorate |
| 17. | jeer | _____ | q. | to polish |
| 18. | vandalize | _____ | r. | a very small amount |
| 19. | fortify | _____ | s. | to exchange information, news, or ideas |
| 20. | murky | _____ | t. | to discourage someone from doing something |

# Word Roots: Unit 5

## ROOTS AND THEIR MEANINGS

| | | | |
|---|---|---|---|
| **path:** | **feeling** | **cred:** | **believe** |
| **uni/mono:** | **one** | **circ/circum:** | **around** |
| **cog(n)** | **to know** | **ac/acr:** | **sharp, bitter** |

## Here are a few examples of some words that use the above roots:

| | |
|---|---|
| empathy: | the ability to understand and share the feelings of another |
| unicycle: | a cycle with one wheel, often used by circus entertainers or acrobats |
| monocle: | a single eyeglass that one wears |
| cognitive: | related to thinking or the mind |
| incredible: | hard to believe; unbelievable |
| circumvent: | to find a way around an obstacle |
| acerbic: | sharp and forthright; bitter or sour tasting |

## Now try to fill in the table below by finding the appropriate root(s) and interpreting the meaning of each word:

| Word | Root(s) | Guessed Meaning | Actual Meaning |
|---|---|---|---|
| sociopath | | | |
| uniform (adj.) | | | |
| circumnavigate | | | |
| credibility | | | |
| acrid | | | |
| incredulous | | | |
| credulous | | | |
| acrimonious | | | |
| monochrome | | | |
| recognize | | | |
| incognito | | | |
| circumlocution | | | |
| circumspect | | | |

# Specific Vocabularies I
## Animal Words

While the standard lessons in this book contain words frequently used in intellectual and academic English, it is also important to realize that certain careers and disciplines have their own specific vocabularies. Many individuals know some words from specific vocabularies, but they may not know a majority of them. Often it is helpful to know such words to be more conversant in specific fields, and some of them may appear frequently on exams with analogy sections. In this book, we aim to furnish you with some specific vocabularies to aid your vocabulary growth.

## Words for Groups of Animals:

- A group of dogs or wolves is called a **pack**
- A group of cats is called a **clowder**
- A group of baby cats is called a **litter**
- A group of fish is called a **school**
- A group of crows is called a **murder**
- A group of birds (in general) is called a **flock**
- A group of lions is called a **pride**
- A group of monkeys is called a **troop** or **cartload**
- A group of bees is called a **swarm**
- A group of buffalo, moose, buffalo, ox, deer, sheep, yak, alpaca, or cattle is called a **herd**
- A sudden panicked rush of horses or other cattle is called a **stampede**

## Words for Baby Animals:

- A baby dog is called a **pup (puppy)**
- A baby cat is called a **kitten**
- A baby kangaroo is called a **joey**
- A baby goat is called a **kid**
- A baby pig is called a **piglet**
- A baby bear is called a **cub**
- A baby sheep is called a **lamb**, **lambkin**, or **cosset**

## Some Male and Female Animal Terms:

- A male chicken is called a **rooster**

- A female chicken is called a **hen**
- A male deer is often called a **buck** or **stag**
- A female deer is often called a **doe**
- A baby male horse is called a **colt**
- A baby female horse is called a **filly**

## Words for Enclosures Containing Certain Animals:

- A large cage or enclosure for keeping birds in is called an **aviary**
- A place where bees are kept is called an **apiary**
- A place that bees construct as a locus of activity is called a **hive**
- A place that hornets or wasps construct as a locus of activity is called a **nest**
- A cage or pen confining poultry is called a **coop**
- An enclosure for pigs is a **sty** or **pen**

## Terms to Describe Category or Likeness of an Animal:

- The term **canine** concerns something of, relating to, or resembling a dog or dogs
- The term **feline** concerns something of, relating to, or resembling a cat or cats, or members of the cat family
- The term **vulpine** concerns something of, relating to, or resembling a fox or foxes
- The term **lupine** concerns something of, relating to, or resembling a wolf or wolves
- The term **porcine** concerns something of, relating to, affecting, or resembling a pig or pigs
- The term **bovine** concerns something of, relating to, or resembling a cattle (especially cows)
- The term **piscine** concerns something of, relating to, or resembling a fish or fish

## Some Miscellaneous Animal Terms:

- The process of change or transformation by which a caterpillar becomes a butterfly or a tadpole becomes a frog is called **metamorphosis**
- An informal term referring to a dead animal that has been hit by a vehicle (often on a highway or high-speed road) is called **road kill**
- The claw on a bird of prey is called a **talon**
- The needles on a porcupine used for self-defense are called **quills**
- A small horse is called a **pony**
- An animal with a backbone is called a **vertebrate**
- An animal lacking a backbone is called an **invertebrate**

## NEW WORDS

**plausible**
ˈplôzəbəl

**devoted**
diˈvōtid

**amble**
ˈambəl

**gale**
gāl

**crude**
krood

# Lesson 51

## A SUMMER ADVENTURE

It was sunny outside and perfect for a pleasant **amble** along the beach, so the young couple decided to go to the coast for the afternoon. Though they were **devoted** parents, they felt this beautiful weather provided the perfect opportunity to spend some time by themselves. Two hours later, they were finally walking down the narrow stony beach. Suddenly the clouds gathered; a strong **gale** and pouring rain followed seconds later. The couple ran and hid under a **crude** shelter made of fallen branches. It was **plausible** that the summer storm would be short; therefore, they kept their high spirits while looking at the water.

**Definitions:**    Try matching the words in the list with the appropriate definitions.  If you are stuck, check the glossary in the back of the book or the passage at the top of the page.

| | | | | |
|---|---|---|---|---|
| 1. | plausible | _____ | a. | to walk or move at a slow, relaxed pace |
| 2. | devoted | _____ | b. | very loving and loyal |
| 3. | amble | _____ | c. | an argument or statement that seems reasonable or logical |
| 4. | gale | _____ | d. | 1. in a natural or raw state; unrefined; 2.constructed in a rudimentary way; 3. (of a person) especially offensive or rude, especially in a sexual way |
| 5. | crude | _____ | e. | a very strong wind |

**Sentences:**    Try to use the words above in a sentence below.  Remember that a word ending may be changed or its figure of speech slightly altered.

6.    Kenneth _____ his way to the country club gate and greeted the guests.

7.    Gerald's _____ language alienated his superiors, who refused to work with him.

8.    It is difficult to guide a boat through a(n) _____: often a strong wind will cause a boat to capsize.

9.    Jake is so _____ to his career that he sleeps and showers in a room right above his restaurant.

10.    That James was late to work because his car broke down is indeed a(n) _____ excuse for his tardiness.

# Lesson 52

## THE TURNAROUND

The **cupidity** of the new company director would eventually **erode** the company's moral principles. Gradually, money became the sole motivating agent in everyone's actions. While the atmosphere had been **placid** and warm before, now there was a **thorough** turnaround in the employees' relationships. The company kept up the **fiction** that everything was going as usual, but soon clients could see deterioration in the quality of its products.

**Definitions:** Try matching the words in the list with the appropriate definitions. If you are stuck, check the glossary in the back of the book or the passage at the top of the page.

1. cupidity _____ a. prose literature in the form of novels that describes imaginary people and events
2. thorough _____ b. a person or animal not easily upset or excited; (of a place or stretch of water) calm and peaceful, with little movement or activity
3. placid _____ c. greed for money or possessions
4. fiction _____ d. to gradually wear away (usually of water, wind, or other natural elements)
5. erode _____ e. complete with regard to every detail

**Sentences:** Try to use the words above in a sentence below. Remember that a word ending may be changed or its figure of speech slightly altered.

6. That there were once unicorns in Asia is indeed _____: unicorns have never existed!
7. Though the waters on Kebo Lake are usually rough, today they are uncharacteristically _____.
8. Dr. Park did a(n) _____ job of critiquing my paper and provided detailed feedback on both my writing and its footnotes.
9. While having money is important, Laura's _____ made her friends think that it was the *raison d'être* of her existence.
10. Over time the Colorado River _____ land in Northern Arizona, thus helping form the Grand Canyon.

# Lesson 53

## THE QUASI GURU

### NEW WORDS

**concede**
kənˈsēd

**tact**
takt

**nonessential**
ˌnänəˈsenCHəl

**terrestrial**
təˈrestrēəl, -ˈresCHəl

**bide**
bīd

He was considered a highly spiritual man but, at the **terrestrial** level, he often showed a lack of **tact** and offended the people around him. His devotees would **bide** their time near him because they believed he was a holy man. They saw his insults as **nonessential** compared to the great wisdom that they believed he imparted to them. They would never **concede** that, in truth, he was simply a grumpy old man with some charisma and an inflated ego.

**Definitions:** Try matching the words in the list with the appropriate definitions. If you are stuck, check the glossary in the back of the book or the passage at the top of the page.

1. concede _____ a. not absolutely necessary
2. tact _____ b. 1. to admit that something is true or valid after first denying or resisting it; 2. to surrender or yield something that one possesses or desires
3. nonessential _____ c. sensitivity in dealing with others or with difficult issues
4. terrestrial _____ d. relating to the land or the Earth
5. bide _____ e. to remain or stay somewhere

**Sentences:** Try to use the words above in a sentence below. Remember that a word ending may be changed or its figure of speech slightly altered.

6. After a hard fought campaign, it was difficult for the losing candidate to _____ the election to her opponent.
7. Paul's lack of _____ has repulsed many of his friends, who have been personally insulted by his directness.
8. Humans are _____ creatures: they dwell and work on the land.
9. Green food coloring is a(n) _____ ingredient in the recipe to make mint ice cream.
10. Joanna _____ her time at the beach while her sister was selling tacos downtown.

# Lesson 54

## ATTEMPTING TO NARRATE A CRIME

The police asked the victim to **narrate** the crime. Unfortunately, it was so **odious** to the victim that he could hardly speak without crying. Remembering that night filled him with anger and **anxiety**. As he told his story, he put the **emphasis** on the intense emotional pain that he had to bear. There was a **consensus** among the police officers that the victim was too emotionally jarred at that moment to talk, so they waited a few days before interrogating him again.

**Definitions:**    Try matching the words in the list with the appropriate definitions. If you are stuck, check the glossary in the back of the book or the passage at the top of the page.

| | | | | | |
|---|---|---|---|---|---|
| 1. | anxiety | _____ | a. | a general agreement | |
| 2. | consensus | _____ | b. | special importance, value, or prominence given to something | |
| 3. | emphasis | _____ | c. | a feeling of worry, unease, or nervousness, typically about an imminent event or one with an uncertain outcome | |
| 4. | narrate | _____ | d. | extremely unpleasant; repulsive | |
| 5. | odious | _____ | e. | to give a spoken or written account of something | |

**Sentences:**    Try to use the words above in a sentence below. Remember that a word ending may be changed or its figure of speech slightly altered.

6.   If a charismatic person is chosen to _____ the tale, its message will resonate more potently with the audience.

7.   Leslie has a great fear of theme park rides, so it was no surprise that he had great _____ about getting in line to ride a giant roller coaster.

8.   There is a general _____ in America that getting a college education will aid one's career prospects.

9.   While some mathematics books choose to highlight drills and practice problems, the _____ of this one is on conceptual understanding.

10.  Many faculty members in the law school find the head secretary to be a disorganized and _____ person.

## NEW WORDS

**allay**
əˈlā

**animosity**
ˌanəˈmäsitē

**destitute**
ˈdestiˌt(y)oot

**catastrophe**
ˈkəˈtastrəfē

**proficient**
prəˈfiSHənt

# Lesson 55

## CHOOSING A PATH IN LIFE

Shanine lived in a poor neighborhood with many **destitute** children walking on the streets. The sight of their sad faces and torn clothes broke her heart. She often gave them food in order to **allay** their hunger. She felt a certain **animosity** in them, as if they didn't completely trust her. To her, that loss of childhood innocence was a **catastrophe**. She decided that when she goes to college, she will study social work and become more **proficient** at helping such children — this became her life goal.

**Definitions:**     Try matching the words in the list with the appropriate definitions. If you are stuck, check the glossary in the back of the book or the passage at the top of the page.

1.     allay     _____     a.     an event causing great and often sudden damage or suffering
2.     animosity     _____     b.     (of a fear, suspicion, or worry) to diminish or put at rest
3.     destitute     _____     c.     competent or skilled in doing or using something
4.     catastrophe _____     d.     lacking the basic necessities in life
5.     proficient     _____     e.     strong hostility

**Sentences:**     Try to use the words above in a sentence below. Remember that a word ending may be changed or its figure of speech slightly altered.

6.     Because Frieda had not saved any money during her career, she found herself almost _____ upon retirement.
7.     It is unfortunate when there is _____ between a child's parents during a divorce: often such harsh feelings can cause serious emotional damage to the child.
8.     Three tornadoes swept through town causing a great _____.
9.     If one is not _____ in the English language, it will be difficult to succeed at an American university.
10.     Unfortunately, Donna could to little to _____ Leslie's fear of heights: Leslie refused to go to the top of the skyscraper despite all of Donna's efforts.

# Lesson 56

## A BLEAK FUTURE

As his health was quickly deteriorating, the king became more lethargic and irritable. He dismissed his responsibilities as **banal** and tedious tasks, he often drifted in a fitful **doze** during the day, and he did not hesitate to **banish** those who opposed his decisions. Since there was no suitable inheritor to the throne, **domestic** violence between factions to gain political power was inevitable. The fate of the kingdom was placed in grave **jeopardy.**

## NEW WORDS

**domestic**
də'mestik

**banal**
'bānl, bə'nal, -'näl

**banish**
'baniSH

**doze**
dōz

**jeopardy**
'jepərdē

**Definitions:**     Try matching the words in the list with the appropriate definitions. If you are stuck, check the glossary in the back of the book or the passage at the top of the page.

| | | | | |
|---|---|---|---|---|
| 1. | domestic | _____ | a. | 1. of or relating to running a home or family relations; 2. existing or occurring inside a particular country |
| 2. | banal | _____ | b. | lacking in originality and thus being obvious or boring |
| 3. | banish | _____ | c. | to send someone away from a country or place as official punishment |
| 4. | doze | _____ | d. | to sleep lightly |
| 5. | jeopardy | _____ | e. | danger of loss, harm, or failure |

**Sentences:**     Try to use the words above in a sentence below. Remember that a word ending may be changed or its figure of speech slightly altered.

6. The queen _____ the traitor from her kingdom after he and his comrades plotted to kill her.

7. Telling high school graduates that they are the future of the world is a rather _____ statement.

8. I am more concerned with _____ issues such as tax rates and racial equality than with international politics.

9. Many Europeans enjoy taking a(n) _____ in the middle of the afternoon to refresh them for evening work.

10. Bertha's life was put in _____ when the brakes on her motorbike suddenly failed her.

## NEW WORDS

**yearn**
yərn

**facilitate**
fəˈsiliˌtāt

**fruitful**
ˈfro͞otfəl

**awkward**
ˈôkwərd

**boycott**
ˈboiˌkät

### DEFENDING ONE'S RIGHTS

Employees for the national airline have announced that they are going on strike following the company's **awkward** and unfair decision to cut salaries by 40% in response to the recent drop in revenue. Consequently, two airline workers' unions have convened to find a strategy defending rights to fair payment for the workers. The union delegates **yearn** to reach to an agreement that will **facilitate** a **fruitful** resolution to these problems. If such a resolution cannot be reached, chances are high that customers may **boycott** the airlines because of its unfair worker treatment.

**Definitions:**     Try matching the words in the list with the appropriate definitions. If you are stuck, check the glossary in the back of the book or the passage at the top of the page.

| | | | | |
|---|---|---|---|---|
| 1. | yearn | _____ | a. | producing much fruit, fertile; producing good or helpful results |
| 2. | facilitate | _____ | b. | 1. causing difficulty, hard to do or deal with; 2. causing or feeling embarrassment or inconvenience; 3. not smooth or grateful |
| 3. | fruitful | _____ | c. | to make an action or process easier |
| 4. | awkward | _____ | d. | (n.) a punitive ban that forbids relations with certain groups, cooperation with a policy, or the handling of goods; (v.) to withdraw from commercial or social relations with a country, organization, or person as punishment or protest |
| 5. | boycott | _____ | e. | to have an intense feeling of longing for something or someone, especially if one is separated from it |

**Sentences:**     Try to use the words above in a sentence below. Remember that a word ending may be changed or its figure of speech slightly altered.

6.     Unfortunately, I am unable to _____ in helping you transition into a new career as I lack both the skills and the time to commit.

7.     Many girls _____ to become princesses and live happily ever after.

8.     Often the best way to demonstrate against a company's abuses is to _____ that company's products.

9.     There was a(n) _____ silence when Meghan's fiancé let out a loud, stinky fart at the dinner table.

10.     It is not _____ to lament the past when such energy can be devoted to building an amazing future.

# Lesson 58

**LIFE CHANGES**

Jackson had tremendous **stamina**, so moving to a place by the ocean with a different climate did not bother him. At first he was fine with the **humidity** and the permanent sweating. However, he had a **penchant** for drinking and he felt extra dehydrated after a night out partying. He began to experience a tiredness that **debilitated** his ability to concentrate for long time periods. He was no longer able to focus on something as **trivial** as a brief newscast.

**Definitions:**     Try matching the words in the list with the appropriate definitions.  If you are stuck, check the glossary in the back of the book or the passage at the top of the page.

| | | | | |
|---|---|---|---|---|
| 1. | stamina | _____ | a. | a strong and habitual liking for something or tendency to do something |
| 2. | humidity | _____ | b. | concerning the amount of water vapor in the air |
| 3. | penchant | _____ | c. | 1. to make someone weak and infirm; 2. to hinder, delay, or weaken |
| 4. | debilitate | _____ | d. | of little value or importance; (of a person) concerned only with trifling or unimportant things |
| 5. | trivial | _____ | e. | the ability to sustain prolonged physical or mental effort |

**Sentences:**     Try to use the words above in a sentence below.  Remember that a word ending may be changed or its figure of speech slightly altered.

6.     I wish I had the _____ that I had twenty years ago; I do not think I could still run a marathon at my age.

7.     Kimberly always had a(n) _____ for cooking, so it is only natural that she has tried to establish herself as a chef in a luxury restaurant downtown.

8.     Understanding Einstein's Theory of Relativity is no _____ matter; the concepts involved are quite intricate and advanced.

9.     Unfortunately an automobile accident ten years ago left my uncle _____; that is why he occasionally needs a wheelchair.

10.     Rainforests are noted to have climates with high _____ because they have regular precipitation.

# NEW WORDS

**allege**
əˈlej

**abase**
əˈbās

**bulge**
bəlj

**adage**
ˈadij

**familial**
fəˈmilēəl, -ˈmilyəl

## CORRUPTION EXPOSED

His opponent sought to **allege** that Senator Sam took substantial sums of money in bribes and used his **familial** and political connections to buy his son a governmental job. Sam insisted that he would not **abase** himself by admitting a crime he did not commit. An investigation, however, soon confirmed the accusations. Meanwhile, his son also got caught shoplifting when an employee noticed an unusual **bulge** in his pocket. As the old **adage** goes, "Like father, like son" — both Sam and his son were imprisoned for their greed.

**Definitions:** Try matching the words in the list with the appropriate definitions. If you are stuck, check the glossary in the back of the book or the passage at the top of the page.

| | | | | |
|---|---|---|---|---|
| 1. | allege | _____ | a. | (n.) a rounded swelling or protuberance that distorts a flat surface; (v.) to swell or protrude to an unnatural or incongruous extent |
| 2. | abase | _____ | b. | to behave in such a way as to degrade or belittle someone |
| 3. | bulge | _____ | c. | a proverb or short statement expressing a general truth |
| 4. | adage | _____ | d. | of, relating to, or concerning a family and its members |
| 5. | familial | _____ | e. | to claim or assert that someone has done something illegal or wrong, typically without proof |

**Sentences:** Try to use the words above in a sentence below. Remember that a word ending may be changed or its figure of speech slightly altered.

6. Discussions concerning personal finances are more often than not _____ matters.

7. A(n) old _____ goes, "A penny saved is a penny earned."

8. It is easy to _____ that my landlord stole money out of my room because he is the only person I know with a key to the front door.

9. Typically when a woman is pregnant, one can recognize an obvious _____ in her stomach.

10. Despite being thrown out of graduate school, Oriana did not _____ her reputation with colleagues at other universities.

# Lesson 60

## THE MAN WITH A GUN

The **putrid** smell coming from the basement indicated that there was rotten meat below. It was against the law to kill animals in that mountainous region, and the police officer had a **legitimate** reason to check the smell. However, he remained **calm** and did not say a word. He saw that the owner of the house had a crazed look in his eyes; the owner looked unstable and was holding a gun. Caution, or perhaps **cowardice**, overcame the police officer and he backed away. The officer realized that government authorities needed to **reform** the law and do background checks on the people that want to buy a gun.

### NEW WORDS

**reform**
ri'fôrm

**legitimate**
li'jitəmit

**cowardice**
'kou-ərdəs

**calm**
kä(l)m

**putrid**
'pyootrid

**Definitions:** Try matching the words in the list with the appropriate definitions. If you are stuck, check the glossary in the back of the book or the passage at the top of the page.

1. reform _____ a. (adj.) conforming to the law or rules; (v.) to justify or make lawful

2. legitimate _____ b. (n.) the action of making changes in something (typically a social, political, or economic institution or practice) in order to improve it (v.) to make changes in something (typically a social, political, or economic institution or practice) in order to improve it

3. cowardice _____ c. (adj.) 1. (of a person) not showing signs of anger, nervousness, or other emotions, 2. pleasantly free from wind; (n.) 1. the absence of violent confrontational activity within a place or group; 2. the absence of wind; (v.) to make someone quiet; soothe

4. calm _____ d. lack of bravery

5. putrid _____ e. characteristic of rotting matter and having a foul smell

**Sentences:** Try to use the words above in a sentence below. Remember that a word ending may be changed or its figure of speech slightly altered.

6. One of my father's best attributes is that he is able to keep _____ in the midst of unsettling events.

7. After fifty successful years, the Italian restaurant is looking to _____ some of its business practices.

8. Elaine's _____ rendered her too timid to take risks and speak out.

9. It often can be tough to tell if a signature is _____ or is a forgery.

10. Because Brad did not empty his trash, a(n) _____ smell filled the room.

# Crossword Puzzle
## Lessons 51-60

ACROSS

1 (adj.) a person or animal not easily upset or excited; (of a place or stretch of water) calm and peaceful, with little movement or activity
4 (adj.) very loving and loyal
6 (adj.) 1. of or relating to running a home or family relations; 2. existing or occurring inside a particular country
8 (n.) prose literature in the form of novels that describes imaginary people and events
10 (n.) special importance, value, or prominence given to something
11 (v.) to behave in such a way as to degrade or belittle someone
13 (adj.) 1. to make someone weak and infirm; 2. to hinder, delay, or weaken
15 (n.) a feeling of worry, unease, or nervousness, typically about an imminent event or one with an uncertain outcome
18 (adj.) an argument or statement that seems reasonable or logical
19 (adj.) 1. (of a person) not showing signs of anger, nervousness, or other emotions, 2. pleasantly free from wind; (n.) 1. the absence of violent confrontational activity within a place or group; 2.

the absence of wind; (v.) to make someone quiet; soothe
20 (v.) to claim or assert that someone has done something illegal or wrong, typically without proof

DOWN

2 (adj.) 1. causing difficulty, hard to do or deal with; 2. causing or feeling embarrassment or inconvenience; 3. not smooth or grateful
3 (adj.) conforming to the law or rules; (v.) to justify or make lawful
5 (n.) a strong and habitual liking for something or tendency to do something
7 (n.) an event causing great and often sudden damage or suffering
9 (v.) (of a fear, suspicion, or worry) to diminish or put at rest
12 (v.) 1. to admit that something is true or valid after first denying or resisting it; 2. to surrender or yield something that one possesses
14 (adj.) producing much fruit, fertile; producing good or helpful results
16 (n.) sensitivity in dealing with others or with difficult issues
17 (v.) to send someone away from a country or place as official punishment

# Vocabulary Review
## Lessons 51-60

**Directions:** Match each word with its best approximate definition. Note that definitions are not necessarily repeated verbatim from the lesson exercises.

| | | | | | |
|---|---|---|---|---|---|
| 1. | amble | _____ | a. | not absolutely necessary |
| 2. | gale | _____ | b. | greed for possessions or money |
| 3. | cupidity | _____ | c. | decaying or rotting and giving of a foul smell |
| 4. | thorough | _____ | d. | to have an intense feeling of longing for something, often that one has been separated from |
| 5. | nonessential | _____ | e. | to give a spoken or written account of something |
| 6. | terrestrial | _____ | f. | concerning the amount of water vapor present in the air |
| 7. | consensus | _____ | g. | lacking the basic necessities of life |
| 8. | narrate | _____ | h. | to walk or move slowly and with relaxation |
| 9. | animosity | _____ | i. | the ability to sustain mental or physical effort |
| 10. | destitute | _____ | j. | lacking in originality; boring |
| 11. | banal | _____ | k. | exhibiting a lack of bravery |
| 12. | jeopardy | _____ | l. | on, of, or relating to the earth |
| 13. | yearn | _____ | m. | a general agreement |
| 14. | facilitate | _____ | n. | strong hostility |
| 15. | stamina | _____ | o. | concerning a family and its members |
| 16. | humidity | _____ | p. | to make an action or process easy or easier |
| 17. | adage | _____ | q. | complete with regard to all details |
| 18. | familial | _____ | r. | a proverb or short saying expressing a general truth |
| 19. | cowardice | _____ | s. | a very strong wind |
| 20. | putrid | _____ | t. | danger of failure, harm, or loss |

# Word Roots: Unit 6

## ROOTS AND THEIR MEANINGS

| | | | |
|---|---|---|---|
| **dys:** | faulty, bad | **mal:** | bad |
| **homo:** | same | **mis:** | wrong, bad |
| **hetero:** | different | **vers/vert:** | to turn |
| **pan:** | everywhere, all | **ab/abs:** | away from, against |

## Here are a few examples of some words that use the above roots:

dystopia: an imagined place where everything is bad; the opposite of a utopia
homophone: each of two words having the same pronunciation, but with different meanings and spellings
heterosexual: a person sexually attracted to people of the opposite sex
pantheon: all the gods of a religion collectively; a building where the dead of a nation are collectively honored
maladjusted: failing to adapt to the demands of a normal social environment
misanthrope: a person who dislikes mankind and who shuns society
vertigo: a sensation of dizziness or loss of balance, often when looking down from heights
aberration: an anomaly or departure from what is normally expected

## Now try to fill in the table below by finding the appropriate root(s) and interpreting the meaning of each word:

| Word | Root(s) | Guessed Meaning | Actual Meaning |
|---|---|---|---|
| abstain | | | |
| dysfunction | | | |
| homogeneous | | | |
| heterodox | | | |
| malign | | | |
| panacea | | | |
| averse | | | |

| | | | |
|---|---|---|---|
| misnomer | | | |
| heterogeneous | | | |
| pandemonium | | | |
| dyslexic | | | |
| maladroit | | | |
| mistake | | | |
| absolve | | | |
| abnegate | | | |

## NEW WORDS

**somber**
ˈsämbər

**tardy**
ˈtärdē

**subdue**
səbˈd(y)oo

**oath**
ōTH

**cultivate**
ˈkəltəˌvāt

# Lesson 61

### LIFE'S TRIBULATIONS

Nothing could **subdue** Ronald's pain after he was fired from his job. He walked around with a **somber** expression and became **tardy** in doing even the simplest household tasks. Sometimes, instead of responding to a question, he would just utter an **oath** and become silent again. The rest of Ronald's family had to **cultivate** patience in order to deal with his new behavior, but soon he became too unbearable for everyone and they asked him to move out.

**Definitions:** Try matching the words in the list with the appropriate definitions. If you are stuck, check the glossary in the back of the book or the passage at the top of the page.

| | | | | | |
|---|---|---|---|---|---|
| 1. | somber | _____ | a. | a solemn promise, often invoking a divine witness, regarding one's future behavior or action |
| 2. | tardy | _____ | b. | to overcome, calm, or bring under control (a feeling or person) |
| 3. | subdue | _____ | c. | dark or dull in color and tone; gloomy |
| 4. | oath | _____ | d. | 1. to prepare and use land for crops or gardening; 2. to acquire and develop a quality, skill, or sentiment |
| 5. | cultivate | _____ | e. | delaying or delayed beyond the expected time; late |

**Sentences:** Try to use the words above in a sentence below. Remember that a word ending may be changed or its figure of speech slightly altered.

6. Attending a funeral is typically a(n) _____ affair.

7. Jerome is often _____ to class; he usually disrupts lecture when he arrives.

8. In the United States, a new President initially must take a(n) _____ before being able to exercise his or her power.

9. Marla has the amazing ability to _____ a bunch of rowdy kindergarteners and to have them listen to her.

10. Cressida enjoys _____ plants in her new vegetable garden.

93

# Lesson 62

## SERIAL KILLERS

There seem to be certain similarities in the behavior of serial killers. They often **foster** feelings of intense hate towards a certain community, occasionally accompanied by **furious** angry outbursts. They can be **presumptuous** and feel that the world owes them something. They are capable of committing **heinous** murders and can exhibit **brazen** indifference towards what a victim's relatives say in court. The mentality of such people remains a mystery to many people, which may be the reason for a growing number of documentaries and television shows on the subject.

**Definitions:**    Try matching the words in the list with the appropriate definitions.  If you are stuck, check the glossary in the back of the book or the passage at the top of the page.

| | | | | |
|---|---|---|---|---|
| 1. | foster | _____ | a. | (concerning a person and his or her behavior) failing to observe the limits of what is deemed appropriate |
| 2. | presumptuous | _____ | b. | a person, wrongful act, or crime that is utterly odious or wicked |
| 3. | furious | _____ | c. | extremely angry |
| 4. | heinous | _____ | d. | to encourage or promote the development of something; to develop a feeling or idea within oneself |
| 5. | brazen | _____ | e. | bold and without shame |

**Sentences:**    Try to use the words above in a sentence below.  Remember that a word ending may be changed or its figure of speech slightly altered.

6.    Diana was _____ enough to raise her hand in an auditorium of a thousand people and ask the famous movie director for an internship.

7.    Mario acted _____ when he assumed his student was not doing work before checking in with the student first.

8.    When Marilyn's mom heard that her daughter had absconded and gotten married, she was _____.

9.    Lynching, slavery, and segregation are among the many _____ actions plaguing the history of the American South.

10.    Providing young children with good mentors and books is an important part of _____ their education.

## NEW WORDS

**pariah**
pəˈrīə

**sovereign**
ˈsäv(ə)rən

**impose**
imˈpōz

**pester**
ˈpestər

**ensnare**
enˈsner

# Lesson 63

## FUELED BY NATIONALISM

After the war, the country finally escaped from the grip of its colonizer and became a **sovereign** nation. Most celebrated the nation's hard-won independence, but any individual who once fawned over the enemy was treated like a **pariah** and traitor in the community. While the local citizens would often bully and **pester** such individuals with disparaging remarks, the government also **imposed** a stricter control on them. From limiting their property rights to banning them from holding important positions, the new order slowly **ensnared** those who worked for the past colonial government.

**Definitions:**     Try matching the words in the list with the appropriate definitions. If you are stuck, check the glossary in the back of the book or the passage at the top of the page.

| | | | | |
|---|---|---|---|---|
| 1. | pariah | _____ | a. | an outcast |
| 2. | sovereign | _____ | b. | 1. to force something unwelcome or unfamiliar to be accepted or put into place; 2. to take advantage of someone by demanding their attention or commitment |
| 3. | impose | _____ | c. | to trouble or annoy someone with frequent interruptions or requests |
| 4. | pester | _____ | d. | to catch in or as in a trap |
| 5. | ensnare | _____ | e. | (adj.) possessing supreme or ultimate power; (n.) a supreme ruler, especially a monarch |

**Sentences:**     Try to use the words above in a sentence below. Remember that a word ending may be changed or its figure of speech slightly altered.

6.     Ellen _____ the local handyman almost daily by demanding that he look at problems in her home.

7.     The pretty girl's charisma was not enough to _____ Harry into dating her.

8.     Attempting to _____ a tax on cigarettes is one approach to helping curb a smoking epidemic.

9.     The Queen of England is able to rule over her subjects because it is her _____ right to do so.

10.    Pamela did not dress like the other people in her department, and so she was treated like a(n) _____ at many events.

# Lesson 64

## THE SMALL PROVINCIAL THEATER

When the actress accidentally stumbled and fell, the theater broke out in **boisterous** laughter. The audience showed no **compassion** for her; in fact, they welcomed the mishap. After a hard day of work in the factories, the men in the audience could not **omit** the chance to have a laugh at her expense. In fact, whenever they did not like something in the play, the men would hurl **acrid** remarks at the cast. Such casual behavior was certainly **repugnant** to the spirit of theater performances in the city; however, it was the norm in this small industrial town.

## NEW WORDS

**boisterous**
ˈboist(ə)rəs

**omit**
ōˈmit

**acrid**
ˈakrid

**repugnant**
riˈpəgnənt

**compassion**
kəmˈpaSHən

**Definitions:** Try matching the words in the list with the appropriate definitions. If you are stuck, check the glossary in the back of the book or the passage at the top of the page.

| | | | |
|---|---|---|---|
| 1. | boisterous _____ | a. | having an irritatingly strong and unpleasant taste or smell |
| 2. | omit _____ | b. | 1. (of a person, event, or occasion) energetic, noisy, and cheerful; 2. (of wind, weather, or water) wild or stormy |
| 3. | acrid _____ | c. | to leave out or exclude, either intentionally or deliberately |
| 4. | repugnant _____ | d. | extremely distasteful; unacceptable |
| 5. | compassion _____ | e. | sympathetic pity and concern for the suffering and misfortunes of others |

**Sentences:** Try to use the words above in a sentence below. Remember that a word ending may be changed or its figure of speech slightly altered.

6. Always the life of the party, Curran can turn a subdued atmosphere into a(n) _____ one.

7. Most educators should be strict with their students, but it is also important to be stern with _____: criticism should be balanced with an equal amount of care.

8. The lemon chicken looks excellent, but its taste is a bit _____.

9. Many see picking one's nose in public as a(n) _____ habit.

10. If you _____ these ideas from your paper, the strength of your thesis will be greatly diminished.

## NEW WORDS

**wither**
ˈwiTHər

**entertain**
ˌentərˈtān

**indulgent**
inˈdəljənt

**instance**
ˈinstəns

**zenith**
ˈzēniTH

Jack and Jill went to a remote mountain resort to witness the **zenith** of the North Star away from city lights. No one could possibly accuse this young couple of being **indulgent** with their money. Their luxury trip epitomizes an **instance** when ambitious, hard working recent college graduates chose not to let their passion for astronomy **wither** soon after graduation. On the contrary, they chose to **entertain** no thought of giving up on their sky gazing passion. Instead, they rather took it to new heights. Literally.

**Definitions:**     Try matching the words in the list with the appropriate definitions. If you are stuck, check the glossary in the back of the book or the passage at the top of the page.

|     |          |            |     |                                                                                                              |
|-----|----------|------------|-----|--------------------------------------------------------------------------------------------------------------|
| 1.  | wither   | _____ | a.  | the highest point reached by a celestial or other object                                                     |
| 2.  | entertain| _____ | b.  | 1. to provide someone with amusement or enjoyment; 2. to give attention or consideration to an idea, suggestion, or feeling |
| 3.  | indulgent| _____ | c.  | having or indicating a tendency to be overly generous or lenient with someone                                |
| 4.  | instance | _____ | d.  | (of a plant) to become dry and shriveled; (of a person) to become shrunken or wrinkled from age or disease; to cease to flourish |
| 5.  | zenith   | _____ | e.  | an example or single occurrence of something                                                                 |

**Sentences:**     Try to use the words above in a sentence below. Remember that a word ending may be changed or its figure of speech slightly altered.

6.     It appears that the sun is at its _____ at high noon.

7.     Comedies are meant to _____ their viewers, for it is important to laugh in life.

8.     Uncle Morris is really _____: every time I come in town to visit him, he takes me to all of my favorite candy stores and shopping malls.

9.     After several days of not watering my yucca plant, its leaves began to
       _____.

10.    I cannot think of a single _____ when my mother failed to be responsible as a parent.

# Lesson 66

## THE ELDER FROM THE MOUNTAINS

The old man had a **luminous** presence: he seemed so joyful and light, almost out of this world. Many people came to the monastery to see him. He was **hospitable** and gave everyone his attention. His presence seemed to **encompass** everything and everyone. Even though big crowds of people came to visit him from all over the world, there was nothing **pretentious** about him. He remained humble and lived in the same small room with **scant** belongings: just a small bed, a blanket, and a few pieces of clothing.

**Definitions:** Try matching the words in the list with the appropriate definitions. If you are stuck, check the glossary in the back of the book or the passage at the top of the page.

1. luminous _____ 
2. hospitable _____ 
3. encompass _____ 
4. scant _____ 
5. pretentious _____ 

a. friendly and welcoming to guests; (of an environment) pleasant and favorable for living in

b. attempting to impress by assuming greater importance, talent, culture, or credibility than one actually possesses

c. small or insufficient in quantity or amount

d. to surround or enclose within; to include comprehensively

e. full of light; shedding light; bright or shining, especially in the dark

**Sentences:** Try to use the words above in a sentence below. Remember that a word ending may be changed or its figure of speech slightly altered.

6. Usually in the spring when the snow melts and the storms subside, New England's weather becomes increasingly _____.

7. Topics to be discussed at the policy brunch this week _____ a variety of humanitarian issues ranging from child trafficking problems to nutrition and gender equality.

8. My neighbor praised the new pub for its generous portions, but I found my meal there to be quite _____.

9. At deep depths in the ocean there can be found many _____ animals brightening the waters proximate to them.

10. The _____ vixen sauntered into the room as if she owned the venue.

## NEW WORDS

**progressive**
prəˈgresiv

**prudish**
ˈproodiSH

**dissonance**
ˈdisənəns

**sanitary**
ˈsaniˌterē

**replica**
ˈreplikə

### SCHOOL CHANGES

The new school principal hoped to make his institution a much more **progressive** place. Among the changes he wanted to implement was to let students wear clothing of their choice in lieu of school uniforms. Yet pushing to change this policy stirred up **dissonance** between the school's **prudish**, conservative faculty and its newer liberal teachers. The principal also wanted to turn the squalid school cafeteria into a viable study space in late afternoons. He presented a **replica** of the local community college cafeteria space at the last faculty meeting to serve as a model for his vision. Implementing such changes, he asserted, would create not only a better educational environment, but also a more **sanitary** one.

**Definitions:** Try matching the words in the list with the appropriate definitions. If you are stuck, check the glossary in the back of the book or the passage at the top of the page.

1. progressive _____ a. of or relating to conditions affecting health or hygiene

2. prudish _____ b. having the tendency to be easily shocked by matters related to sex or nudity

3. dissonance _____ c. lack of harmony between two or more musical notes; a tension resulting from a combination of two or more unsuitable elements

4. sanitary _____ d. an exact copy or model of something, often on a smaller scale

5. replica _____ e. 1. developing in stages; proceeding step by step; 2. favoring or implementing social reform or new, liberal ideas

**Sentences:** Try to use the words above in a sentence below. Remember that a word ending may be changed or its figure of speech slightly altered.

6. Ideas such as homosexual marriage were considered to be _____ in the 1960s.

7. The _____ between the two professors only grew worse after one claimed that the other's work was plagiarized.

8. If restaurants do not keep their kitchens in _____ condition, the Board of Health may come and shut them down.

9. My aunt has such a(n) _____ attitude: she yelled at me because I was reading a fashion magazine with some provocative photos in it.

10. The Queens Museum has a famous _____ of Manhattan on display.

# Lesson 68

**BLIND BELIEF**

A **preponderance** of people in the kingdom believed that the origins of the new king were **sacred**. After all, the head priest had convinced them that the new king was a divine man. The people had no doubt that the newcomer would **accede** to their requests that he assume the throne. Just the sight of his glamorous attire and his golden scepter would **stupefy** them. They believed that the new king could **evoke** myriad divine powers with his golden scepter and were mortally afraid of him.

## NEW WORDS

**sacred**
ˈsākrid

**preponderance**
priˈpändərəns

**accede**
akˈsēd

**evoke**
iˈvōk

**stupefy**
ˈst(y)oopəˌfī

**Definitions:** Try matching the words in the list with the appropriate definitions. If you are stuck, check the glossary in the back of the book or the passage at the top of the page.

1.  sacred _____ a. to assent or agree to a request, demand, or treaty
2.  preponderance _____ b. 1. religious rather than secular; 2. something connected with God or the gods and thus worthy of veneration; 3. regarded with great reverence and respect
3.  accede _____ c. the fact or quality of being great in number, quantity, extent, or importance
4.  evoke _____ d. to bring or call to mind; to elicit a response; to invoke a spirit or deity
5.  stupefy _____ e. to astonish and shock, often to the point of being unable to think or act properly

**Sentences:** Try to use the words above in a sentence below. Remember that a word ending may be changed or its figure of speech slightly altered.

6.  The Torah is considered to be a(n) _____ object in the Jewish tradition.
7.  It was difficult to get my parents to _____ to my arrangement to spend spring break in the Bahamas.
8.  The eerie music at the beginning of the play _____ a sense of fright that is intended to last throughout the performance.
9.  Albert noted that there was a(n) _____ of sugar in his aunt's cake; it tasted far too sweet for his liking.
10. Harris was _____ when he heard that his sister's boyfriend was a prince.

# NEW WORDS

**process**
ˈpräˌses, ˈpräsəs, ˈprō-

**contempt**
kənˈtem(p)t

**eminent**
ˈemənənt

**mischief**
ˈmisCHif

**stolid**
ˈstälid

# Lesson 69

## THE REBEL

During the legal **process**, Jason had a **stolid** expression in his face, as if nothing mattered to him. He knew that painting the teacher's car was not merely **mischief** and that he had to face the consequences. At the same time, he was barely trying to hide his **contempt** for both the legal system and for the teacher. An **eminent** prankster at his school, Jason was known for his disdain for authority and for his rebellious views about social systems.

**Definitions:**     Try matching the words in the list with the appropriate definitions. If you are stuck, check the glossary in the back of the book or the passage at the top of the page.

1.   process   _____      a.   1. a feeling that a person is beneath consideration, deserving scorn, or unworthy; 2. a disregard for something that should be taken into account

2.   contempt   _____     b.   characterizing one who is calm and showing little emotion

3.   eminent   _____      c.   (n.) series of actions or steps taken in order to achieve a particular end; (v.) to perform a series of mechanical or chemical operations on something in order to change or preserve it

4.   mischief   _____     d.   playful behavior often involved in troublemaking and usually exhibited by children; playfulness intended to tease, mock, and create trouble; harm or trouble caused by something

5.   stolid   _____       e.   characterizing a person who is famous or respected within a certain field or profession

**Sentences:**     Try to use the words above in a sentence below. Remember that a word ending may be changed or its figure of speech slightly altered.

6.   René Descartes (1596-1650) is heralded by scholars as a(n) _____ mathematician in early modern Europe.

7.   The child got into _____ to see how far he could push social norms.

8.   I have nothing but _____ for the people who stole my computer.

9.   Grief is a(n) _____: it takes time to make peace with another's passing.

10.   Dave is a(n) _____ man who did not even cry at his father's funeral.

# Lesson 70

## STAYING TRUE TO YOURSELF

After the **massive** success of his book, the writer was approached by **inquisitive** television producers. They asked him a **variety** of questions, but their main concern was whether he would be willing to turn the book into a movie. They wanted to know if he would **tailor** the plot to a sensation-hungry audience and change some aspects of the original story. The writer agreed to do so, but only if the television producers left him $500,000 as **collateral** for his intellectual property. The writer, however, ultimately declined their offers and declared his intention to stay true to the original narrative.

**Definitions:** Try matching the words in the list with the appropriate definitions. If you are stuck, check the glossary in the back of the book or the passage at the top of the page.

| | | | | |
|---|---|---|---|---|
| 1. | massive | _____ | a. | something pledged as security for repayment of a loan |
| 2. | inquisitive | _____ | b. | (n.) a person whose occupation is to adjust clothing (suits, pants, jackets) to fit individual customers; (v.) 1. to make clothes fit individual customers; 2. to make or adapt for a particular purpose or person |
| 3. | collateral | _____ | c. | the quality of being different or diverse; the absence of sameness; lacking homogeneity |
| 4. | tailor | _____ | d. | curious and asking many questions |
| 5. | variety | _____ | e. | exceptionally large, heavy, solid, or important |

**Sentences:** Try to use the words above in a sentence below. Remember that a word ending may be changed or its figure of speech slightly altered.

6. Because Peter did not have money to pay his mortgage last month, he offered his landlord his designer watch as _____.

7. It is important to have a good _____ to adjust your pants; if you don't they will not fit you well.

8. The moon is a(n) _____ body that orbits the earth.

9. There are a(n) _____ of reasons why I do not like my stepmother: she is cruel, she does not speak to me, and she does not value education.

10. Many scientists believe that macaque monkeys are exceptionally intelligent because of their _____ nature.

# Word Search
## Lessons 41-50

```
O M Y  M N Y A E S Y  G R D S E  M T
T Z Q D P S  G C K T O Z M '  J Y I
M G M Z  G E  G S  G K Q Y  G V E B F
S S S L X S Z O M F E V D Y T B C
K S K N V L S X M M B  G '  Y F J Z
B M D D Q A D A T S S Y '  C I Y Y
O T Y Y C Z E E O E E  G T T C T T
E '  G E M G A  G M B M M M E O T O
K D B M A  G L T O T D V T S E E B
D T K B Y  G D D M S B N A H T T E
K O L O P K L Z E D D N C X F W O
S I W E S X D D S S T P Y L T '  E
Q H A E L S B X T M H F L H Z B B
B D Y O T Z W E C E B I O I V Q F
```

1 (adj.) dart or dizzbn cozor and yonef l zoo, u
; (n.) a soze, n qro, bsemowyen bn2otbnl a
db2bne g bynessmrel ardbnl oneps vi yi re
weha2bor or acybon

x (2.) yo encoi ral e or qro, oye yhe
de2ezoq, eny ovso, eyhbnl f yo de2ezoq a
veezbnl or bdea g byhbn onesezv

3 (adj.) (concernbnl a qerson and hbs or her
weha2bor) vabbnl yo owser2e yhe zb bys ov
g hay bs dee, ed aqqroqrbaye

k (adj.) qossessbnl si qre, e or i zyb aye
qog erf (n.) a si qre, e ri zermesqecbazu a
, onarch

4 (2.) yo yroi wze or annou so, eone g byh
vre6i eny bnyerri qybons or re6i esys

5 (adj.) 1. (ova qersonme2enymor occasbon)
enerl eybcmmobsumand cheervi zf ; . (ov
g bndmg eayhermor g ayer) g bd or syor, u

7 (n.) su, qayheybc qbyu and concern vor yhe
si werbnl and , bsvoryi nes ovoyhers

8 (2.) 1. yo qro2bde so, eone g byh
a, i se, eny or enjou, enyf ; . yo l b2e
ayyenybon or consbderaybon yo an bdeam
si l l esybonmor veezbnl

10 (n.) an e9a, qze or sbnl ze occi rrence ov
so, eyhbnl

11 (adj.) vi zzovzb hyf sheddbnl zb hyf wrbl hy or

shbnbnl mesqecbazu bn yhe dart

1; (adj.) vrbendzu and gezco, bnl yo l i esysf
(ovan en2bron, eny) qzeasany and
va2orawze vor zb2bnl bn

1x (adj.) 1. de2ezoqbnl bn syal esf qroceedbnl
syeq wu syeqf ; . va2orbnl or b, qze, enybnl
socbazrevor, or neg mzowerazbdeas

13 (adj.) ha2bnl yhe yendencu yo we easbu
shocyed wu, ayyers rezayed yo se9 or ni dbyu

1k (adj.) 1. rezb bbi s rayher yhan seci zarf ; .
so, eyhbnl connecyed g byh ' od or yhe
l ods and yhi s g oryhu ov 2enerayonf x.
rel arded g byh l reay re2erence and resqecy

14 (2.) yo wrbnl or cazzy o, bndf yo ezbcby a
resqonsef yo bn2oye a sqbrby or debyu

15 (n.) 1. a veezbnl yhaya qerson bs weneayh
consbderaybonmdeser2bnl scornmor
i ng oryhuf ; . a dbsrel ard vor so, eyhbnl
yhay shoi zd we yayen bnyo accoi ny

17 (adj.) characyerbbbnl one g ho bs caz, m
deqendawze and shog bnl zbyyze, oybon

18 (adj.) ci rbobi s and astbnl , anu 6i esybons

; 0 (n.) a qerson g hose occi qaybon bs yo
adji sycbzoyhbnl (si bysmqanysmjacteys) yo vby
bndb2bdi azci syo, ersf (2.) 1. yo, aye
cazoyhes vby bndb2bdi azci syo, ersf ; . yo
, aye or adaqy vor a qaryboci zar qi rqose or
qerson
```

103
```

# Vocabulary Review
## Lessons 61-70

**Directions: Match each word with its best approximate definition. Note that definitions are not necessarily repeated verbatim from the lesson exercises.**

1. tardy _____    a. concerning conditions related to health or hygiene

2. cultivate _____    b. an outcast

3. furious _____    c. extremely angry

4. brazen _____    d. small or insufficient quantity

5. pariah _____    e. to surround and enclose within; to include comprehensively

6. ensnare _____    f. playful misbehavior or troublemaking, often from children

7. acrid _____    g. catch in or as in a trap

8. repugnant _____    h. to raise or grow (especially plants); to acquire and develop

9. indulgent _____    i. to assent or agree to a demand, request, or treaty

10. zenith _____    j. having a bitter or unpleasant taste or smell

11. encompass _____    k. bold and without shame

12. scant _____    l. extremely distasteful; unacceptable

13. sanitary _____    m. being great in quality, number, or importance

14. replica _____    n. exceptionally large and heavy or solid

15. preponderance _____    o. the highest point reached by a celestial or other object

16. accede _____    p. having a tendency to be too generous with someone

17. eminent _____    q. a person who is famous and respected within his or her profession

18. mischief _____    r. something pledged as repayment for a loan, to be forfeited in case of default

19. massive _____    s. delaying or being delayed beyond the expected time

20. collateral _____    t. an exact copy or model of something, often on a smaller scale

# Word Roots: Unit 7

## ROOTS AND THEIR MEANINGS

| | | | |
|---|---|---|---|
| neo/nov: | new | derm: | skin |
| carn: | flesh | equ(i): | equal |
| extra: | beyond, outside | anti: | against, opposite |

**Here are a few examples of some words that use the above roots:**

| | |
|---|---|
| neophyte: | a novice, a beginner |
| carnage: | the killing of a large number of people |
| extraterrestrial: | from beyond the earth or its atmosphere |
| dermatologist: | a doctor who diagnoses and treats skin disorders |
| equivalent: | equal in value, amount, or function |
| antisocial: | not wanting the company of other people |

**Now try to fill in the table below by finding the appropriate root(s) and interpreting the meaning of each word:**

| Word | Root(s) | Guessed Meaning | Actual Meaning |
|---|---|---|---|
| equanimity | | | |
| carnal | | | |
| extraordinary | | | |
| equivocate | | | |
| reincarnation | | | |
| dermal | | | |
| antithetical | | | |
| extravagant | | | |
| novice | | | |
| antithesis | | | |
| innovate | | | |

# Lesson 71

## THE NIGHT BEFORE THE BATTLE

The knights visited a **seer**, hoping that she would be able to foretell the future of the battle. They were **incredulous** by nature, however, the fear of the impending fight made them less skeptical. The seer stared into her magic ball and told them that they needed to first attack the **sentry** at the castle gate. At the same time, she seemed to **insinuate** that the knights would lose the battle. Driven by anger, the knights told the seer that her vision was **preposterous** and that they would win the fight under all circumstances.

**Definitions:** Try matching the words in the list with the appropriate definitions. If you are stuck, check the glossary in the back of the book or the passage at the top of the page.

1.  preposterous _____      a.  absurd or ridiculous; contrary to common sense
2.  insinuate _____         b.  a person who is able to see what the future holds
3.  sentry _____            c.  to suggest or hint at (something bad or reprehensible) in an unpleasant way
4.  incredulous _____       d.  a soldier stationed to keep guard over a place
5.  seer _____              e.  a person who is unable or unwilling to believe something

**Sentences:** Try to use the words above in a sentence below. Remember that a word ending may be changed or its figure of speech slightly altered.

6.  It is _____ to believe that someone with no knowledge of a foreign language could become fluent in that language in one day.
7.  Two _____ guarded the gate to the palace that I hoped to pass through.
8.  Ingrid was _____ when she saw that she had failed all of her midterm exams.
9.  Willy's boss tried to _____ that his colleagues did not respect him, but such communication fell on deaf ears.
10. Only a(n) _____ can know for sure whether I will live to be one hundred years old.

# Lesson 72

## NEW WORDS

**expenditure**
ik'spendiCHər

**smite**
smīt

**onus**
'ōnəs

**statute**
'staCHoot

**chaff**
CHaf

### DRAMA AT WORK

A key **statute** of the organization prohibited many of Michael's business expenses. About half of his business **expenditure** covered lavish personal hotel and phone bills. When confronted by the board of directors about this matter, Michael tried to place the **onus** of the blame on his personal assistant, who he claimed was not a responsible person. Such accusations would **smite** the assistant's reputation. Ultimately the assistant was terminated, likely because Michael was regarded as an honest, responsible worker. In fact, many of his co-workers liked to **chaff** him for staying at work late. Thus, the assistant felt that his boss blamed him unjustly for his own carelessness.

**Definitions:** Try matching the words in the list with the appropriate definitions. If you are stuck, check the glossary in the back of the book or the passage at the top of the page.

1. expenditure _____     a.  a written law passed by a legislative body; a rule of an organization or institution
2. smite _____     b.  (n.) a heavy blow with a weapon or from the hand; (v.) 1. to strike with a firm blow; 2. to affect severely
3. onus _____     c.  the action of spending funds
4. statute _____     d.  used to refer to something that is one's duty or responsibility
5. chaff _____     e.  to tease

**Sentences:** Try to use the words above in a sentence below. Remember that a word ending may be changed or its figure of speech slightly altered.

6. Most people's basic monthly _____ are on rent and food.
7. The boys joked and _____ with each other about my asking a supermodel on a date.
8. The leader of the rebel army prayed to the gods that divine intervention would _____ their enemies.
9. Often parents bear the _____ of accountability for their children's behavior.
10. In early 2015, Congress was looking to repeal a(n) _____ declaring it illegal to curse in front of women and children.

# Lesson 73

## THE OLD SAGE

Everyone revered the old **sage**. His reputation was **untainted**, as his actions were always regarded as noble and unassuming. Often the look in his eyes would **express** boundless compassion for all beings. He also seemed to possess much **brawn** despite his incredibly advanced age. His name had a positive **connotation** in everyone's recollection: all of the town folk admired him and looked up to him.

**Definitions:** Try matching the words in the list with the appropriate definitions. If you are stuck, check the glossary in the back of the book or the passage at the top of the page.

1. express _____ a. (adj.) operating at high speed; (n.) a rapid moving vehicle or delivery service; (v.) 1. to convey a thought or feeling in words or by gestures and conduct; 2. to send quickly or at high speed

2. brawn _____ b. (adj.) wise; (n.) a profoundly wise (and often old) person

3. connotation _____ c. physical strength (in contrast to intelligence)

4. sage _____ d. an idea or feeling that a word evokes in addition to its literal meaning

5. untainted _____ e. not contaminated or polluted

**Sentences:** Try to use the words above in a sentence below. Remember that a word ending may be changed or its figure of speech slightly altered.

6. It is important to _____ one's feelings eloquently and clearly so that others can comprehend them.

7. Shayna may be the brains behind the operation, but it would not succeed without Douglas' _____ and sheer power.

8. The word "lazy" generally bears a negative _____ because it is associated with a lack of desire to do anything, which is not perceived as positive.

9. Often grandparents are good sources for _____ advice: having lived for quite some time, they know best about how to handle many circumstances.

10. Because of its distance from the metropolis, rural Clarkville remained largely _____ by air pollution and toxins produced in the big city.

## NEW WORDS

**nutritious**
n(y)oo'triSHəs

**brash**
braSH

**forestall**
fôr'stôl

**diminish**
di'miniSH

**phobia**
'fōbēə

Martin's fear of leaving the house after his mother's death turned into a **phobia**. He would sit in his room and rely on his older sister, Amy, for food. Amy tried to alleviate his fears and brought him **nutritious** meals in order to keep him healthy. Despite Amy's help, sometimes Martin made **brash** and rude remarks toward her. He was scared and angry at the whole world. Amy felt that her efforts to help him could not **forestall** his anger. However, Martin's hostility did not **diminish** her resolution to help him overcome their mother's death.

**Definitions:** Try matching the words in the list with the appropriate definitions. If you are stuck, check the glossary in the back of the book or the passage at the top of the page.

1. nutritious _____    a. to prevent an event or action from happening by taking advance action; an act to delay

2. brash _____    b. an extreme or irrational fear of or aversion to something

3. forestall _____    c. to make or become less

4. diminish _____    d. self-assertive in a rude, overbearing, or noisy way; overbearing

5. phobia _____    e. nourishing and efficient as food

**Sentences:** Try to use the words above in a sentence below. Remember that a word ending may be changed or its figure of speech slightly altered.

6. Fruits and vegetables are _____ snacks, for they contain many vitamins that are good for one's health.

7. Feelings of sadness in grieving the loss of a loved one will eventually _____ in time.

8. Unlike her urbane aunt, Nicoletta is _____ and voices her opinion on many matters boldly and self-confidently.

9. Hannah has many _____: she is afraid of cockroaches, the number thirteen, and black cats.

10. The students tried to _____ their math quiz by bombarding their teacher with questions during the entire class period.

# Lesson 75

**A HAPLESS STATE**

The **portentous** fire burned down the only hospital in the region and chaos soon ensued. Without medical equipment and facilities, people who were injured during the fire – covered in burns, wounds, and **char** marks – were left untreated for weeks. With the unstable political climate of the country and a lack of infrastructure, it was impossible for international organizations to **donate** resources in a timely manner; as a result, the injured did not receive **equitable** treatment. The **inextricable** link between poverty and disease had never been more evident.

**Definitions:**     Try matching the words in the list with the appropriate definitions.  If you are stuck, check the glossary in the back of the book or the passage at the top of the page.

| | | | | |
|---|---|---|---|---|
| 1. | donate | _____ | a. | fair and impartial |
| 2. | char | _____ | b. | impossible to disentangle or separate; impossible to escape from |
| 3. | inextricable | _____ | c. | ominously significant or important; momentous |
| 4. | equitable | _____ | d. | to partially burn an object as to blacken its surface |
| 5. | portentous | _____ | e. | 1. to give one's money or goods for a cause, especially a charity; 2. to allow the removal of one's blood or organ(s) from one's body for transplant or transfusion |

**Sentences:**     Try to use the words above in a sentence below.  Remember that a word ending may be changed or its figure of speech slightly altered.

6.   After the dispute, the magistrate hoped to find a(n) _____ solution that could satisfy both parties.

7.   How _____ it was when dark clouds swirled above the battleground in the hours before the slaughter.

8.   It seems that the chef _____ my lunch: my chicken breast is partially black and flaking apart.

9.   Every year my family _____ clothing and canned soup to help the homeless.

10.  For many physicists, the concept of relativity is _____ linked to that of the Bohr model of the atom.

## NEW WORDS

**enormous**
i'nôrməs

**prestidigitation**
ˌprestəˌdijə'tāSHən

**appropriate**
ə'prōprē-it (adj.); -ˌāt (v.)

**negligent**
'negləjənt

**populate**
'päpyəˌlāt

### CORRUPT OFFICIAL

Despite the fact that Ricky was a **negligent** official who preferred sitting on the veranda and smoking cigars to doing his work, he exerted **enormous** power in the small colonial community. Through remarkable **prestidigitation**, he was able to replace genuine business contracts filed at the county office with counterfeit ones, thus enabling him to control many of the local establishments and **appropriate** the largest part of their profits. His power seemed to be boundless. However, as more educated families began to **populate** the area, Ricky found that he could no longer maintain his position through deception and dangerous charisma.

**Definitions:**     Try matching the words in the list with the appropriate definitions. If you are stuck, check the glossary in the back of the book or the passage at the top of the page.

1.   enormous _____     a.   to fill with people; to form the population of a particular town, area, or country
2.   prestidigitation _____     b.   slight of hand; legerdemain
3.   appropriate _____     c.   very large in size, quantity, or extent
4.   negligent _____     d.   failing to take proper care in doing something
5.   populate _____     e.   (adj.) suitable or proper in the circumstances; (v.) 1. to take something for one's use, typically without permission; 2. to devote money or assets to a special purpose

**Sentences:**     Try to use the words above in a sentence below. Remember that a word ending may be changed or its figure of speech slightly altered.

6.   Because Rochelle was _____, he cousin crawled onto a hot stove and burnt his hand.
7.   Over 300,000 people _____ the state of California in the years 1848-55 after James W. Marshall discovered gold at Sutter's Mill in Coloma.
8.   With careful _____, the magician made the coin disappear right before my eyes.
9.   The new house being built at the cul-de-sac is _____: it appears to have at least a dozen bedrooms!
10.   It is not _____ to wear a swimsuit and lei to an American funeral.

# Lesson 77

**YOU REAP WHAT YOU SOW**

The newspaper was full of misinformation and **propaganda**. Journalists had the liberty to **concoct** any story they wished, as long as it reflected the paper's ideology. One day, someone threatened to sue the newspaper based on the **fallacy** of the information that the paper printed. The newspaper office suddenly became so quiet that one could hear the **somnolent** hum of grasshoppers outside. Eventually, the court issued a **requisition** to the newspaper for the payment of $10,000 to the plaintiff.

**NEW WORDS**

**propaganda**
ˌpräpəˈgandə

**concoct**
kənˈkäkt

**somnolent**
ˈsämnələnt

**fallacy**
ˈfaləsē

**requisition**
ˌrekwəˈziSHən

**Definitions:**     Try matching the words in the list with the appropriate definitions. If you are stuck, check the glossary in the back of the book or the passage at the top of the page.

| 1. | propaganda _____ | a. | a mistaken belief, especially one founded on unsound argument |
| 2. | concoct _____ | b. | sleepy or drowsy |
| 3. | somnolent _____ | c. | (n.) an official order laying claim to the use of property or materials; (v.) to demand the use or supply of, especially by official order and for military or public use |
| 4. | fallacy _____ | d. | 1. to make a dish or meal by combining various ingredients; 2. to create or devise a story or plan |
| 5. | requisition _____ | e. | information that is typically biased or misleading that is used to promote or publicize a particular political cause or point of view |

**Sentences:**     Try to use the words above in a sentence below. Remember that a word ending may be changed or its figure of speech slightly altered.

6. The library has obtained permission to _____ three paintings from the local art gallery.

7. Often governments will use _____ to get others to believe their creed.

8. It is a(n) _____ to believe everything that the media says: even news companies have their own biases in outlook and hires.

9. My _____ boss kept dozing off at work this morning; I'm not sure if he slept last night!

10. Lydia _____ a story about why she did not show up at work yesterday; sadly, I'm not sure that anyone believed it.

## NEW WORDS

**dormant**
ˈdôrmənt

**ideal**
 īˈdē(ə)l

**exist**
igˈzist

**scathing**
ˈskāTHiNG

**unswerving**
ˌənˈswərviNG

## THE AWAKENING

A sense of social justice was **dormant** in Jerome for many years. He knew he was treated unfairly at work, but he needed the money to feed his family. Long ago, as a child, Jerome had believed in an **ideal** world – a society in which everyone was equal. After so many years, during a company meeting, the **scathing** remarks of his boss finally woke Jerome up. Jerome was surprised to see that dignity and self-respect could still **exist** in him. Feeling humiliated by his boss, he immediately left his job. For the first time in his adult life, Jerome was filled with an **unswerving** commitment to follow his own sense of justice.

**Definitions:**     Try matching the words in the list with the appropriate definitions. If you are stuck, check the glossary in the back of the book or the passage at the top of the page.

1.   dormant   _____   a.   steady or constant; unchanging or unwavering

2.   ideal   _____   b.   severely critical or scornful

3.   exist   _____   c.   1. to have objective reality or being; 2. to live (under especially adverse conditions)

4.   scathing   _____   d.   1. (of an animal) having normal physical functions suspended as if in a deep sleep; 2. (of a volcano) temporarily inactive; 3. (of a disease) showing no symptoms but liable to recur

5.   unswerving   _____   e.   (adj.) satisfying one's conception of what is perfect or most suitable; (n.) a person or thing regarded as perfect; a standard of perfection or principle to be aimed at

**Sentences:**     Try to use the words above in a sentence below. Remember that a word ending may be changed or its figure of speech slightly altered.

6.   The volcano on that island has been _____ for nearly four decades.

7.   My _____ girlfriend would be attractive, honest, communicative, altruistic, and dedicated to her work.

8.   Though rare, it is true that four-leaf clovers do _____: perhaps one in every 10,000 clovers has four leaves.

9.   The senator's _____ remarks left his government colleagues speechless and offended.

10.   Sasha's _____ commitment to her studies should help her earn a spot at a top university.

# Lesson 79

## WITH BATED BREATH

As soon as the news broke that James would not follow into the family **tradition** of becoming a perfume creator, members of his family wondered what had **transpired** that caused him to make this decision. Indeed, hey waited with bated breath to hear about James' career choice. They were **ravenous** to know what new use James's impeccable **olfactory** senses would be put to. Knowing what a rare and nuanced sense of smell James has, I would not put it past his family to **connive** a plan that forces James to reconsider his career options in favor of his good old perfume designer destiny.

**Definitions:**     Try matching the words in the list with the appropriate definitions.  If you are stuck, check the glossary in the back of the book or the passage at the top of the page.

| | | | | |
|---|---|---|---|---|
| 1. | transpire | _____ | a. | to occur or happen |
| 2. | tradition | _____ | b. | extremely hungry |
| 3. | ravenous | _____ | c. | the transmission of customs and beliefs from one generation to the next |
| 4. | connive | _____ | d. | of or relating to the sense of smell |
| 5. | olfactory | _____ | e. | to secretly allow something immoral, illegal, wrong, or harmful to occur (often conspiring with others) |

**Sentences:**     Try to use the words above in a sentence below.  Remember that a word ending may be changed or its figure of speech slightly altered.

6.     When one has a common cold, _____ senses may be suppressed.

7.     I do not know what _____ when I was on vacation last week; that is why I'm asking my assistant to fill me in on the details of all transactions.

8.     The dog was so _____ that he devoured food as soon as it was set out for him.

9.     Out of spite, the employees are _____ to get their boss fired.

10.    It is a family _____ to go to the beach on Independence Day.

## NEW WORDS

**shun**
SHən

**null**
nəl

**malicious**
məˈliSHəs

**ransack**
ˈranˌsak, ranˈsak

**adept**
əˈdept

### PAINFUL MEMORIES

The marriage was now **null** and void, and Deborah tried to **shun** any attempt on Tom's part to visit the apartment and retrieve his belongings. Deborah had always been **adept** at avoiding unpleasant situations. It was not that she was purposefully **malicious** and wanted to deprive Tom of things that held sentimental value for him. She simply could not bear to see Tom **ransack** their old home looking for memories. She knew this would be too painful for her.

**Definitions:**     Try matching the words in the list with the appropriate definitions. If you are stuck, check the glossary in the back of the book or the passage at the top of the page.

1.  shun     _____   a.   to persistently avoid, ignore, or reject someone or something through antipathy or caution

2.  null     _____   b.   characterized by an intention to do harm

3.  malicious     _____   c.   to move hurriedly through a place stealing things and causing damage

4.  ransack     _____   d.   very skilled or proficient at something

5.  adept     _____   e.   1. having no legal or binding force; invalid; 2. having or associated with the value zero

**Sentences:**     Try to use the words above in a sentence below. Remember that a word ending may be changed or its figure of speech slightly altered.

6.    Jill _____ her ex-boyfriend's attempt to try and rebuild their relationship.

7.    In some societies' history, marriage between people of two different races was deemed to be _____.

8.    One has to be _____ with numbers if he or she desires an actuarial career.

9.    The unruly children _____ the doctor's home on Halloween, destroying her mailbox and stealing all of her holiday candy.

10.   Only a(n) _____ person would try to sabotage another person's career for fun.

# Crossword Puzzle
## Lessons 71-80

ACROSS

7  (adj.) of or relating to the sense of smell
11 (v.) to prevent an event or action from happening by taking advance action; to delay
12 (adj.) impossible to disentangle or separate; impossible to escape from
13 (adj.) very large in size, quantity, or extent
16 (adj.) satisfying one's conception of what is perfect or most suitable; (n.) a person or thing regarded as perfect; a standard of perfection or principle to be aimed at
17 (n.) used to refer to something that is one's duty or responsibility
18 (v.) 1. to have objective reality or being; 2. to live under adverse conditions
20 (n.) an extreme or irrational fear of or aversion to something

DOWN

1  (v.) to fill with people; to form the population of a particular town, area, or country
2  (v.) to secretly allow something immoral, illegal, wrong, or harmful to occur
3  (n.) a mistaken belief, especially one founded on unsound argument
4  (n.) information that is typically biased or misleading that is used to promote or publicize a particular political cause or point of view
5  (adj.) absurd or ridiculous; contrary to common sense
6  (adj.) fair and impartial
8  (n.) the action of spending funds
9  (n.) an idea or feeling that a word evokes in addition to its literal meaning
10 (adj.) not contaminated or polluted
14 (v.) to move hurriedly through a place stealing things and causing damage
15 (n.) a person who is able to see what the future holds
19 (v.) to persistently avoid, ignore, or reject someone or something through antipathy or caution

# Vocabulary Review
## Lessons 71-80

**Directions:** Match each word with its best approximate definition. Note that definitions are not necessarily repeated verbatim from the lesson exercises.

1. sentry _____ 
2. incredulous _____ 
3. statute _____ 
4. chaff _____ 
5. brawn _____ 
6. sage _____ 
7. nutritious _____ 
8. diminish _____ 
9. char _____ 
10. portentous _____ 
11. prestidigitation _____ 
12. negligent _____ 
13. concoct _____ 
14. somnolent _____ 
15. scathing _____ 
16. unswerving _____ 
17. transpire _____ 
18. ravenous _____ 
19. malicious _____ 
20. adept _____ 

a. physical strength in contrast to intelligence
b. concerning a warning that something bad is likely to happen
c. steady, constant; steadfast
d. to occur or happen
e. failing to take proper care in doing something
f. sleight of hand
g. a soldier stationed to keep guard or to control access to a place
h. characterized by an intention to do harm
i. very skilled or proficient at something
j. sleepy or drowsy
k. to make or become less
l. extremely critical or scornful
m. lighthearted joking or banter
n. a written law that is passed by a legislative body
o. to partially burn an object or to blacken its surface
p. extremely hungry
q. unwilling or unable to believe something
r. to make up something (a dish, meal, or lie) by combining various ingredients
s. something that is efficient as food; nourishing
t. showing wisdom; a profoundly wise man

# Word Roots: Unit 8

## ROOTS AND THEIR MEANINGS

| | | | |
|---|---|---|---|
| **dign/dian:** | **worth (value)** | **in/en/em/im:** | **into** |
| **nai/nas/nat:** | **to be born** | **phon:** | **sound** |
| **gen:** | **type, birth** | **fac:** | **to do; to make** |
| **ad/at:** | **to, toward** | **cli:** | **to lean** |

## Here are a few examples of some words that use the above roots:

| | |
|---|---|
| dignity: | the state of equality in being worthy of honor or respect |
| renaissance: | the rebirth of something, usually art or music |
| genotype: | the genetic composition of an organism |
| advance: | to move forward or make progress, typically with an expressed purpose |
| immerse: | to submerge in a liquid |
| incarnate: | embodied in human form or in the flesh |
| telephone: | an instrument by which one can communicate with others at a distance |
| facilitate: | to make a process or an action easier |
| inclination: | a natural tendency to act or behave in a certain way |

## Now try to fill in the table below by finding the appropriate root(s) and interpreting the meaning of each word:

| Word | Root(s) | Guessed Meaning | Actual Meaning |
|---|---|---|---|
| factory | | | |
| phonetics | | | |
| nationality | | | |
| proclivity | | | |
| nascence | | | |
| attain | | | |
| genealogy | | | |
| engaged | | | |
| generic | | | |
| engrossing | | | |
| decline | | | |

## NEW WORDS

**felon**
'felən

**exotic**
ig'zätik

**stifle**
'stīfəl

**provocative**
prə'väkətiv

**benefactor**
'benə,faktər, ,benə'faktər

# Lesson 81

## THE REVENGE

The **felon**, Mr. Joyce, had to **stifle** his anger in the court. He knew that if he became enraged in front of the judge, his penalty would become even more severe. As far as he was concerned, the victim – a young native boy – had acted in an emotionally **provocative** manner with his **exotic** story about his unhappy childhood and gang history. The boy had made Mr. Joyce feel like his **benefactor**. Thus, when the boy ran away with Mr. Joyce's money, it seemed justified that Mr. Joyce would chase him down and try to seek revenge.

**Definitions:**     Try matching the words in the list with the appropriate definitions. If you are stuck, check the glossary in the back of the book or the passage at the top of the page.

| | | | | |
|---|---|---|---|---|
| 1. | felon | _____ | a. | to suffocate; to stop one from acting on an emotion; to restrain or prevent |
| 2. | exotic | _____ | b. | deliberately evoking annoyance, anger, or another strong reaction; deliberately attempting to arouse sexual desire |
| 3. | stifle | _____ | c. | a person who gives money or other aid to a person or cause |
| 4. | provocative | _____ | d. | originating in or characteristic of a foreign country; appealing because of having come from a far away place |
| 5. | benefactor | _____ | e. | a person who has been convicted of a felony |

**Sentences:**     Try to use the words above in a sentence below. Remember that a word ending may be changed or its figure of speech slightly altered.

6.     Maria did not realize that she was _____ her students' interest in mathematics by refusing to answer more advanced questions than what the textbook taught.

7.     The only reason an actress would wear a(n) _____ outfit like that is to get the attention of the media or of some man.

8.     For most Americans, _____ birds are fascinating because local varieties neither have brightly colored plumage nor can squawk out words.

9.     As one of the _____ of the school, I strongly believe in helping people develop the ability to help themselves learn.

10.     The _____ escaped from jail in the middle of the night and was unable to be apprehended by authorities.

# Lesson 82

## A LIFE CRISIS

It seemed that nothing could **impede** Bob's oncoming existential crisis.   No matter how much he tried to **refrain** from thinking, Bob could not forget that in just a few days his superiors would **demote** him to the lower rank of a junior officer.  His future now seemed like an open **abyss**: it seemed that if he looked down, he would drown.  It was not until many months later that Bob was able to forgive himself for his misdeed and take **tentative** steps back to positivity and self-belief.

**Definitions:**       Try matching the words in the list with the appropriate definitions.  If you are stuck, check the glossary in the back of the book or the passage at the top of the page.

| | | | | |
|---|---|---|---|---|
| 1. | impede | _____ | a. | to stop oneself from doing something |
| 2. | refrain | _____ | b. | not certain or fixed; provisional |
| 3. | demote | _____ | c. | to give someone a lower rank or less senior position, usually as a punishment |
| 4. | abyss | _____ | d. | to delay or prevent someone or something by preventing him, her, or it |
| 5. | tentative | _____ | e. | a deep or seemingly bottomless chasm |

**Sentences:**       Try to use the words above in a sentence below.  Remember that a word ending may be changed or its figure of speech slightly altered.

6. It is important to _____ from talking during a movie.
7. Though a difficult decision to make, the company decided to _____ three of its managers because they were not performing up to par.
8. It seems that almost nothing can _____ the growth of the city; prices are cheap, jobs are abundant, and there is much to do downtown.
9. That canyon is so deep that it feels like a(n) _____.
10. I have _____ plans to go to the zoo on Friday to draw animals, but if need be I could alter those arrangements.

## NEW WORDS

**confusion**
kən'fyooZHən

**genteel**
jen'tēl

**prediction**
pri'dikSHən

**annex**
ə'neks, 'aneks

**falsetto**
fôl'setō

### TROUBLES IN THE COMPANY

Whenever Philip got angry, he sang in an unusually high, unpleasant **falsetto**. Philip was a man of **genteel** upbringing and he felt that it was beneath him to deal with the financial matters of the company. Just bringing up money issues made him lose his temper. Therefore, hearing a report that the company was on the verge of bankruptcy caused him much anger and **confusion**. The report included the **prediction** that the bankruptcy would happen before the end of the month. As usual, Philip began to sing at his colleagues in his high-pitched voice and did not bother to read the **annex** to the report. As it turned out later, the annex contained some useful information on how to avoid the bankruptcy and save the company.

**Definitions:** Try matching the words in the list with the appropriate definitions. If you are stuck, check the glossary in the back of the book or the passage at the top of the page.

1. confusion _____ a. 1. a lack of understanding; uncertainty; 2. the state of being bewildered or unclear in one's mind about something

2. genteel _____ b. a forecast or estimation of future events

3. prediction _____ c. polite, refined, or respectable, often in an affected or ostentatious way

4. annex _____ d. (n.) a building joined to or associated with a main building; an addition to a document; (v.) to append or add as a subordinate part (especially of a document or a territory)

5. falsetto _____ e. for a male singer to sing notes higher than normal in range

**Sentences:** Try to use the words above in a sentence below. Remember that a word ending may be changed or its figure of speech slightly altered.

6. It was funny watching Atisha sing a girly song in a(n) _____ voice.

7. Oliver's _____ upbringing led him to always open doors for ladies.

8. When the fire alarm blared in the mall, mass _____ broke out among the shoppers.

9. The French apothecary and clairvoyant Nostradamus (1503-66) made _____ about the Great Fire of London (1666), the French Revolution (1789), and the advent of the atomic bomb.

10. Upon completion of the _____, the war artifacts will be housed there.

# Lesson 84

### THE DETERMINED LOVER

Kyle decided to **douse** the cake with rich chocolate sauce in order to give the dessert that he cooked a more aphrodisiacal taste. Linda had not warmed up to his advances in their five previous dates; however, Kyle was a **tenacious** suitor. He showered her with **munificent** gifts. He would **extract** much pleasure from watching her admire the gifts. **Contrary** to everyone's opinion, Kyle believed that he could make Linda forget her ex-husband and fall in love with him.

**Definitions:**    Try matching the words in the list with the appropriate definitions. If you are stuck, check the glossary in the back of the book or the passage at the top of the page.

| | | | | |
|---|---|---|---|---|
| 1. | tenacious | _____ | a. | (n.) 1. a short passage taken from a piece of writing, music, or film; 2. a preparation containing the active ingredient of a substance in concentrated form; (v.) to remove or take out, especially by force |
| 2. | contrary | _____ | b. | (of a gift or sum of money) greater or more generous than is necessary |
| 3. | extract | _____ | c. | (adj.) 1. opposite in nature, direction, or meaning; 2. perversely inclined to do the opposite of what is expected or desired; (n.) the opposite |
| 4. | munificent | _____ | d. | tending to keep a firm hold of something; not readily relinquishing a position, principle, or course of action |
| 5. | douse | _____ | e. | to pour a liquid over, to drench |

**Sentences:**    Try to use the words above in a sentence below. Remember that a word ending may be changed or its figure of speech slightly altered.

6.    My doctor successfully managed to _____ an ingrown toenail last week; I feel much less pain now!

7.    David was very _____, refusing to give up on his dreams of being a rock star despite numerous attempts to steer him in a different direction.

8.    Firefighters _____ the flames in the apartment after a fire broke out.

9.    The _____ prince provided his subjects a free buffet brunch.

10.    Though Most Americans think it is difficult to become rich, I believe that the _____ is true: hard work and pragmatism can help one thrive.

## NEW WORDS

**concur**
kən'kər

**associate**
ə'sōsē͟ˌāt, -SHē-

**prose**
prōz

**primitive**
'primətiv

**divisive**
di'vīsiv

## THE PROVOCATIVE FRIEND

Even though Donald was good-natured, he enjoyed speaking about **divisive** topics that provoked anger among his friends. Last week, for example, he decided to discuss the topic of lung cancer with his friend Gerry, a chain smoker. While Gerry could politely **concur** that smoking was problematic, he could hardly stand being lectured about its health risks. In fact, such talk made Gerry not want to **associate** any further with Donald. In fact, tears welled up in Gerry's eyes as Donald spoke. Though his **primitive** instincts made him want to punch Donald, Gerry instead went home and wrote a beautiful piece of **prose** to Donald expressing his feelings about their relationship.

**Definitions:** Try matching the words in the list with the appropriate definitions. If you are stuck, check the glossary in the back of the book or the passage at the top of the page.

1. concur _____ a. 1. concerning the character of an early stage in the evolutionary or historical development of something; 2. not developed or derived from anything else

2. associate _____ b. 1. to be of the same opinion, to agree; 2. to happen at the same time

3. prose _____ c. written or spoken language in its typical form, without metrical structure

4. primitive _____ d. tending to cause disagreement or hostility between people

5. divisive _____ e. (adj.) joined or connected with an organization or business; (n.) a partner or colleague in business or at work; 2. a person with limited or subordinate membership in an organization; (v.) to connect someone or something with something else in one's mind

**Sentences:** Try to use the words above in a sentence below. Remember that a word ending may be changed or its figure of speech slightly altered.

6. Ruth's beautiful _____ was engrossing and earned her many accolades.

7. Often people of different social classes do not _____ with each other.

8. One might argue that _____ calculators have existed ever since the abacus appeared in Mesopotamia about five thousand years ago.

9. Many people would _____ that poaching safari animals is a crime.

10. Abortion is a(n) _____ issue in the United States today; people are deeply split among whether it is a woman's choice to end the life of her unborn child.

# Lesson 86

## THE OLD CIRCUS DIRECTOR

Driven by **avarice**, the circus director habitually underpaid his employees. He let them live in **miserable** conditions. Sometimes they asked for their payment, but the director would **procrastinate** and let them go hungry for days. Naturally, everyone hated him. They had no idea that he once was a **jovial** young man, full of hopes and dreams. Little by little, however, the harsh reality of being a traveling entertainer succeeded at hardening him. Aside from becoming **corrupt** and taking bribes from circus sponsors, the director's only hope for living a luxurious lifestyle and saving a hefty retirement was to prey upon his underlings at work.

## NEW WORDS

**miserable**
ˈmiz(ə)rəbəl

**avarice**
ˈavəris

**jovial**
ˈjōvēəl

**corrupt**
kəˈrəpt

**procrastinate**
prəˈkrastəˌnāt, prō-

**Definitions:** Try matching the words in the list with the appropriate definitions. If you are stuck, check the glossary in the back of the book or the passage at the top of the page.

1. miserable _____ a. (adj.) having or showing a willingness to act dishonestly in return for money or personal gain; (v.) to cause to act dishonestly in return for money or personal gain

2. avarice _____ b. cheerful and friendly

3. jovial _____ c. to delay or postpone action; to put off doing something

4. corrupt _____ d. extreme greed for material gain or wealth

5. procrastinate _____ e. 1. concerning one who is or a situation that is extremely unhappy or uncomfortable; 2. pitiably small or inadequate

**Sentences:** Try to use the words above in a sentence below. Remember that a word ending may be changed or its figure of speech slightly altered.

6. A _____ police officer will decide to put his or her own interests before the law.

7. Tracy's _____ led to her demise: she abandoned her friends, family, and hobbies all in pursuit of money.

8. Elmira _____ and did not begin her weekend homework assignments until late Sunday evening.

9. Sherman was a(n) _____ guy: he always enjoyed talking and joking with people at his construction company.

10. Our neighbor is _____: she quarrels with everybody and always complains about life.

## NEW WORDS

**merit**
'merit

**merge**
mərj

**palatable**
'palətəbəl

**precarious**
pri'ke(ə)rēəs

**animate**
'anə,mit (adj.); -māt (v.)

# Lesson 87

## THE MERGE

The future of the company seemed too **precarious** on its own; therefore, the CEO decided that it needed to **merge** with a similar company to become a larger establishment. Eventually the CEO found a good fit: the other company's **merit** seemed undoubted. However, the idea of losing a part of his own power was not so **palatable** to the CEO. Nevertheless, the merge seemed to **animate** the business and things were going well. The CEO thought that now was the time to consolidate his powerful position in the new company.

**Definitions:**    Try matching the words in the list with the appropriate definitions. If you are stuck, check the glossary in the back of the book or the passage at the top of the page.

1.    merit    _____    a.    not securely held in position; dependent on chance, uncertain

2.    merge    _____    b.    1. food or drink that is pleasant to taste; 2. an action or proposal that is acceptable or satisfactory

3.    palatable    _____    c.    to combine or cause to combine into a single entity

4.    precarious    _____    d.    (adj.) alive or having life; (v.) 1. to bring to life; to give encouragement, vigor, or renewed vigor to; 2. to give a movie or a character the appearance of movement using artistic techniques

5.    animate    _____    e.    (n.) the quality of being good or worthy; (v.) to deserve or be worthy of (typically a reward, punishment, or attention)

**Sentences:**    Try to use the words above in a sentence below. Remember that a word ending may be changed or its figure of speech slightly altered.

6.    Jacqueline earned a promotion based on her own _____: because of her industry and pragmatism, she earned a directorship position.

7.    Rather than considering the ideas of Geoffrey and Andrea separately, I'd like to _____ their insights in order to create something truly innovative.

8.    When the municipal government reduced funding for the subway system, the latter's survival was put in a(n) _____ state.

9.    The hotel food is _____: I especially love the chocolate croissants!

10.    Only when I saw the still cockroach begin to move was I convinced that it was a(n) _____ creature.

125

# Lesson 88

**MORE THAN SKIN DEEP**

When Arlene fell in love with Hakim, she knew that her conservative family would **castigate** her. In fact, they probably would **expunge** her name from the family will. The fact that an Orthodox Jewish heir to a large trust fund would consider marriage to a **swarthy** Muslim, irrespective of his highly reputable profession and philanthropic endeavors, was problematic. Even pondering such an option did much to **contradict** their entrenched belief systems, and refused to **abjure** under any circumstance. All this would not stop Arlene from marrying her true love.

## NEW WORDS

**castigate**
ˈkastəˌgāt

**expunge**
ikˈspənj

**swarthy**
ˈswôrTHē

**abjure**
abˈjoor

**contradict**
ˌkäntrəˈdikt

**Definitions:**    Try matching the words in the list with the appropriate definitions. If you are stuck, check the glossary in the back of the book or the passage at the top of the page.

|     |            |            |     |     |
|-----|------------|------------|-----|-----|
| 1.  | castigate  | _____ | a.  | to erase or remove completely |
| 2.  | expunge    | _____ | b.  | to reprimand someone severely |
| 3.  | swarthy    | _____ | c.  | to solemnly renounce a belief, cause, or claim |
| 4.  | abjure     | _____ | d.  | dark-skinned |
| 5.  | contradict | _____ | e.  | to deny the truth of something by asserting the opposite; to assert the opposite of a statement made by someone |

**Sentences:**    Try to use the words above in a sentence below. Remember that a word ending may be changed or its figure of speech slightly altered.

6.    Tuan _____ his life in fashion and became an ascetic Buddhist monk.

7.    Javier's parents _____ him for staying out past his curfew and bringing a woman home with him.

8.    Vanessa's claim that she doesn't need a vacation seems to _____ the fact that she just bought a three-week travel package to tour the Alps.

9.    Even though Tonya missed two credit cards payments, she wrote to her credit union in an attempt to see if her late payments could be _____ from her record.

10.    Often villains in cartoons are depicted as enigmatic, _____ characters lurking in the shadows.

## NEW WORDS

**speculate**
ˈspekyəˌlāt

**cycle**
ˈsīkəl

**apex**
ˈāpeks

**tamper**
ˈtampər

**pittance**
ˈpitns

### REALITIES OF GRADUATE SCHOOL

At the **apex** of his graduate career, John received an abundant academic stipend from the university. However, after paying for research travel fees and archival access, the money was reduced to a mere **pittance**. Unfortunately, John soon fell into a vicious **cycle** of working low-paid jobs and procrastinating the completion of his degree so that he could survive financially. He tried to **speculate** about how many more years he would need in order to finish his dissertation under these conditions. He did not want to **tamper** with progressing toward his degree; thus he had no choice but to work invidious jobs in order to pay the bills.

**Definitions:**     Try matching the words in the list with the appropriate definitions. If you are stuck, check the glossary in the back of the book or the passage at the top of the page.

1.   speculate   _____   a.   a very small or inadequate amount of money paid to someone as an allowance or wage

2.   cycle   _____   b.   the top or highest point of something

3.   apex   _____   c.   to interfere with something in order to cause damage or make unauthorized alterations

4.   tamper   _____   d.   to form a theory about something without having firm evidence

5.   pittance   _____   e.   (n.) 1. a series of events that are regularly repeated in the same order; 2. a bicycle or tricycle; (v.) 1. to move in or follow a regularly repeated sequence of events; 2. to ride a bicycle or tricycle

**Sentences:**     Try to use the words above in a sentence below. Remember that a word ending may be changed or its figure of speech slightly altered.

6.   When Gareth finally reached the _____ of the mountain, he took several panoramic pictures of the view.

7.   It is easy to _____ that housing prices in Singapore will rise if the population of the island-nation keeps increasing at the current rate.

8.   Tiffany was paid a(n) _____ for her many hours of hard work at the factory.

9.   Every year the Earth experiences a(n) _____ of seasons.

10.   Police detectives are not supposed to _____ with evidence in a criminal investigation.

# Lesson 90

## THE SECRET LIFE OF A DANCER

With his natural talent as a dancer, Yannis was **poised** for professional success. Everyone saw in him the next dance superstar. Nobody suspected that Yannis led a **dual** life. After each dancing performance, he would **seclude** himself in his room and take out a notebook and a pen. Writing was not only a **hobby** for him but also way to become centered. The silent process of putting his thoughts on a page would **exhilarate** him in a quiet way. He sometimes felt more alive in his room than when he was dancing on the big stage.

**Definitions:** Try matching the words in the list with the appropriate definitions. If you are stuck, check the glossary in the back of the book or the passage at the top of the page.

| | | | | |
|---|---|---|---|---|
| 1. | poised | _____ | a. | having a composed and self-assured manner |
| 2. | dual | _____ | b. | an activity one regularly does in one's leisure time for pleasure |
| 3. | hobby | _____ | c. | to keep (someone) away from other people |
| 4. | seclude | _____ | d. | to make (someone) feel very happy, animated, or elated |
| 5. | exhilarate | _____ | e. | consisting of two parts, elements, or aspects |

**Sentences:** Try to use the words above in a sentence below. Remember that a word ending may be changed or its figure of speech slightly altered.

6. Niveh has _____ roles in the university: she is both a professor who teaches and a dean who makes important administrative decisions.

7. When I was a child, my favorite _____ was collecting baseball cards.

8. Lisa felt _____ upon hearing that her father would be taking her to New York City on his upcoming business trip.

9. Given all of his corporate successes, Herman is _____ to become the next CEO of the company.

10. After losing the election, Orrin decided to _____ himself in his forest home to regroup and reassess.

# Word Search

## Lessons 81-90

```
P N E X T R A C T W N H O B B Y
R T O D E J L R T O A B J U R E
O N Q I X X U B I I G V P T L T
C E T R T C P S S E R I J S B J
R C J E N C U U V T T E U V Y D
A I J O V F I I N T I O M M K K
S F C D N I S D A G I F I Y M M
T I M O Y I T N E R E S L S Y D
I N C D V I C A A R E W E E Z L
N U B I M E N C T R P C D E L W
A M D P Z O E P A N L P L M D T
T V E P L R K B R U E C N N B X
E D D E P R L M D M Y T L R R Q
E M F K R E Y E N C Z L J T B M
```

1 (n.) a person who has been convicted of a felony
2 (v.) to suffocate; to stop one from acting on an emotion; to restrain or prevent
3 (v.) to delay or prevent someone or something by preventing him, her, or it
4 (adj.) not certain or fixed; provisional
5 (n.) 1. a lack of understanding; uncertainty; 2. the state of being bewildered or unclear in one's mind about something
6 (n.) a forecast or estimation of future events
7 (n.) 1. a short passage taken from a piece of writing, music, or film; 2. a preparation containing the active ingredient of a substance in concentrated form; (v.) to remove or take out, especially by force
8 (adj.) (of a gift or sum of money) greater or more generous than is necessary
9 (v.) 1. to be of the same opinion, to agree; 2. to happen at the same time
10 (adj.) tending to cause disagreement or hostility between people
11 (adj.) 1. concerning one who is or a situation that is extremely unhappy or uncomfortable; 2. pitiably small or inadequate
12 (v.) to delay or postpone action; to put off doing something
13 (n.) the quality of being good or worthy; (v.) to deserve or be worthy of (typically a reward, punishment, or attention)
14 (adj.) not securely held in position; dependent on chance, uncertain
15 (v.) to erase or remove completely
16 (v.) to solemnly renounce a belief, cause, or claim
17 (n.) 1. a series of events that are regularly repeated in the same order; 2. a bicycle or tricycle; (v.) 1. to move in or follow a regularly repeated sequence of events; 2. to ride a bicycle or tricycle
18 (n.) a very small or inadequate amount of money paid to someone as an allowance or wage
19 (n.) an activity one regularly does in one's leisure time for pleasure
20 (v.) to keep someone away from other people

# Vocabulary Review
## Lessons 81-90

Directions: Match each word with its best approximate definition.  Note that definitions are not necessarily repeated verbatim from the lesson exercises.

1. provocative _____ a. polite, refined, or respectable, often in an ostentatious way

2. benefactor _____ b. a deep or seemingly bottomless pit

3. refrain _____ c. written or spoken language in ordinary form

4. abyss _____ d. having dark skin

5. genteel _____ e. opposite in meaning or nature

6. falsetto _____ f. friendly and cheerful

7. tenacious _____ g. a male voice singing notes higher than normal range

8. contrary _____ h. deliberately trying to evoke anger, annoyance, or some other strong reaction

9. prose _____ i. a person who gives money (or something else) to help another person or cause

10. primitive _____ j. to combine into a single entity

11. avarice _____ k. to form a theory about something without having solid evidence

12. jovial _____ l. the top or highest part of something

13. merge _____ m. to reprimand severely

14. palatable _____ n. concerning the early stage in the evolutionary development of something

15. castigate _____ o. consisting of two parts, elements, or actions

16. swarthy _____ p. extreme greed

17. speculate _____ q. being composed and self-assured

18. apex _____ r. keeping a firm hold of something; not easy to relinquish a position, principle, or course of action

19. poised _____ s. food or drink that tastes pleasant; an action or proposal that seems satisfactory

20. dual _____ t. to stop oneself from doing something

# Word Roots: Unit 9

## ROOTS AND THEIR MEANINGS

| | | | |
|---|---|---|---|
| cur/cour: | to run | tens/ten: | to stretch |
| ob: | against, toward in front of | vor: | to eat |
| techn: | tools, skill | magna/magni: | big, great |

## Here are a few examples of some words that use the above roots:

| | |
|---|---|
| courier: | a messenger who transports goods or documents (eg. carries documents between places) |
| obviate: | to avoid; prevent; remove a specific difficulty |
| technology: | the application of scientific knowledge and/or machinery for practical purposes |
| tenuous: | very weak or slight |
| voracious: | wanting or devouring great quantities of something, often food |
| magnanimous: | very generous or forgiving |

## Now try to fill in the table below by finding the appropriate root(s) and interpreting the meaning of each word:

| Word | Root(s) | Guessed Meaning | Actual Meaning |
|---|---|---|---|
| carnivore | | | |
| technocracy | | | |
| tensile | | | |
| attenuate | | | |
| obscure | | | |
| magnificent | | | |
| current | | | |
| omnivore | | | |
| obstinate | | | |

# Specific Vocabularies 2
## Transportation Words

## Some Boat Terms:

- The left side of a ship when facing forward is called the **port** side
- The right side of a ship when facing forward is called the **starboard** side
- The main body of a ship, including the bottom and sides (but not including the masts or engines) is called the **hull**
- The kitchen in a boat or ship is called the **galley**
- The paddles that one uses in a boat are called **oars**
- The person in charge of a large boat or ship is called a **captain**
- A tall upright post, spar, or other structure on a boat or ship is called a **mast**

## Some Airplane and Airport Terms:

- The person in charge of the airplane is called the **pilot**
- The part of the plane where the pilot sits to navigate the plane is called the **cockpit**
- The part of an airport where one picks up luggage is called a **baggage claim**
- The place at an airport where officials check passports, luggage, and goods is called **customs and immigration**
- A **layover** is a period of rest before a further stage of a journey, in the case of flying, it is a middle or intermediary location (airport) where one rests in between flights

## Some Train Terms:

- The person in charge of the train is called a **conductor**
- Each car on a train is called a **coach**
- The final car on a train can be called a **caboose**
- Sometimes a train station is called a **depot**

## Some Driving Terms:

- A driver whose job is to drive a limousine or town car is called a **chauffeur**
- A truck driver is called a **teamster**
- The driver's compartment of a truck, bus, or train can be called a **cab**
- The device on a vehicle that measures speed on a vehicle is called a **speedometer**
- The device on a vehicle that measures the total distance traveled is called an **odometer**

# Key Words With Multiple Definitions

Often in intellectual writing and on standardized tests, words are used that bear multiple definitions. Not knowing alternate meanings of such words can interfere with one's comprehension of a text. Below is a chart of some common words that are used in sophisticated writing. Certain commonly-understood definitions are provided as well as some less common definitions. For the latter case, they are used in sentences. Do note that this list is neither exhaustive of words with multiple definitions nor necessarily exhaustive of every definition for each word below.

| Word | More Common Definition(s) | Less Common Definition(s) and Sentence Usage |
|---|---|---|
| **arrest** | (n.) the act of seizing someone to take into custody; (v.) to seize (someone) by legal authority and take into custody | (n.) the stoppage or sudden cessation of motion; (v.) to stop or check (progress or a process)<br><br>Mackenzie's parents sought to **arrest** their daughter's growing obsession with video games by throwing out all of her gaming consoles and limiting her computer use. |
| **base** | (n.) the main place where a person works or stays; (v.) to have as the foundation for (something); to use as a point from which something can develop | (adj.) evil; sordid; wicked; dishonest<br><br>The **base** queen poisoned all of her enemies to ensure that all of her subjects would revere her. |
| **coin** | (n.) a flat and usually round piece of metal used as currency | (v.) to invent or devise a new word or phrase<br><br>The English playwright William Shakespeare (1564-1616) **coined** the phrase "dead as a doornail" in *Henry VI, Part II*. |
| **comb** | (n.) a utensil with a row of narrow teeth used for untangling or arranging the hair | (v.) to search carefully and systematically<br><br>Georgia realized that she would have to **comb** through all of her papers in order to locate the receipt for the television she had purchased last summer. |

| | | |
|---|---|---|
| **conviction** | (n.) declaration of guilt, sentence, or judgment | (n.) a firmly held belief or opinion<br><br>My mathematics teacher said with great **conviction** that if students do not do their homework regularly, then they will struggle with the concepts. |
| **founder** | (n.) the creator, originator, founding father, or prime mover, or inventor of something | (v.) to sink; to collapse, backfire, or fall through; to trip up<br><br>After a cannon pierced its hull, the sloop **foundered** and sank in the bay. |
| **gravity** | (n.) the force that attracts a body toward the center of the earth | (n.) extreme or alarming importance<br><br>Though he heard that Jared was injured in a car accident, Bennett did not realize the **gravity** of the matter until he saw Jared in a wheelchair at the hospital. |
| **marshal** | (n.) 1. an officer of the highest rank in the armed forces of some countries; 2. a federal or municipal law officer; 3. A head of a police or fire department; 4. an official responsible for supervising public events (e.g. sports events or parades) | (v.) to arrange or assemble (a group of people, especially soldiers) in order<br><br>The captain began to **marshal** his forces to send relief to the victims of the recent earthquake. |
| **parochial** | (adj.) of or relating to a church parish | (adj.) having a limited or narrow outlook or scope<br><br>Unlike uncle Ned, who is open-minded and liberal, aunt Marge holds a **parochial** worldview and expects everyone to make life choices that are similar to her life choices. |
| **pedestrian** | (n.) a person walking along a road or in a developed area | (adj.) lacking inspiration or excitement; dull<br><br>A date consisting of simply dinner and a movie is an awfully **pedestrian** idea. |
| **plastic** | (n.) a synthetic material made from a wide range of polymers that can be molded into shape when soft and then set into rigid form | (adj.) (of a substance or materials) easily shaped or molded<br><br>The human brain is somewhat **plastic**; when people learn new things or memorize new information, long lasting functional changes in the brain occur. |

| | | |
|---|---|---|
| **qualify** | (v.) to be entitled to a particular benefit or privilege by fulfilling a necessary condition | (v.) to make (a statement or assertion) less absolute; to add reservations to<br><br>Although Kyle's mother told him that he could go out partying with his friends, she **qualified** the statement by saying that he could only do so if he finished his homework and research paper first. |
| **sanction** | (n.) a threatened penalty for disobeying a law or rule | (v.) to give official permission or approval for (an action)<br><br>After a much-heated debate, the aldermen **sanctioned** dog walking in all municipal parks. |
| **sound** | (n.) vibrations that travel through air (or another medium) that can be heard when they reach one's ear | (adj.) 1. in good condition; not damaged, diseased, or injured; 2. based on reason, judgment, or sense; 3. financially secure<br><br>It is **unsound** to drive your car home from a party if you are drunk.<br><br>Martha made a **sound** decision to invest in her education rather than taking all of her hard earned cash to the local casino. |
| **trace** | (n.) 1. A mark or object or indication of the existence or passing of something; (v.) 1. to find or discover by investigation; 2. To copy (a drawing, map, or design) by drawing over its lines on a superimposed and partially transparent sheet of paper | (n.) a very small quantity of something, especially one that is too small to be measured accurately<br><br>Only **traces** of argon can be found in the earth's atmosphere, which is composed primarily of nitrogen and oxygen. |

# Lesson 91

## THE DILIGENT ART STUDENT

Maria prided herself on being an **intellectual** who could **embrace** new and diverse opinions on art. Moreover, she was **diligent** in her studies of new artistic trends. Whenever she had an essay to write, she did not like to **generalize**; on the contrary, she would research many specific details about the issue in question. She knew that artistic tastes were quite **fickle** and could change very quickly. Thus, Maria strove to keep herself updated on artistic topics so that she could be an effective critic.

### NEW WORDS

**intellectual**
ˌintlˈekCHoͻəl

**embrace**
emˈbrās

**generalize**
ˈjenərəˌlīz

**fickle**
ˈfikəl

**diligent**
ˈdiləjənt

**Definitions:** Try matching the words in the list with the appropriate definitions. If you are stuck, check the glossary in the back of the book or the passage at the top of the page.

1. intellectual _____     a. changing one's loyalties, interests, or affection frequently

2. embrace _____     b. (n.) the act of holding someone closely in one's arms; (v.) 1. to hold someone closely in one's arms; 2. to accept or support a belief, theory, or change willingly and enthusiastically; 3. to include or contain something as a constituent part

3. generalize _____     c. to make a general or broad statement by inferring from specific cases; to make something more widespread or common

4. fickle _____     d. (adj.) of or relating to use of mental faculties; possessing highly developed mental faculties; (n.) a person with highly developed mental faculties

5. diligent _____     e. having or showing care and conscientiousness in one's work or duties

**Sentences:** Try to use the words above in a sentence below. Remember that a word ending may be changed or its figure of speech slightly altered.

6. Universities are excellent places to have myriad _____ discussions.

7. Dale is _____ and changes her mind about nearly everything.

8. Seeing the twins _____ each other after a long separation was moving.

9. It is hard to _____ whether a student will be successful in my history course based on one five-minute quiz.

10. As a(n) _____ realtor, Annette previews the properties that she sells.

## NEW WORDS

**wax**
waks

**noisome**
ˈnoisəm

**beneficial**
ˌbenəˈfiSHəl

**optimal**
ˈäptəməl

**encumber**
enˈkəmbər

### DISCORD AT THE FASHION COMPANY

The conflict between the two designers would **wax** very quickly and they often threw **noisome** and hurtful remarks at each other. This constant discord was not **beneficial** for anyone at the office. Because the two did not work together well, the company could not operate at an **optimal** level. The arguments between the two main designers would greatly **encumber** the creative process and the company's popularity slowly waned.

**Definitions:**     Try matching the words in the list with the appropriate definitions. If you are stuck, check the glossary in the back of the book or the passage at the top of the page.

1.   wax   _____   a.   to restrict or burden someone or something in such a way that free action or movement is difficult; to saddle a person with debt or mortgage; to fill or block up (a place)

2.   noisome   _____   b.   favorable or advantageous; resulting in good

3.   beneficial   _____   c.   best or most favorable

4.   optimal   _____   d.   to become larger or stronger

5.   encumber   _____   e.   having an extremely offensive smell; disagreeable; unpleasant

**Sentences:**     Try to use the words above in a sentence below. Remember that a word ending may be changed or its figure of speech slightly altered.

6.   Research shows that, in general, the _____ amount of sleep time for humans is eight hours.

7.   Philippa's interest in the mayoral race _____ as she heard that her best friend would be seeking office.

8.   When a skunk feels threatened, it emits a _____ scent.

9.   It is _____ to eat healthfully and to exercise daily.

10.   It is important not to let your workload _____ you.

# Lesson 93

## A GOOD MATCH

David possesses an almost **celestial** beauty – a **ruddy** tan that accentuates his lean and strong muscles, beautiful blonde locks that are carelessly brushed back, and piercing blue eyes that soften every time he smiles. Add to the mix his cheerful **disposition** and a wisdom that tends to **accrue** with each passing day. With such traits, David can easily **enthrall** most women that he meets. His girlfriend Jane often wonders why he fell in love with her, without realizing that her unique charm, intelligence, and sense of humor are just as attractive as David's.

**Definitions:** Try matching the words in the list with the appropriate definitions. If you are stuck, check the glossary in the back of the book or the passage at the top of the page.

| | | | | |
|---|---|---|---|---|
| 1. | celestial | _____ | a. | 1. a person's inherent qualities of mind and character; 2. the way in which something is placed or arranged, especially in relation to other things |
| 2. | ruddy | _____ | b. | (adj.) having a healthy red or reddish color; (v.) to make reddish in color |
| 3. | enthrall | _____ | c. | to capture the fascinated attention of |
| 4. | accrue | _____ | d. | (of sums of money or benefits) to be received by someone in regular or increasing amounts over time |
| 5. | disposition | _____ | e. | of or pertaining to the sky or the heavens |

**Sentences:** Try to use the words above in a sentence below. Remember that a word ending may be changed or its figure of speech slightly altered.

6. Interest will _____ in most savings accounts if left untouched over time.

7. Laney was _____ with the idea of being promoted to a chair on the board of directors for her company.

8. Mars is called "the red planet" because of its _____ appearance.

9. Part of the reason that Shikha is so likeable is because of her warm and pleasant _____.

10. Though astronomy and astrology both concern _____ matters, the former is a science while the latter is used to assess the influence of heavenly bodies on human affairs.

## NEW WORDS

**manipulate**
mə'nipyə‚lāt

**linchpin**
'linCH‚pin

**erroneous**
i'rōnēəs

**enlighten**
en'lītn

**hasten**
'hāsən

The famous politician was the **linchpin** of the newly found party. Thus when he got involved in a scandal, other political parties tried to **manipulate** the situation and discredit the whole organization. To think that the party would completely fall apart was an **erroneous** assumption, however. The new party's spokespeople did indeed **hasten** to refute the accusations. They did their best to **enlighten** the public about important details regarding the scandal that dissociated the party itself from the politician's actions.

**Definitions:**     Try matching the words in the list with the appropriate definitions. If you are stuck, check the glossary in the back of the book or the passage at the top of the page.

| | | | |
|---|---|---|---|
| 1. | manipulate _____ | a. | a person or thing vital to an enterprise or organization |
| 2. | linchpin _____ | b. | to give (someone or several people) greater knowledge and understanding about a subject or situation |
| 3. | erroneous _____ | c. | to be quick to do something; to move hurriedly |
| 4. | enlighten _____ | d. | wrong, incorrect |
| 5. | hasten _____ | e. | 1. to handle or control (a tool, mechanism, etc.) in a skillful manner; to edit, alter, or move text or data on a computer; 2. to control or influence a person or situation cleverly, unscrupulously, or unfairly; to alter data or present statistics so as to mislead |

**Sentences:**     Try to use the words above in a sentence below. Remember that a word ending may be changed or its figure of speech slightly altered.

6.     In an effort to _____ the progress of building the skyscraper, workers were given increased hours and salaries.

7.     The cunning politician tried to _____ other people into voting for him by making false promises in his campaign speeches.

8.     Margot is the _____ that holds this academic program together; if she retires, its fate will be put into question.

9.     The purpose of the conference is to _____ people about the importance of receiving a university education.

10.     Marlene had to defend herself against _____ claims that she had stolen her sister's wallet and money.

# Lesson 95

### THE DOWN-TO-EARTH ARTIST

The young dancer often received ample **praise** for her **lithe** body and graceful movements.  However, she did not let those flatteries go to her head. She continued to focus on her work and improvement.  She knew that praise and fame were a part of the show business **gloss**.  She was also aware that in the world of show business sincerity was **scarce**.  Therefore, she was not surprised when criticisms came; in fact, she was able to **weather** all such negative remarks with the same calm and determined attitude with which she received all positive feedback.

**Definitions:**      Try matching the words in the list with the appropriate definitions.  If you are stuck, check the glossary in the back of the book or the passage at the top of the page.

1.    lithe    _____    a.    (of food, money, or another resource) insufficient for the demand; occurring in small numbers or quantities

2.    praise    _____    b.    (n.) a shine or luster on a smooth surface; (v.) to conceal or disguise something by treating it briefly or representing it misleadingly

3.    weather    _____    c.    (n.) the state of the atmosphere at a place and time as regards heat, precipitation, humidity, etc.; (v.) 1. to wear away and change the texture of something by long exposure to the atmosphere; 2. to come safely through a storm or turbulent situation

4.    gloss    _____    d.    (especially of a person's body) thin, supple, graceful

5.    scarce    _____    e.    (n.) the expression of approval or admiration of someone or something; (v.) to express warm approval of

**Sentences:**      Try to use the words above in a sentence below.  Remember that a word ending may be changed or its figure of speech slightly altered.

6.    Funke was disappointed when her professor _____ over her paper instead of giving it a thorough read.

7.    The _____ in equatorial regions is warmer than it is in arctic regions.

8.    People with _____ bodies are able to stretch well in exercises.

9.    Though not impossible to find, albino individuals are truly _____.

10.    Receiving _____ from Joan is a big deal, as she rarely ever gives anyone or anything a compliment.

140

## NEW WORDS

**warp**
wôrp

**resuscitate**
ri'səsə,tāt

**endeavor**
en'devər

**mendicant**
'mendikənt

**ferocious**
fə'rōSHəs

A policeman was trying to **resuscitate** a **mendicant** who had fallen unconscious on the street. The officer made many an **endeavor** to revive him, but to no avail. Though this policeman's determination to save the man was **ferocious**, it seemed that the homeless guy was too weak to overcome the hunger and dehydration sapping his vitality. Though bystanders were bewildered by the officer's ardor, optimism was the cornerstone of the policeman's personal philosophy. For him, neither stereotypes nor negative prior experiences with homeless people could **warp** his vision that all humans are created equal and deserve a fair shot at life.

**Definitions:**    Try matching the words in the list with the appropriate definitions. If you are stuck, check the glossary in the back of the book or the passage at the top of the page.

1. warp _____ a. savagely fierce, cruel, or violent
2. resuscitate _____ b. (adj.) given to begging; (n.) a beggar
3. endeavor _____ c. to revive someone from unconsciousness or apparent death; to make an idea or enterprise vigorous again
4. mendicant _____ d. (n.) an attempt to achieve a goal; an enterprise or undertaking; (v.) to try hard to do or achieve something
5. ferocious _____ e. to bend or cause to become bent out of shape, typically because of dampness

**Sentences:**    Try to use the words above in a sentence below. Remember that a word ending may be changed or its figure of speech slightly altered.

6. The _____ approached me on the sidewalk and asked if I could donate a dollar to him.

7. If someone has a heart attack, the goal of emergency medical services is to _____ that person.

8. Most people view tigers and lions as _____ animals, but they also have a soft and caring side.

9. Monsoon rains have caused the wood panels on my dining room floor to _____.

10. Julian is _____ to create a health clinic in Da Nang; if his vision materializes, he will have a flourishing health center in a few years.

# Lesson 97

**MAYORAL ADDRESS**

Tomorrow afternoon, citizens will **convene** at City Hall and listen to the mayor's speech. The talk is especially important because the town has recently endured numerous problems: **harsh** rains, two fires, and a measles outbreak. It is expected that the mayor will be **articulate** in his oration, focusing on pragmatic solutions to the recent problems rather than lofty, **theoretical** issues. Hopefully his presentation will **blend** a sense of action together with a hope that, together, the community can overcome recent tribulations.

**NEW WORDS**

**articulate**
är'tikyəlit

**harsh**
härSH

**blend**
blend

**convene**
kən'vēn

**theoretical**
THēə'retikəl

**Definitions:** Try matching the words in the list with the appropriate definitions. If you are stuck, check the glossary in the back of the book or the passage at the top of the page.

1.  articulate _____  a.  (adj.) having the ability to speak fluently and coherently; (v.) to express an idea or feeling fluently and coherently

2.  harsh _____  b.  concerned with or involving the abstract ideas of a field or study rather than its practical application

3.  blend _____  c.  (n.) a mixture of different things or qualities; (v.) to mix a substance with another so that they meld together as a mass; to put abstract things together; a harmonious combination

4.  convene _____  d.  unpleasantly jarring to the senses or rough; cruel or severe

5.  theoretical _____  e.  to come or bring together for a meeting or activity; to assemble

**Sentences:** Try to use the words above in a sentence below. Remember that a word ending may be changed or its figure of speech slightly altered.

6.  The décor of the new bodega constitutes a(n) _____ of Spanish colonial imagery and California flora.

7.  Grounding a child for a year for not doing homework seems _____.

8.  Most professors have a solid grasp of _____ ideas in their field; many, however, cannot implement such ideas in the real world.

9.  It is important for celebrities to be _____ about issues that impassion them, for a well-known voice can go a long way in helping implement change.

10.  Educators will _____ at the resort hotel next week to discuss educational opportunities in the Pacific Rim.

## NEW WORDS

**antisocial**
ˌantēˈsōSHəl, ˌantī-

**raze**
rāz

**relish**
ˈreliSH

**caliber**
ˈkaləbər

**incur**
inˈkər, iNG-

# Lesson 98

## THE LONER ARCHITECT

Jack is an architect of the highest **caliber**, as he possesses rare design talents, innovation, and creativity. However, others often do not **relish** his company. Often they find Jack's **antisocial** nature and condescending airs discomforting, and they do not wish to **incur** hostility stemming from unnecessary interactions with him. When state officials decided to **raze** the abandoned church — Jack's first and most memorable architectural project — for a public parking lot, some of Jack's coworkers feared his bitterness and quit their job because of it.

**Definitions:**     Try matching the words in the list with the appropriate definitions. If you are stuck, check the glossary in the back of the book or the passage at the top of the page.

| | | | | |
|---|---|---|---|---|
| 1. | antisocial | _____ | a. | to become subject to (something unwelcome or unpleasant) as a result of one's own behavior or actions |
| 2. | raze | _____ | b. | to enjoy greatly |
| 3. | relish | _____ | c. | 1. the quality of someone's character or the level of someone's ability; 2. the internal diameter or bore of a gun barrel |
| 4. | caliber | _____ | d. | 1. not friendly; not wanting the company of others; 2. contrary to the laws and customs of society |
| 5. | incur | _____ | e. | to completely destroy (a building, town, or other site) |

**Sentences:**     Try to use the words above in a sentence below. Remember that a word ending may be changed or its figure of speech slightly altered.

6.     Only students of high _____ are admitted to the competitive preparatory school down the road.

7.     Next week construction companies will _____ the dilapidated building across the street.

8.     Jose _____ numerous late fees when he forgot to pay any of his bills on time.

9.     Lolita's friends construed her isolation as a sign that she had become _____; in reality, she had hidden herself away to write a book.

10.     I don't just enjoy eating a gooey chocolate chip cookie; I _____ it.

# Lesson 99

## THE COMPETITORS

In the morning, the club owner found **graphic** obscenities drawn all over the narrow corridor that provided the **egress** from the nightclub to the street. He knew that this **ignoble** act was **deliberate**. He was convinced that the perpetrators were not random club goers, but instead were professionals hired by his competition. From the moment he opened his club and attracted much of the other club's visitors, he knew that conflict with the neighboring establishment would be **imminent**.

**Definitions:**     Try matching the words in the list with the appropriate definitions. If you are stuck, check the glossary in the back of the book or the passage at the top of the page.

| | | | | |
|---|---|---|---|---|
| 1. | deliberate | _____ | a. | about to happen |
| 2. | graphic | _____ | b. | (adj.) 1. of or related to visual art; 2. giving a vivid picture with explicit detail; (n.) a pictorial item displayed on a screen or stored as data |
| 3. | ignoble | _____ | c. | (adj.) done consciously and intentionally; (v.) engage in long and careful consideration |
| 4. | egress | _____ | d. | not honorable in character or in purpose |
| 5. | imminent | _____ | e. | an exit |

**Sentences:**     Try to use the words above in a sentence below. Remember that a word ending may be changed or its figure of speech slightly altered.

6.     If you need to evacuate the building, the _____ point is located behind the stairwell to the right.

7.     The movie *Pulp Fiction* (1994) is noted for its _____ scenes and intense plot.

8.     The jury is _____ about whether the defendant is guilty of first-degree murder.

9.     It is _____ for a ruler to maliciously kill his own honest and supportive citizens.

10.    It seems that the announcement of a new pontiff is _____, as there is white smoke emanating from the Sistine chapel.

## NEW WORDS

**summit**
'səmit

**extravagant**
ik'stravəgənt

**candid**
'kandid

**mar**
mär

**alternate**
'ôltər‚nāt

### NEWFOUND APLOMB

The fashion designer had reached the **summit** of fame. As a result, he grew in self-confidence and his collections became more and more **extravagant**. Yet the designer's boss was not happy about the former's huge expenditures and thus gave the designer his **candid** opinion on the matter. Despite this criticism, tensions with his boss could not **mar** the designer's newfound confidence. He knew that his work had become very valuable in the market and that his boss could not easily find an **alternate** for him.

**Definitions:**     Try matching the words in the list with the appropriate definitions. If you are stuck, check the glossary in the back of the book or the passage at the top of the page.

| | | | | | |
|---|---|---|---|---|---|
| 1. | summit | _____ | a. | truthful and straightforward; frank | |
| 2. | extravagant | _____ | b. | to impair the appearance, to disfigure; to impair the quality of | |
| 3. | candid | _____ | c. | 1. the highest point of a hill or mountain; 2. a meeting between heads of government | |
| 4. | mar | _____ | d. | (adj.) 1. every other; every second; 2. taking the place of; (n.) a person who acts as a substitute; (v.) to occur in turn repeatedly | |
| 5. | alternate | _____ | e. | lacking restraint in spending money or resources; exceeding what is reasonable or appropriate | |

**Sentences:**     Try to use the words above in a sentence below. Remember that a word ending may be changed or its figure of speech slightly altered.

6.     Unlike Jake, who is superficial and fake, Corey is _____.

7.     A climate change _____ will be held in Mexico City next month; leaders of many nations are expected to attend.

8.     Because I want to save money, I do not live a(n) _____ lifestyle.

9.     Do you have any _____ ideas if we are unable to travel to New Orleans for Mardi Gras?

10.     The unruly teenager attempted to _____ his neighbor's reputation by saying mean things about her.

# Crossword Puzzle
## Lessons 91-100

ACROSS

2 (adj.) best or most favorable
6 (v.) to impair the appearance, to disfigure; to impair the quality of
10 (n.) 1. the highest point of a hill or mountain; 2. a meeting between heads of government
11 (adj.) unpleasantly jarring to the senses or rough; cruel or severe
13 (v.) to become subject to (something unwelcome or unpleasant) as a result of one's own behavior or actions
15 (v.) (of sums of money or benefits) to be received by someone in regular or increasing amounts over time
16 (v.) to revive someone from unconscious or apparent death; to make an idea or enterprise vigorous again
18 (n.) the act of holding someone closely in one's arms; (v.) 1. to hold someone closely in one's arms; 2. to accept or support a belief, theory, or change willingly and enthusiastically; 3. to include or contain something as a constituent part
19 (adj.) savagely fierce, cruel, or violent

DOWN

1 (v.) to make a general or broad statement by inferring from specific cases; to make something more widespread or common
3 (adj.) concerned with or involving the abstract ideas of a field or study rather than its practical application
4 (adj.) 1. not friendly; not wanting the company of others; 2. contrary to the laws and customs of society
5 (n.) a shine or luster on a smooth surface; (v.) to conceal or disguise something by treating it briefly or representing it misleadingly
7 (v.) 1. to handle or control (a tool, mechanism, etc.) in a skillful manner; to edit, alter, or move text or data on a computer; 2. to control or influence a person or situation cleverly, unscrupulously, or unfairly; to alter data or present statistics so as to mislead
8 (adj.) about to happen
9 (v.) to be quick to do something; to move hurriedly
12 (adj.) 1. of or related to visual art; 2. giving a vivid picture with explicit detail; (n.) a pictorial item displayed on a screen or stored as data
14 (n.) the expression of approval or admiration of someone or something; (v.) to express warm approval of
16 (adj.) having a healthy red or reddish color; (v.) to make reddish in color
17 (v.) to become larger or stronger

# Vocabulary Review
## Lessons 91-100

**Directions: Match each word with its best approximate definition. Note that definitions are not necessarily repeated verbatim from the lesson exercises.**

1. fickle _____
2. diligent _____
3. noisome _____
4. beneficial _____
5. celestial _____
6. enthrall _____
7. linchpin _____
8. erroneous _____
9. lithe _____
10. scarce _____
11. warp _____
12. mendicant _____
13. articulate _____
14. convene _____
15. raze _____
16. relish _____
17. ignoble _____
18. egress _____
19. extravagant _____
20. candid _____

a. wrong, false, incorrect
b. having the ability to speak or to speak fluently and coherently
c. a person or thing vital to an organization or enterprise
d. lacking restraint in spending money or resources
e. a beggar
f. to capture the attention of and fascinate
g. positioned in or relating to the sky or heavens
h. occurring in limited numbers or quantities; insufficient for the demand
i. having an offensive smell
j. to completely destroy (a building or site)
k. showing care or conscientiousness in one's abilities
l. to bring together for a meeting or activity; to assemble
m. truthful and straightforward; frank
n. thin, supple, graceful (concerning one's body)
o. to become or cause to become bent, usually as a result of dampness or heat
p. favorable or advantageous
q. an exit
r. to enjoy greatly
s. dishonorable in character or purpose
t. changing one's loyalties, interests, or affection frequently

# Word Roots: Unit 10

## ROOTS AND THEIR MEANINGS

| | | | |
|---|---|---|---|
| **hyper:** | over | **fic/fig:** | to make; to do |
| **epi:** | upon | **vid/vis:** | to see |
| **hypo:** | under | **dem:** | people |

## Here are a few examples of some words that use the above roots:

| | |
|---|---|
| hyperactive: | abnormally or extremely active |
| epidemic: | widespread occurrence of infectious disease in a community |
| hypothermia: | condition of having a low body temperature |
| figment: | something one believes to be real, but that he or she makes up in imagination |
| visual: | of or related to sight or seeing |
| demography: | the study of populations and changes in populations (especially as related to births, deaths, income, and disease) |

## Now try to fill in the table below by finding the appropriate root(s) and interpreting the meaning of each word:

| Word | Root(s) | Guessed Meaning | Actual Meaning |
|---|---|---|---|
| hypersensitive | | | |
| video | | | |
| demographics | | | |
| hypothyroidism | | | |
| fictional | | | |
| epithet | | | |
| figurative | | | |
| epidermis | | | |
| hypertension | | | |
| figure (v.) | | | |

## NEW WORDS

**variance**
ˈve(ə)rēəns

**vague**
vāg

**deficiency**
diˈfiSHənsē

**kiln**
kiln, kil

**reception**
riˈsepSHən

### THE OLD BRICK MAKER

There was not much **variance** in the routine of the old brick maker. Every morning he put the new clay bricks in the **kiln** to bake and then laid them out in the yard to cool. His bricks always met with a warm **reception** – they were considered to be the best ones in the area. Recently, however, he began to feel a **vague** pain in his chest that made it harder to work. His doctor insisted that it was likely a vitamin **deficiency**, but the old brick maker felt that there was something wrong with his heart. With proper care, the old brick maker healed and continued his routine at his typical pace.

**Definitions:** Try matching the words in the list with the appropriate definitions. If you are stuck, check the glossary in the back of the book or the passage at the top of the page.

1. variance _____ a. of uncertain, indefinite, or unclear character or meaning

2. vague _____ b. the fact or quality of being different, divergent, or inconsistent

3. deficiency _____ c. 1. the action or process of receiving something sent, given, or inflicted; 2. a formal social occasion held to welcome someone or to celebrate a particular event; 3. the area in a hotel, office, or establishment where guests and visitors are greeted and dealt with

4. kiln _____ d. a furnace or oven for burning, baking, or drying, especially one for firing pottery

5. reception _____ e. a lack or shortage

**Sentences:** Try to use the words above in a sentence below. Remember that a word ending may be changed or its figure of speech slightly altered.

6. There is much _____ in how people interpret important novels.

7. I only have a(n) _____ idea of what I may be doing with my life twenty years from now.

8. After having made racist remarks, the journalist was welcomed at the annual banquet with a frigid _____.

9. Individuals with a reading _____ may experience difficulty comprehending prose or parsing the words contained in that prose.

10. When I took a pottery class last winter, Gary taught me how to use the _____ to fire my creations.

# Lesson 102

**KIDNAPPED**

Frank woke up and found himself in the awful **predicament** of being kidnapped. He was able to **notice** only a locked door and a window in the room, the latter of which was big enough for him to climb through and escape. Yet, since Frank was chained up in shackles, he was not **ambulatory** and could not flee. After many hours of waiting, the **noxious** kidnapper finally entered to check on him. He threatened Frank to be obedient, and left a bowl of some **bland** soup behind. Frank quickly devoured the soup, but was unable to quench his anxiety about the future.

**Definitions:** Try matching the words in the list with the appropriate definitions. If you are stuck, check the glossary in the back of the book or the passage at the top of the page.

1. notice _____ a. a difficult, unpleasant, or embarrassing situation

2. noxious _____ b. lacking strong features or characteristics and therefore uninteresting; food or drink that is mild and insipid; a person lacking strong emotion and unremarkable

3. predicament _____ c. harmful, poisonous, or very unpleasant

4. bland _____ d. (n.) 1. attention, observation; 2. notification or warning of something, especially to allow preparations to be made; 3. a displayed sheet giving news or information; (v.) to become aware of

5. ambulatory _____ e. related to or adapted to walking

**Sentences:** Try to use the words above in a sentence below. Remember that a word ending may be changed or its figure of speech slightly altered.

6. Certain pesticides are _____ and thus have the potential to greatly erode human health.

7. After weeks of being practically bedridden, Sonya was finally _____ enough to walk to the grocery store.

8. It was hard not to _____ the orange stain that appeared on Natalie's white shirt this afternoon: she accidentally had spilled marinara sauce on her top at lunch.

9. Usually the Malaysian food at this restaurant is spicy, but today it seems to taste rather _____.

10. Jeremy found himself in a(n) _____ when his dissertation adviser passed away and there was nobody remaining who was capable of supervising his research.

150

## NEW WORDS

**heirloom**
ˈe(ə)rˌloom

**pose**
pōz

**pathetic**
pəˈTHetik

**instantaneous**
ˌinstənˈtānēəs

**forlorn**
fərˈlôrn, fôr-

## THE DISAPPOINTING WILL

James was convinced that he would inherit the old Chinese vase, which was his family's most valuable **heirloom**. He was **forlorn** when he found out that the vase was gifted to the local museum. When the estate lawyer finished reading the will, James' **instantaneous** reaction was to protest. He struck a **pose** of defiance; however, his **pathetic** effort to change the situation was completely futile.

**Definitions:**  Try matching the words in the list with the appropriate definitions. If you are stuck, check the glossary in the back of the book or the passage at the top of the page.

1.  heirloom  _____  a.  arousing pity, especially through vulnerability or sadness; miserable; inadequate

2.  pose  _____  b.  (n.) 1. a way of standing or sitting, usually adopted in order to be photographed, drawn, or painted; 2. a particular way of behavior adopted in order to give others a false impression or to impress others; (v.) 1. to present or constitute (a problem, danger, or difficulty); 2. to assume a particular attitude in order to be photographed, drawn, or painted; 3. to behave affectedly in order to impress others

3.  pathetic  _____  c.  occurring or done immediately

4.  instantaneous  _____  d.  a valuable object that has belonged to a family for several generations

5.  forlorn  _____  e.  pitifully sad, abandoned, or lonely; miserable; inadequate

**Sentences:**  Try to use the words above in a sentence below. Remember that a word ending may be changed or its figure of speech slightly altered.

6.  That necklace is a family _____ that belonged to my mother's parents.

7.  Unlike in the nineteenth century, in the digital world communication between people living far away can occur almost _____.

8.  Ike's attempt to ask Paloma out was _____: rather than addressing Paloma directly, he had his friends suggest that the two meet for tea because he was lonely.

9.  Often reporters _____ questions to celebrities and leaders during major events.

10.  Larry became _____ when he realized that his puppy ran away.

# Lesson 104

## BUSINESS NEGOTIATIONS

Negotiations between the two companies reached a critical **juncture**. There was a **tacit** agreement between the two that the current market could handle only one of them since their products were **akin**. According to the younger company, which had modeled its products on the older one, a merger would **suffice** to clear the situation. Representatives of the older company, however, felt that the younger company had violated copyright laws and needed to pay a large sum of money to its **predecessor**. The two companies squabbled for weeks before finally settling their differences and merging.

## NEW WORDS

**tacit**
ˈtasit

**akin**
əˈkin

**juncture**
ˈjəNGkCHər

**suffice**
səˈfīs

**predecessor**
ˈpredəˌsesər, ˈprē-

**Definitions:** Try matching the words in the list with the appropriate definitions. If you are stuck, check the glossary in the back of the book or the passage at the top of the page.

1. tacit _____ a. to be enough or adequate; to meet the needs of
2. akin _____ b. a person who held a job or office before another; a thing that has been followed or replaced by another
3. juncture _____ c. understood or implied without being stated
4. suffice _____ d. a particular point in events or time; a place where things join
5. predecessor _____ e. of similar character

**Sentences:** Try to use the words above in a sentence below. Remember that a word ending may be changed or its figure of speech slightly altered.

6. Not voting in an election is _____ to not caring about the political future of the country.
7. Though I prefer job candidates to have a physics degree, candidates holding a mathematics degree will also _____.
8. One might argue that a typewriter is a _____ of the modern word processor.
9. At this _____, you have important decisions to make about your future, for they will dictate your future path in life.
10. Unlike Gordon, who talked endlessly about gun control, Felicia remained _____ on the issue.

## NEW WORDS

**yield**
yēld

**bard**
bärd

**clone**
klōn

**repress**
ri'pres

**conspicuous**
kən'spikyooəs

# Lesson 105

## A BARD IN LOVE

Though the **bard** typically enjoyed expressing poetic thoughts about the ladies he met, he quit doing so after he met Julia. Private and introverted by nature, Julia begged him not to publicize their relationship in his art or to **clone** the private love notes that he wrote to her. Though he **yielded** to her wishes, it was difficult for him to **repress** his feelings. And although Julia did not want people knowing about their relationship, their courtship became **conspicuous** after townsfolk saw the pair out dining together – the couple's privacy could not remain hidden forever.

**Definitions:**    Try matching the words in the list with the appropriate definitions. If you are stuck, check the glossary in the back of the book or the passage at the top of the page.

1.   yield   _____   a.   (n.) an identical copy of something; (v.) to make an identical copy of

2.   bard   _____   b.   a poet, especially one conveying epics in an oral tradition

3.   clone   _____   c.   to subdue someone or something by force; to restrain, prevent, or inhibit

4.   repress   _____   d.   (n.) the full amount of an agricultural or industrial product; (v.) 1. to produce or provide; to generate; 2. to give way to arguments, demands, pressure, or traffic

5.   conspicuous   _____   e.   standing out so as to be clearly visible

**Sentences:**    Try to use the words above in a sentence below. Remember that a word ending may be changed or its figure of speech slightly altered.

6.   This year our _____ of apples was over two thousand tons!

7.   Dolly the sheep was the first living mammal to be _____.

8.   It was _____ that the teacher did not prepare for class because he could not deliver the lecture without being completely dependent on his notes.

9.   The eloquent _____ told the story of his kingdom in a melodramatic fashion.

10.   It was hard for Michael to _____ his feelings at the funeral; he tried to hold back, but tears eventually flowed profusely from his eyes.

153

# Lesson 106

## THE TRUTH WILL OUT

The management style of the new science fiction film director was quite **erratic**. It resulted in chaos on the set, especially from the actors playing **galactic** warriors who spent hours each day getting made up as extraterrestrials for their roles. Such awful leadership resulted in **innumerable** contract details that needed to be resolved and an increasingly chaotic morale. Despite such bedlam, the director's prior employer did **vouch** for him: they said he had been their best director. They obviously had lied, and the new movie company's representatives simply stood **aghast** at the sight of the director's sheer incompetence.

## NEW WORDS

**erratic**
iˈratik

**galactic**
gəˈlaktik

**aghast**
əˈgast

**innumerable**
iˈn(y)oomərəbəl

**vouch**
vouch

**Definitions:** Try matching the words in the list with the appropriate definitions. If you are stuck, check the glossary in the back of the book or the passage at the top of the page.

| | | | | |
|---|---|---|---|---|
| 1. | erratic | _____ | a. | filled with shock or horror |
| 2. | galactic | _____ | b. | of or relating to galaxies, especially the Milky Way |
| 3. | aghast | _____ | c. | too many to be counted (used often in exaggeration) |
| 4. | innumerable | _____ | d. | uneven in pattern or movement |
| 5. | vouch | _____ | e. | to assert or confirm from one's experience that something is true or accurately as described |

**Sentences:** Try to use the words above in a sentence below. Remember that a word ending may be changed or its figure of speech slightly altered.

6. It is important to have others _____ for your character, accomplishments, and credibility when an employer solicits references.

7. Jacob's _____ attendance in class probably explains why his grades are not as high as they could be.

8. There are _____ grains of sand on that beach; one could never fathom counting them all.

9. The new movie provides viewers with a(n) _____ experience, showing them the vast star systems in the Milky Way.

10. Artie was _____ when he heard that someone had broken his favorite piano.

## NEW WORDS

**lore**
lôr

**tumult**
ˈt(y)oo͵məlt

**arbitrator**
ˈärbi͵trātər

**retract**
riˈtrakt

**adroit**
əˈdroit

### AN ACT OF BETRAYAL

After acquiring the elixir – which could extend life according to traditional **lore** – from the chief of the Kanbu tribe, the King decided to **retract** his words. He refused to sign the peace treaty and concede part of his land to the tribe as he promised, inciting political **tumult**. An **arbitrator** was sent to settle the conflict, but his **adroit** persuasion still failed to appease the irate chief.

**Definitions:**    Try matching the words in the list with the appropriate definitions. If you are stuck, check the glossary in the back of the book or the passage at the top of the page.

1. lore _____ a. an independent person or body officially appointed to settle a dispute

2. tumult _____ b. to draw or be drawn back in; withdraw

3. arbitrator _____ c. a body of traditions and knowledge on a subject or held by a particular group, typically transmitted by word of mouth

4. retract _____ d. a loud confused noise, especially one caused by a mass of people; confusion or disorder

5. adroit _____ e. clever or skillful in using the hands or mind

**Sentences:**    Try to use the words above in a sentence below. Remember that a word ending may be changed or its figure of speech slightly altered.

6. Sitting in her apartment, Shaolaine heard the _____ as protests broke out in the park.

7. According to Norse _____, Thor is the god of thunder.

8. Colleen was so _____ with her hands that she stole her friend's wallet without the latter even noticing.

9. When disputes become nasty, they often require a(n) _____ to help resolve them.

10. Realizing that he had, perhaps, promised to deliver too much, Mark asked if he could _____ his last offer in the business negotiation.

# Lesson 108

## BEHIND THE CURTAINS

The **merger** between the two theater companies was a task of **herculean** proportions. There was an **inclination** on both sides to resist cooperation. The companies' representatives responsible for the merger felt that there was no **antidote** to the inflated egos of the artists. Each of the two groups of actors would try to **abash** the other by sneering and making disparaging remarks during the meetings. The merger was doomed to fail from the beginning.

**Definitions:**    Try matching the words in the list with the appropriate definitions. If you are stuck, check the glossary in the back of the book or the passage at the top of the page.

| | | | | |
|---|---|---|---|---|
| 1. | abash | _____ | a. | a medicine taken to counteract a particular poison |
| 2. | antidote | _____ | b. | requiring great strength or effort |
| 3. | inclination | _____ | c. | a combination of two things (usually companies) into one |
| 4. | herculean | _____ | d. | to cause to feel embarrassed, disconcerted, or ashamed |
| 5. | merger | _____ | e. | 1. a person's natural tendency to act in a particular way; a propensity or disposition; 2. a slope or slant; 3. the angle at which a straight line or plane intersects another |

**Sentences:**    Try to use the words above in a sentence below. Remember that a word ending may be changed or its figure of speech slightly altered.

6.    It was a(n) _____ task to move all of my stuff from my old house to my new one.

7.    The _____ between the two companies will offer new business opportunities, but the employees from the respective companies must get along first.

8.    Allegra felt _____ when her parents discussed her previous boyfriends with her fiancé and his family.

9.    Often the best _____ for the common cold is a bowl of piping hot chicken soup.

10.    Because I have little _____ to study robotics for months, I do not think I should be helping you build intelligent machines.

## NEW WORDS

**shirk**
SHərk

**pigment**
ˈpigmənt

**brevity**
ˈbrevitē

**conduit**
ˈkänˌd(y)oōət, ˈkänd(w)ət

**iniquity**
iˈnikwitē

# Lesson 109

## ON OBTAINING A BLUE HUE

In Renaissance Italy, obtaining a deep blue **pigment** was a costly endeavor. This is because the stone providing this color – lapis lazuli – had to be transported from far away (present-day Afghanistan). Because the Renaissance era lacked modern transport, delivery of such stones was a process that lacked **brevity**. Access to merchants, of course, served as a main **conduit** through which such stones could eventually be obtained and delivered. But if a merchant was inclined to **shirk** his responsibility, such stones may never arrive and the purchaser would lose his or her money in the purchase. For this reason, selecting a merchant with credibility was very important, and any display of **iniquity** in the trading community was broadcast widely and could easily damage one's career.

**Definitions:**     Try matching the words in the list with the appropriate definitions. If you are stuck, check the glossary in the back of the book or the passage at the top of the page.

1.  shirk     _____     a.  to avoid or neglect a duty or responsibility
2.  pigment     _____     b.  the natural coloring of plant or animal tissue; a substance used for coloring or painting, especially a dry powder that, when mixed with water or oil, forms a paint or ink
3.  brevity     _____     c.  immoral or grossly unfair behavior
4.  conduit     _____     d.  concise and exact use of words in speech; shortness of time
5.  iniquity     _____     e.  a channel for conveying a fluid; a person or organization that acts as a channel for the transmission of something

**Sentences:**     Try to use the words above in a sentence below. Remember that a word ending may be changed or its figure of speech slightly altered.

6.    Only years of penitence could help mitigate the old man's _____.
7.    The _____ for the red color in that painting comes from the stones that I bought in the market last week.
8.    The Detroit River serves as a(n) _____ that connects the larger bodies of water Lake Erie and Lake St. Clair.
9.    Good writing should be praised not only for its clarity but also for its _____: it is best to be eloquent in as few words as possible
10.    If you _____ your responsibilities, there may be negative repercussions.

157

# Lesson 110

## RALPH AND THE YACHT

When Ralph's parents agreed to **grant** him access to the family yacht after he graduated from college, a **priceless** expression of glee appeared on his face. Ralph had wanted to ride the yacht ever since he was six, and each year his family would **convey** to him that the boat was reserved only for adults. Finally old enough to travel himself, Ralph joyously guided the yacht out to sea for the first time. He found the **drone** of the boat's motor so relaxing that he fell asleep for hours. Twelve hours later he woke up stranded at sea in the middle of the night. He had to phone his family for help, and thus felt compelled to **prevaricate** about what had happened when pressed by his parents for an explanation.

**Definitions:**     Try matching the words in the list with the appropriate definitions. If you are stuck, check the glossary in the back of the book or the passage at the top of the page.

| | | | |
|---|---|---|---|
| 1. | grant _____ | a. | to speak or act in an evasive way |
| 2. | priceless _____ | b. | so precious that its value cannot be determined |
| 3. | convey _____ | c. | (n.) a sum of money given by an organization, especially a government, for a particular purpose; (v.) 1. to agree to give or allow (something requested) to; 2. to agree or admit to someone that something is true |
| 4. | prevaricate _____ | d. | to transport or carry from place to place; to make an idea, impression, or feeling known or understandable to someone |
| 5. | drone _____ | e. | (n.) a low, continuous humming sound; (v.) to make a continuous low humming sound; to speak tediously in a monotonous tone |

**Sentences:**     Try to use the words above in a sentence below. Remember that a word ending may be changed or its figure of speech slightly altered.

6.    Often in fairy tales, a genie will _____ his or her master three wishes.

7.    Stephanie shut the window to help drown out the _____ of the vehicle motors.

8.    It was difficult for the lost child to _____ his gratitude to the strangers who helped reunite him with his parents.

9.    While clothing, cars, and fine dining are costly, developing a relationship with your child is indeed a(n) _____ experience.

10.   When asked about his business intentions, the lobbyist chose to _____ to the media about them.

158

# Word Search

## Lessons 101-110

```
L N N R N Y D R A B N N V D X T
C O Z R N R Y N Z K I A E X I Q
O M R Y J K T Z W K R C T U Y D
N T N E M G I P A I I K D J X B
S U O E N A T N A T S N I L A Y
P L Z T L Y Q N O N O D N R E R
I R J N N B C N F C X M B V M J
C W Z A B E A O D X K I N P L J
U M E R G E R R N G T O W L T R
O B S G J L N W E R C W Y S I K
U L M U O B L T A M A T A Z J K
S A K R F Q D T P B U H V K M G
T N N Q R F O P A Y G N N N J Y
L D B K R R I S P A L Z N P R J
V M Q M R D H C J L R P L I J N
V K Y D R B V D E N M X W L R K
```

1  (n.) the fact or quality of being different, divergent, or inconsistent
2  (n.) a furnace or oven for burning, baking, or drying, especially one for firing pottery
3  (n.) 1. attention, observation; 2. notification or warning of something, especially to allow preparations to be made; 3. a displayed sheet giving news or information; (v.) to become aware of
4  (adj.) lacking strong features or characteristics and therefore uninteresting; food or drink that is mild and insipid; a person lacking strong emotion and unremarkable
5  (adj.) occurring or done immediately
6  (adj.) pitifully sad, abandoned, or lonely
7  (adj.) of similar character
8  (v.) to be enough or adequate; to meet the needs of
9  (n.) a poet, especially one conveying epics in an oral tradition
10 (adj.) standing out so as to be clearly visible
11 (adj.) filled with shock or horror
12 (adj.) too many to be counted (used often in exaggeration)
13 (n.) a body of traditions and knowledge on a subject or held by a particular group, typically transmitted by word of mouth
14 (n.) an independent person or body officially appointed to settle a dispute
15 (v.) to cause to feel embarrassed, disconcerted, or ashamed
16 (n.) a combination of two things (usually companies) into one
17 (n.) the natural coloring of plant or animal tissue; a substance used for coloring or painting, especially a dry powder that, when mixed with water or oil, forms a paint or ink
18 (n.) a channel for conveying a fluid; a person or organization that acts as a channel for the transmission of something
19 (n.) a sum of money given by an organization, especially a government, for a particular purpose; (v.) 1. to agree to give or allow (something requested) to; 2. to agree or admit to someone that something is true
20 (v.) to transport or carry from place to place; to make an idea, impression, or feeling known or understandable to someone

# Vocabulary Review
## Lessons 101-110

**Directions: Match each word with its best approximate definition. Note that definitions are not necessarily repeated verbatim from the lesson exercises.**

1. vague _____
2. deficiency _____
3. predicament _____
4. ambulatory _____
5. heirloom _____
6. pathetic _____
7. tacit _____
8. juncture _____
9. yield _____
10. clone _____
11. erratic _____
12. galactic _____
13. tumult _____
14. adroit _____
15. antidote _____
16. herculean _____
17. brevity _____
18. iniquity _____
19. priceless _____
20. prevaricate _____

a. a place where things join; a particular point in events or time
b. loud confused noise typically caused by a mass of people; confusion or disorder
c. sinfulness; immoral behavior
d. concise and exact use of words in speech; shortness of time
e. to speak or act in an evasive way
f. relating to or adapted to walking
g. not even or regular in pattern or movement
h. to give way to arguments, demands or pressure; to produce or provide a natural or agricultural product
i. so precious its value cannot be determined
j. to make an identical copy; a person or thing that is an identical copy of another
k. a valuable object belonging to a family for several generations
l. medicine taken to counteract a poison
m. a difficult, embarrassing, or unpleasant situation
n. arousing pity, especially through sadness or vulnerability; miserable; inadequate
o. relating to galaxies, especially the Milky Way
p. requiring great strength or effort
q. clever in using the hands or mind
r. implied or understood without being stated
s. a lack or shortage
t. uncertain or indefinite in character or meaning

# Word Roots: Unit 11

Here are a few examples of some words that use the above roots:

## ROOTS AND THEIR MEANINGS

| | | | |
|---|---|---|---|
| pro: | forward, supporting | pon/pos: | to put; to place |
| eu: | pleasing | voc: | to call |
| sequ/secu: | to follow | luc/lum: | light, bright |

## Here are a few examples of some words that use the above roots:

| | |
|---|---|
| proactive: | creating or controlling a situation by being active rather than passive after it has taken place |
| euphoric: | characterized by feeling of intense excitement and happiness |
| consequential: | following as a result or effect of something; important or substantive |
| deposit (v.): | to put or set down something (usually money) in a specific place, often for safekeeping |
| vocal: | expressing feelings loudly |
| luminous: | full of shedding light; very bright |

## Now try to fill in the table below by finding the appropriate root(s) and interpreting the meaning of each word:

| Word | Root(s) | Guessed Meaning | Actual Meaning |
|---|---|---|---|
| sequence | | | |
| postpone | | | |
| lucid | | | |
| provocative | | | |
| deposit | | | |
| eulogy | | | |
| consecutive | | | |

# Lesson 111

## THE ART HISTORY LECTURE

The teacher gave an **oration** in which she attempted to **illustrate** the value of Victorian art. She discussed the **detrimental** effects of social taboos on artistic expression during that time period. She cited the standard experts on Victorian art as well as some **additional** sources, which she found to be illustrative in proving her point. She explained to the students that many artists from that time period were considered **impudent** if their work was too sexually explicit for the conservative Victorian public.

## NEW WORDS

**illustrate**
ˈiləˌstrāt

**oration**
ôˈrāSHən

**additional**
əˈdiSHənl

**detrimental**
ˌdetrəˈmentl

**impudent**
ˈimpyəd(ə)nt

**Definitions:**    Try matching the words in the list with the appropriate definitions. If you are stuck, check the glossary in the back of the book or the passage at the top of the page.

1.    illustrate  _____    a.    1. to provide (a book, newspaper, etc.) with pictures; 2. to explain or make something clear by way of charts, pictures, and other visuals; 3. to serve as an example of

2.    oration  _____    b.    tending to cause harm

3.    additional  _____    c.    not showing due respect for another person

4.    detrimental  _____    d.    a formal speech, ordinarily one that is given on a ceremonial occasion

5.    impudent  _____    e.    added, extra, or supplementary to what is already given

**Sentences:**    Try to use the words above in a sentence below. Remember that a word ending may be changed or its figure of speech slightly altered.

6.    The chairman's _____ was truly moving: his words inspired me to be a better worker.

7.    Without someone to _____ my children's book, the text will be devoid of images to complement the text.

8.    If anybody in the audience has _____ questions, such persons should feel free to contact me by email after the presentation.

9.    Lack of exercise can be _____ to one's physical health and mental stability.

10.    The _____ student castigated his teachers and walked out of school.

## NEW WORDS

**lexicon**
ˈleksiˌkän, -kən

**brusque**
brəsk

**paltry**
ˈpôltrē

**recognize**
ˈrekigˌnīz, ˈrekə(g)ˌnīz

**incoherent**
ˌinkōˈhi(ə)rənt, ˌiNG-, -ˈher-

## GOING BACK TO THE VILLAGE

The old man was lying on the bed almost unconscious. Stephen listened to his **incoherent** mumble, trying to figure out what his father was saying. After so many years, he could only **recognize** some of the words in his father's **lexicon**, which was full of **brusque** and often offensive expressions typical of the local villagers. Stephen remembered why he left this village such a long time ago: everything about his father's farm, including his manner of speaking, struck him as **paltry** and outdated.

**Definitions:** Try matching the words in the list with the appropriate definitions. If you are stuck, check the glossary in the back of the book or the passage at the top of the page.

| | | | | |
|---|---|---|---|---|
| 1. | lexicon | _____ | a. | abrupt or offhand in speech or manner |
| 2. | brusque | _____ | b. | the vocabulary of a person, language, or branch of knowledge |
| 3. | paltry | _____ | c. | a small or meager amount of something; petty; trivial |
| 4. | recognize | _____ | d. | expressed in an incomprehensible or confusing way |
| 5. | incoherent | _____ | e. | 1. to identify (someone or something) from having a previous encounter; 2. to acknowledge the existence, validity, or legality of |

**Sentences:** Try to use the words above in a sentence below. Remember that a word ending may be changed or its figure of speech slightly altered.

6. Static on the telephone made my friend's words sound _____.
7. Nitya's _____ comments put off his sweet and caring girlfriend.
8. It was hard to _____ that the girl in the costume was actually my sister.
9. Though I speak fluent English, I am not well acquainted with the _____ of the shipping industry.
10. To work nine hours for a(n) _____ three dollars is exploitive.

# Lesson 113

## THE ART CUSTOMS OF AN ISLAND COMMUNITY

The **mores** of the island community encouraged artists to seek a wealthy **patron** to support their endeavors. Such values supported the **opinion** that artistic endeavors should be a spontaneous and **joyous** process and thus should not be influenced by an artist's monetary concerns. A patron could sponsor his or her favorite artist; however, the financial support also had to be within a reasonable **margin**. The community believed that the artist needed to remain humble and grounded as well if he or she was to produce authentic art.

**NEW WORDS**

**patron**
ˈpātrən

**mores**
ˈmôrˌāz

**margin**
ˈmärjən

**opinion**
əˈpinyən

**joyous**
ˈjoiəs

**Definitions:**    Try matching the words in the list with the appropriate definitions. If you are stuck, check the glossary in the back of the book or the passage at the top of the page.

| | | | | |
|---|---|---|---|---|
| 1. | patron | _____ | a. | the fundamental customs and conventions of a community |
| 2. | mores | _____ | b. | a view or judgment formed about something, not necessarily based on fact or knowledge; a formal statement by an expert rendering advice or judgment on a matter |
| 3. | margin | _____ | c. | 1. a person who gives financial support to another individual, a cause, an organization, or an activity; 2. a customer (typically a regular one) |
| 4. | opinion | _____ | d. | 1. the edge or border of something; 2. the amount by which a thing is won or falls short |
| 5. | joyous | _____ | e. | full of happiness and excitement |

**Sentences:**    Try to use the words above in a sentence below. Remember that a word ending may be changed or its figure of speech slightly altered.

6.    Often in seventeenth-century books, readers can find handwriting in the
_____ of a page.

7.    I am a special _____ of the Thai restaurant on the peninsula.

8.    To a Westerner, some of the _____ of the Cambodian people seem quite alien.

9.    Usually Christmas is a(n) _____ holiday for me, but for some reason I feel somewhat down this holiday season.

10.    In my _____, students who do not do their homework do not deserve a tutor.

## NEW WORDS

**scalpel**
ˈskalpəl

**goodwill**
ˌgoodˈwil

**gainsay**
ˌgānˈsā, ˈgānˌsā

**buffet**
bəˈfā (n.); ˈbəfit (v.)

**facile**
ˈfasəl

# Lesson 114

### NURTURE

Jim saw it as a gesture of **goodwill** to invite his students to a **buffet** before their final exam. No one on campus, in fact, could **gainsay** that Jim was one of the kindest mentors who always tried to **facilitate** a rapport between him and his students. Jim always knew that a good mentoring relationship entailed more than just pedagogy. Though he likened providing incisive analysis on student papers with his red pen to a surgeon operating with a **scalpel**, Jim made it a priority to be a supportive presence for his students in more ways than one.

**Definitions:** Try matching the words in the list with the appropriate definitions. If you are stuck, check the glossary in the back of the book or the passage at the top of the page.

1. scalpel _____ a. a surgical knife
2. goodwill _____ b. (n.) a meal consisting of several dishes in which guests serve themselves; (v.) to strike repeatedly; to batter; to knock someone over or off course
3. gainsay _____ c. easily achieved or effortless; superficial
4. buffet _____ d. friendly, helpful, or cooperative feelings or attitude
5. facile _____ e. to deny or contradict a fact or statement

**Sentences:** Try to use the words above in a sentence below. Remember that a word ending may be changed or its figure of speech slightly altered.

6. The defendant tried to _____ the plaintiff's accusations with evidence and testimony.
7. On account of Marisa's _____, she was given an internship at the local design studio.
8. The Sunday morning _____ at the hotel is fabulous: I love the endless flow of drinks, carving station, and curry corner.
9. For a mathematician, adding numbers is a(n) _____ task.
10. One cannot perform a successful operation if one does not have a(n) _____ handy.

# Lesson 115

## THE SPENDTHRIFT SALES MANAGER

The sales manager sometimes made **frivolous** purchases. For instance, he had a weakness for purchasing **newfangled** gadgets that the company could do without. Yet despite these acquisitions, he was able to **operate** the business well and it make it a profit. This was primarily because he liked to **collaborate** with people from other departments. He was also quite **discreet** about his extravagant purchases. Overall, the CEO appreciated the sales manager's work, and the latter's unorthodox spending practices seemed not to undermine executive support for him.

## NEW WORDS

**discreet**
dis'krēt

**newfangled**
'n(y)oo'faNGgəld, -ˌfaNG-

**collaborate**
kəˈlabəˌrāt

**frivolous**
'frivələs

**operate**
'äpəˌrāt

**Definitions:** Try matching the words in the list with the appropriate definitions. If you are stuck, check the glossary in the back of the book or the passage at the top of the page.

1. discreet _____
2. newfangled _____
3. collaborate _____
4. frivolous _____
5. operate _____

a. to work jointly on an activity, especially to produce something

b. 1. to control the functioning of a machine, process, or system; 2. to manage and run a business; 3. to perform a surgical procedure

c. not having any serious purpose or value

d. careful and circumspect in one's speech or actions, especially in order to avoid causing offense or to gain an advantage

e. different from what one is used to; objectionably new

**Sentences:** Try to use the words above in a sentence below. Remember that a word ending may be changed or its figure of speech slightly altered.

6. The _____ video game console allows players to experience virtual reality unlike any machine that came before it.

7. Bennett and Thao tried to be _____ about their relationship at work, for they did not want colleagues knowing that they were dating.

8. Going to the casino, to me, is not only a(n) _____ activity, but also a potentially dangerously expensive one, too.

9. I am learning how to _____ a crane so that I can become more experienced in construction.

10. Both professors are trying to _____ and write a history of Kazakhstan.

166

## NEW WORDS

**ascertain**
ˌasərˈtān

**evacuate**
iˈvakyəˌwāt

**objectionable**
əbˈjekSHənəbəl

**extol**
ikˈstōl

**solid**
ˈsälid

# Lesson 116

### GABOR'S DOUBLE LIFE

Gabor had a **solid** reputation in his neighborhood. Everyone would look at him with admiration and **extol** him for all the free services he provided his neighbors through his company. This is why people did not find it **objectionable** when they did not see Gabor's children leave the house for days. No one suspected anything. However, a social worker visiting the house was immediately able to **ascertain** that the children looked very nervous and bothered. The social worker knew that she needed to **evacuate** the children from the house immediately and take them to a safe place in order to interrogate them.

**Definitions:**     Try matching the words in the list with the appropriate definitions. If you are stuck, check the glossary in the back of the book or the passage at the top of the page.

1.     ascertain _____     a.     (adj.) 1. firm and stable in shape, not liquid or fluid; 2. not hollow; 3. dependable, reliable; (n.) a substance that is firm and stable in shape and not a liquid or fluid

2.     evacuate _____     b.     to find something out for certain; to make sure of

3.     objectionable _____     c.     arousing distaste or opposition; unpleasant or offensive

4.     extol _____     d.     to praise

5.     solid _____     e.     1. to remove someone (or several people) from a place of danger to a safe place; 2. to remove air, water, or other contents from a container

**Sentences:**     Try to use the words above in a sentence below. Remember that a word ending may be changed or its figure of speech slightly altered.

6.     After a conflagration broke out in the kitchen, the chef was forced to _____ the restaurant.

7.     It is difficult to _____ the meaning of ancient Egyptian hieroglyphic texts.

8.     If the student had received _____ support from his supervisors, he would not be struggling so much with his research.

9.     I find Travis' behavior _____: he was rude to my parents and offended my little brother.

10.     It is easy to _____ the virtues of America's founding fathers.

# Lesson 117

## THE WARRING SPOUSES

A weekend getaway with **splendid** views of the countryside was a promising **oasis** in their recently troubled marriage. Yet the husband seemed to be making a **unilateral** effort to save the marriage. His wife kept arguing with him during the trip, and their child served as a **buffer** between the warring couple. Whenever the husband pointed out that his wife simply did not want to cooperate, the wife would **repudiate** these claims and transfer the blame onto him.

**Definitions:**    Try matching the words in the list with the appropriate definitions. If you are stuck, check the glossary in the back of the book or the passage at the top of the page.

| | | | | |
|---|---|---|---|---|
| 1. | splendid | _____ | a. | to refuse to accept or be associated with; to deny the truth or validity of |
| 2. | oasis | _____ | b. | 1. (of an action or decision) performed by or affecting only one person, group, or country involved in a particular situation, without the agreement of another or the others; 2. relating to, occurring on, or affecting only one side of an organ or structure, or of the body |
| 3. | buffer | _____ | c. | (n.) a person or thing that prevents incompatible or antagonistic people or things from coming into contact with or harming each other; (v.) to lessen or moderate the impact of something |
| 4. | unilateral | _____ | d. | a fertile spot in a desert where water is found |
| 5. | repudiate | _____ | e. | magnificent; very impressive |

**Sentences:**    Try to use the words above in a sentence below. Remember that a word ending may be changed or its figure of speech slightly altered.

6.    The caravan stopped at a(n) _____ to drink, bathe, and relax.

7.    The St. Louis Gateway Arch is a(n) _____ monument: it provides an example of modern architecture and has a great view from the top.

8.    Barry _____ every effort the girl made to ask him on a date.

9.    It was a(n) _____ decision to expel the student who plagiarized his essay.

10.   Jill erected a fence to serve as a(n) _____ between herself and her neighbor.

## NEW WORDS

**fanatic**
fəˈnatik

**copious**
ˈkōpēəs

**traumatic**
trəˈmatik, trou-, trô-

**effectual**
iˈfekCHo͞oəl

**negative**
ˈnegətiv

# Lesson 118

## SHATTERED DREAMS

Max used to be a swimming **fanatic** who trained for hours each day and acquired **copious** medals for his talents. However, after a car crash damaged his vertebrae, swimming became an impossible task for Max. After visiting many hospitals, none offered an **effectual** remedy. The **traumatic** accident, as well as Max's realization that he might never be able to swim again, left Max with **negative** thoughts and some depression.

**Definitions:** Try matching the words in the list with the appropriate definitions. If you are stuck, check the glossary in the back of the book or the passage at the top of the page.

1. fanatic _____ a. emotionally disturbing or distressing

2. copious _____ b. (typically of something abstract or inanimate) successful in producing a desired or intended result; effective

3. traumatic _____ c. 1. consisting in or characterized by the absence rather than the presence of distinguishing features; 2. not desirable or optimistic; 3. characterizing a number less than zero

4. effectual _____ d. abundant in supply or quantity

5. negative _____ e. a person filled with excessive single-minded passion, often for an extreme religious or political cause

**Sentences:** Try to use the words above in a sentence below. Remember that a word ending may be changed or its figure of speech slightly altered.

6. The court stenographer took _____ notes during this morning's divorce trial.

7. Being mugged can be a(n) _____ experience that takes some time and therapy to recover from.

8. The religious _____ told the crowd that unless they became more spiritual immediately, they would all be damned.

9. Often _____ people complain about everything and refuse to better themselves.

10. The law proved to be _____ and, after its passing, women were granted suffrage rights.

# Lesson 119

### BECOMING INDEPENDENT

George's first company was a total **fiasco**. It went bankrupt in less than a year. Consequently, George's father employed him in his own company. The old man saw this as a **convenient** way to keep an eye on his son, who had become quite sullen and depressed. He knew George needed a daily **dose** of encouragement and support. Yet even though George seemed to be getting better, the memory of his failure remained as a **scourge** in his mind. George had always craved to see himself as a separate **entity** from his family, but he was still working for his father's business. This filled him with sadness and a quiet resolution to try and start a new company in the future.

## NEW WORDS

**convenient**
kən'vēnyənt

**fiasco**
fē'askō

**dose**
dōs

**entity**
'entitē

**scourge**
skərj

**Definitions:**     Try matching the words in the list with the appropriate definitions. If you are stuck, check the glossary in the back of the book or the passage at the top of the page.

1. convenient _____
2. fiasco _____
3. dose _____
4. entity _____
5. scourge _____

a. a person or thing that causes great trouble or suffering

b. a complete failure, usually in a ludicrous or humiliating way

c. (n.) a quantity of a medicine or drug (or something analogous and unpleasant) recommended to be taken at a particular time; (v.) to administer a quantity of a medicine or drug to someone

d. fitting in well with one's needs, activities, and/or plans

e. a thing with a distinct, independent existence

**Sentences:**     Try to use the words above in a sentence below. Remember that a word ending may be changed or its figure of speech slightly altered.

6. For many Italians, Benito Mussolini (1883-1945) and his fascist regime was a(n) _____ upon democracy.

7. The Supreme Court is the highest legal _____ in the United States.

8. It is not _____ for me to drive across town just to deliver you one dollar.

9. A(n) _____ emerged as the waiter tripped and dropped the couple's dinner all over their clean clothing.

10. It is important to take a(n) _____ of your medicine every six hours to heal you from your infection.

170

## NEW WORDS

**rupture**
ˈrəpCHər

**vogue**
vōg

**strive**
strīv

**wan**
wän

**warrant**
ˈwôrənt, ˈwä-

# Lesson 120

## TROUBLE AT THE PHARMACY

The police issued a **warrant** for the pharmacist's arrest, which caused a social **rupture** within the office. Half of his fellow pharmacists believed that their colleague was innocent, as his character seemed pure: he never would have sold medications on the black market. The rest of his fellow pharmacists were convinced that he was guilty, as his **wan** complexion at the sight of the cops intimated wrongdoing. Nevertheless, fellow coworkers' feelings ran so deep that both sides had to **strive** to make the pharmacy succeed amidst these legal troubles. Only the hope of running an organized office and carrying **vogue** medications bound the pharmacy team together.

**Definitions:**     Try matching the words in the list with the appropriate definitions. If you are stuck, check the glossary in the back of the book or the passage at the top of the page.

1.   rupture   _____   a.   (usually of a pipe, vessel, or bodily organ) to break or burst suddenly

2.   vogue   _____   b.   (of skin) pale and weak, giving the impression of illness or exhaustion

3.   strive   _____   c.   (n.) a document issued by a legal or government official authorizing the police or some other body to make an arrest, search premises, or execute some other action to carry out justice; (v.) to justify or necessitate course of action

4.   wan   _____   d.   to make great efforts to achieve or obtain something

5.   warrant   _____   e.   (adj.) popular; fashionable; (n.) the prevailing fashion or style at a particular time

**Sentences:**     Try to use the words above in a sentence below. Remember that a word ending may be changed or its figure of speech slightly altered.

6.   After obtaining a(n) _____, the detective entered the suspect's home to search for the murder weapon.

7.   It is important to _____ for your goals: without effort and hard work, it is hard to accomplish great things.

8.   When the pipe _____ last week, sewage spilled all over the street.

9.   During the 1950s, the hula hoop was in _____ internationally.

10.   Eva's _____ complexion made me wonder whether she might be ill.

# Crossword Puzzle
## Lessons 111-120

ACROSS

2  (adj.) (of skin) pale and weak, giving the impression of illness or exhaustion
3  (adj.) full of happiness and excitement
5  (adj.) popular; fashionable; (n.) the prevailing fashion or style at a particular time
11 (v.) to refuse to accept or be associate with; to deny the truth or validity of
13 (n.) a formal speech, ordinarily one that is given on a ceremonial occasion
15 (adj.) arousing distaste or opposition; unpleasant or offensive
19 (adj.) emotionally disturbing or distressing
20 (adj.) 1. (of an action or decision) performed by or affecting only one person, group, or country involved in a particular situation, without the agreement of another or the others; 2. relating to, occurring on, or affecting only one side of an organ or structure, or of the body.

DOWN

1  (n.) a complete failure, usually in a ludicrous or humiliating way
4  (v.) 1. to control the functioning of a machine, process, or system; 2. to manage and run a business; 3. to perform a surgery
6  (adj.) tending to cause harm
7  (adj.) different from what one is used to; objectionably new
8  (n.) a person or thing that causes great trouble or suffering
9  (v.) to find something out for certain; to make sure of
10 (n.) friendly, helpful, or cooperative feelings or attitude
12 (adj.) expressed in an incomprehensible or confusing way
14 (adj.) (typically of something abstract or inanimate) successful in producing a desired or intended result; effective
16 (adj.) abrupt or offhand in speech or manner
17 (n.) 1. a person who gives financial support to another individual, a cause, an organization, or an activity; 2. a customer (typically a regular one)
18 (adj.) easily achieved or effortless

# Vocabulary Review
## Lessons 111-120

**Directions: Match each word with its best approximate definition. Note that definitions are not necessarily repeated verbatim from the lesson exercises.**

| | | | | | |
|---|---|---|---|---|---|
| 1. | additional | _____ | a. | abundant in quantity or supply |
| 2. | impudent | _____ | b. | not containing serious value or purpose |
| 3. | lexicon | _____ | c. | to praise enthusiastically |
| 4. | paltry | _____ | d. | a person with excessive zeal for something |
| 5. | mores | _____ | e. | (of a pipe, vessel, or other body part) to break or burst suddenly |
| 6. | margin | _____ | f. | to deny or contradict a statement |
| 7. | scalpel | _____ | g. | the edges or border of something |
| 8. | gainsay | _____ | h. | to work jointly on an activity, typically to create something |
| 9. | collaborate | _____ | i. | a surgical knife |
| 10. | frivolous | _____ | j. | vocabulary of a person, language, or field |
| 11. | evacuate | _____ | k. | to remove (a person) from a place of danger to a safe spot |
| 12. | extol | _____ | l. | fitting well with one's needs, plans, or activities |
| 13. | splendid | _____ | m. | added, extra, or supplementary to what is present or available |
| 14. | oasis | _____ | n. | not showing respect for another |
| 15. | fanatic | _____ | o. | a thing with a distinct and independent existence |
| 16. | copious | _____ | p. | a spot on the desert that is fertile and where water is found |
| 17. | convenient | _____ | q. | the essential characteristic customs of a community |
| 18. | entity | _____ | r. | magnificent or very impressive |
| 19. | rupture | _____ | s. | to take great efforts to achieve or attain something |
| 20. | strive | _____ | t. | small or meager (of an amount) |

# Word Roots: Unit 12

## ROOTS AND THEIR MEANINGS

| | | | |
|---|---|---|---|
| her/hes: | to stick | tract: | to drag, pull draw |
| scrib/script: | to write | port: | to carry |
| mut: | to change | ven/vent: | to come |

## Here are a few examples of some words that use the above roots:

cohesive:           the quality of sticking together or forming a united whole
scripted:           something written out and then enacted
mutate:             to change or cause to change in form
retract:            to draw or be pulled back in; to withdraw
transport:          to move from one place to another by means of a vehicle
invent:             to create or design (to come upon) an idea

## Now try to fill in the table below by finding the appropriate root(s) and interpreting the meaning of each word:

| Word | Root(s) | Guessed Meaning | Actual Meaning |
|---|---|---|---|
| immutable | | | |
| coherent | | | |
| airport | | | |
| traction | | | |
| convene | | | |
| prescribe | | | |
| scribal | | | |
| portal | | | |

## NEW WORDS

**shrewd**
SHrood

**scour**
skou(ə)r

**pompous**
ˈpämpəs

**ingenious**
inˈjēnyəs

**incision**
inˈsiZHən

# Lesson 121

## AMAZING VETERINARIAN

William is an accomplished veterinarian who, on many occasions in his career, demonstrated how **shrewd** and sophisticated he was. Remember that **ingenious incision** he made to save a pregnant cow that had been swallowed whole by a python? A less savvy doctor would have chosen to chop up the snake, but William disregarded his older colleagues' **pompous** claims that he was wasting his time. He quickly got to work and made a long incision in the snake. He then extracted the cow and proceeded to **scour** the latter with hydrogen peroxide. Finally, he performed another operation – this time on the cow – and extracted a perfectly healthy calf. It was truly a remarkable feat.

**Definitions:**    Try matching the words in the list with the appropriate definitions. If you are stuck, check the glossary in the back of the book or the passage at the top of the page.

1.    shrewd    _____    a.    (n.) the action of cleaning or brightening the surface of something by rubbing it hard, typically with an abrasive or a detergent; (v.) to clean or brighten the surface of something by rubbing it hard, typically with an abrasive or a detergent; 2. to subject a place or text to a thorough search in order to try to locate something
2.    scour    _____    b.    affectedly and irritatingly self-important or grand
3.    pompous    _____    c.    having or showing sharp powers of judgment; astute
4.    ingenious    _____    d.    a surgical cut made into the skin or flesh
5.    incision    _____    e.    clever, original, and inventive

**Sentences:**    Try to use the words above in a sentence below. Remember that a word ending may be changed or its figure of speech slightly altered.

6.    The surgeon made a(n) _____ into the patient's stomach during the surgery.
7.    An intelligent person who is _____ is a real turnoff; I much prefer smart individuals who are humble about their abilities.
8.    The maid _____ the bathtub until it was clean and sparkly.
9.    Placing electrical cords along the restaurant wall for customers to charge their electronic equipment is a(n) _____ idea.
10.    Sometimes entrepreneurs must be _____ and manipulate people in order to create revenue for their company.

# Lesson 122

## THE LIFE CHANGING DECISION

Jacob eventually got tired of performing **menial** jobs and decided to go in **pursuit** of a higher education degree that would allow him to find a stable career. His **fidelity** to the family tradition of working in restaurants had kept him from realizing his potential for too long. He had always let the desire to please his parents **usurp** his own feelings about what he wanted to do. Moreover, working in restaurants for so many years had turned him into a **gourmand** and he needed to get out of that environment for health reasons as well. Now he was going to make changes in his life.

**Definitions:**     Try matching the words in the list with the appropriate definitions.  If you are stuck, check the glossary in the back of the book or the passage at the top of the page.

| | | | | | |
|---|---|---|---|---|---|
| 1. | gourmand | _____ | a. | the act of following or chasing someone or something | |
| 2. | fidelity | _____ | b. | (of work) not requiring much skill and of little prestige | |
| 3. | menial | _____ | c. | faithfulness to a person, cause, or belief as exhibited by continuing loyalty and support; faithfulness to a spouse | |
| 4. | pursuit | _____ | d. | one who enjoys eating and who often eats too much | |
| 5. | usurp | _____ | e. | to take a position of power or importance illegally or by force | |

**Sentences:**     Try to use the words above in a sentence below.  Remember that a word ending may be changed or its figure of speech slightly altered.

6.     For someone with a doctorate, having a career of cleaning toilets may feel like a(n) _____ career.

7.     Those who spend their entire lives in _____ of happiness may never actually obtain it.

8.     Lack of _____ in a marriage can lead to serious problems, even divorce.

9.     The insurgents tried to _____ power from the established leadership.

10.    Jo is such a _____: she delights in food and all cuisines and typically stuffs her face.

## NEW WORDS

**acquiesce**
ˌakwēˈes

**choreography**
ˌkôrēˈägrəfē

**grovel**
ˈgrävəl, ˈgrə-

**laceration**
ˌlasəˈrāSHən

**incorrigible**
inˈkôrijəbəl, -ˈkär-

### FOR THE SAKE OF ART

The new theater director's daring **choreography** included dancing around real pieces of broken glass. Anne knew that this would increase the dramatic effect in the play; however, she was well aware that a piece of glass could cause a **laceration** of the dancers' feet, especially when they had to **grovel** on the ground in part of the act. Unfortunately, the director had an **incorrigible** interest in dangerous stunts and Anne simply had to **acquiesce** to his decision. After all, he was much more famous and powerful than her.

**Definitions:**    Try matching the words in the list with the appropriate definitions.  If you are stuck, check the glossary in the back of the book or the passage at the top of the page.

| | | | | |
|---|---|---|---|---|
| 1. | acquiesce _____ | a. | a deep cut in the skin or flesh |
| 2. | choreography _____ | b. | the sequence of steps and movements in dance or figure skating |
| 3. | grovel _____ | c. | to accept something reluctantly and without protest |
| 4. | laceration _____ | d. | (of a person or his or her tendencies) unable to be corrected, reformed, or improved |
| 5. | incorrigible _____ | e. | to lie or move abjectly on the ground with one's face downward |

**Sentences:**    Try to use the words above in a sentence below.  Remember that a word ending may be changed or its figure of speech slightly altered.

6.    After hours of trying to persuade Danya to go to Hawaii with me, she finally

_____.

7.    The _____ behind that dance routine is genius: I love the sounds and rhythms involved.

8.    Often a smoking habit is a(n) _____ habit, and people continue to smoke until they die.

9.    I never knew that Shri had a(n) _____ on her back until I saw her in a swimsuit.

10.    The dictator forced his subjects to _____ whenever they needed his approval for something.

# Lesson 124

## THE MYSTERIOUS STRANGER

The gypsy **nomad** was wearing a gorgeous red **frock** that took Lionel's breath away. Pleasant music was coming out of a strange **appliance** on the floor near her that looked like a hand-made radio. As the gypsy gracefully danced to the music, her movements created a deep feeling of **euphoria** in Lionel. He wondered if the girl was married. Listening to the sound of the music and watching the beautiful girl dance, for a moment Lionel forgot all about the world and any **atrocity** that had derailed his life.

### NEW WORDS

**atrocity**
əˈträsitē

**appliance**
əˈplīəns

**euphoria**
yooˈfôrēə

**frock**
fräk

**nomad**
ˈnōˌmad

**Definitions:** Try matching the words in the list with the appropriate definitions. If you are stuck, check the glossary in the back of the book or the passage at the top of the page.

| | | | | |
|---|---|---|---|---|
| 1. | atrocity | _____ | a. | an extremely wicked or cruel act, often involving physical violence or injury |
| 2. | appliance | _____ | b. | a feeling or state of intense happiness or excitement |
| 3. | euphoria | _____ | c. | a device or piece of equipment designed to perform a specific task, typically a domestic one |
| 4. | frock | _____ | d. | a woman's dress |
| 5. | nomad | _____ | e. | a person or a member of a people who travel from place to place |

**Sentences:** Try to use the words above in a sentence below. Remember that a word ending may be changed or its figure of speech slightly altered.

6. A refrigerator is a necessary _____ for any modern kitchen.
7. It is a(n) _____ to burn a flag.
8. After Hattie won the lottery she was in a state of _____.
9. If you want my honest opinion, that _____ does not suit Erin very well.
10. After thirty years of working a desk job, Irving packed his bag to become a(n) _____ and explore the world

## NEW WORDS

**memento**
mə'men̪to̪

**illegible**
i(l)'lejəbəl

**migrate**
'mī̪grāt

**rendezvous**
'rändi̪voo, -dä-

**detour**
'dē̪toor

## THE NEVER FORGOTTEN PAST

Jackson had kept one letter from his former fiancée as a **memento** of their love. After years of carrying it in his wallet, the letter had become almost **illegible**. A decade ago, when he had to **migrate** to another continent, he left the girl behind. Since then, whenever he returned to his home country, he would always take a **detour** to avoid her hometown. He was terrified at the prospect of a chance **rendezvous** with her. He could not bear the thought of looking into her eyes and experiencing feelings of guilt and remorse for leaving without her.

**Definitions:**      Try matching the words in the list with the appropriate definitions. If you are stuck, check the glossary in the back of the book or the passage at the top of the page.

1.   memento _____   a.   an object kept as a reminder or souvenir of a person or event

2.   illegible _____   b.   a meeting at a specific time and place (typically between two people)

3.   migrate _____   c.   not clear enough to be read

4.   rendezvous _____   d.   (n.) a long and roundabout route taken to avoid something or to visit somewhere along the way; (v.) to take a long or roundabout route

5.   detour _____   e.   to move from one region or habitat to another (often seasonally); to move from one country to another; to move from one part of something to another

**Sentences:**      Try to use the words above in a sentence below. Remember that a word ending may be changed or its figure of speech slightly altered.

6.      Because of the highway construction, drivers were forced to take a thirty-mile _____ through Connecticut's suburbs.

7.      That photograph of my mother is the only _____ I still have of my childhood.

8.      The archivist had great difficulty trying to discern the _____ handwriting of the letters of French polymath Pierre Gassendi (1592-1655).

9.      Anthropologists believe that humans _____ from Asia to North America across what is now the Bering Strait approximately 15,000 years ago.

10.     The crab shack at the end of the road is a favorite _____ of Gene and his girlfriend.

# Lesson 126

## A MATTER OF PRINCIPLE

The mayor's office offered to give a **subsidy** to the NGO for cleaning up the city parks. To its surprise, NGO representatives were quick to **rebuff** the proposal. The NGO refused to work with the mayor, who had previously shown support for **malevolent** racist organizations and who had spoken with **levity** about serious issues such as the growing homelessness in the town. According to the NGO representatives, to work with this mayor would have been a **blasphemy** towards everything that the NGO stood for: after all, it was an organization fully dedicated to social justice and helping the poor.

**Definitions:**    Try matching the words in the list with the appropriate definitions. If you are stuck, check the glossary in the back of the book or the passage at the top of the page.

1.    malevolent _____    a.    to reject someone or something in an abrupt or ungracious manner

2.    blasphemy _____    b.    the act of speaking sacrilegiously about God or things that are sacred

3.    levity _____    c.    having a desire to harm or do evil to others

4.    subsidy _____    d.    a sum of money granted by the government or a public body to assist an industry or business so that the price of a commodity will remain affordable

5.    rebuff _____    e.    humor or frivolity; often treating a serious matter in a manner lacking due respect

**Sentences:**    Try to use the words above in a sentence below. Remember that a word ending may be changed or its figure of speech slightly altered.

6.    It is _____ against the Hindu religion to eat beef, as cows are considered sacred.

7.    The _____ witch tried to poison the princess in an attempt to gain power over the kingdom.

8.    The narcissistic dowager _____ the young man's attempts to secure a date with her.

9.    Often students receive a(n) _____ from the government to assist them with their studies.

10.    I miss my childhood, for it was a time of _____ when I had few worries in life.

## NEW WORDS

**flabbergast**
ˈflabərˌgast

**clash**
klaSH

**idiom**
ˈidēəm

**fling**
fliNG

**famine**
ˈfamən

# Lesson 127

## LIFE'S TRIALS AND TRIBULATIONS

The way his sudden outbursts of aggression would **clash** with his usual cheerfulness was something that indeed did **flabbergast** her. When he was angry he would **fling** objects across the room, which scared her. Also, he would utter an **idiom** in his native language that she found very vulgar. Perhaps the recent **famine** in the region, which came as a result of a period of severe drought, had greatly unnerved him. Still, it could not justify his unacceptable behavior.

**Definitions:**     Try matching the words in the list with the appropriate definitions. If you are stuck, check the glossary in the back of the book or the passage at the top of the page.

1.    flabbergast _____     a.    to greatly surprise someone, to astonish
2.    clash _____     b.    an extreme scarcity of food
3.    idiom _____     c.    a group of words having an established meaning that is not deducible from the words themselves
4.    fling _____     d.    (n.) a short period of enjoyment or wild behavior; (v.) to throw or hurl forcefully
5.    famine _____     e.    1. a violent confrontation; 2. a color mismatch; 3. a loud, jarring sound made by clashing metal objects together

**Sentences:**     Try to use the words above in a sentence below. Remember that a word ending may be changed or its figure of speech slightly altered.

6.     I was _____ when I arrived home from a long day's work only to find that my wife had cooked me a lovely meal.

7.     "Going postal" is a(n) _____ that refers to going completely crazy, often to the point of harming innocent bystanders in one's way.

8.     The objective of the game is to _____ a ring onto a stick.

9.     Last year's _____ resulted in the death of over six hundred undernourished children.

10.     The secretary and treasurer have personalities that _____: they cannot be together for more than ten minutes without getting into an explosive argument.

# Lesson 128

## THE HOMELESS BELIEVER

Joseph had a **constant**, unwavering faith in his church. Whenever life on the street became too challenging, he would **cling** to his faith. He kept a small icon in a **cavity** in the wall by his bed. Whenever one of the other homeless people in the shelter would **ruffle** him, Joseph took out the icon and would talk to in in a low voice. He loved Christmas best of all: on that day, a huge crowd of people would **amass** in his church and for that one day Joseph felt as if he was not alone in the world.

## NEW WORDS

**constant**
ˈkänstənt

**cling**
kliNG

**cavity**
ˈkavitē

**ruffle**
ˈrəfəl

**amass**
əˈmas

**Definitions:**    Try matching the words in the list with the appropriate definitions. If you are stuck, check the glossary in the back of the book or the passage at the top of the page.

| | | | | |
|---|---|---|---|---|
| 1. | constant | _____ | a. | continuous and unchanging; remaining the same over a period of time; referring to a person who is faithful |
| 2. | cling | _____ | b. | to gather together or accumulate over a time period; to gather together in a group or crowd |
| 3. | cavity | _____ | c. | an empty space within a solid object, especially the human body; the decayed part of a tooth |
| 4. | ruffle | _____ | d. | to hold on tightly to; to remain stubbornly persistent or faithful to something |
| 5. | amass | _____ | e. | to disturb the smoothness or tranquility of; to disorder or disarrange |

**Sentences:**    Try to use the words above in a sentence below. Remember that a word ending may be changed or its figure of speech slightly altered.

6.    In order to have an early retirement, it is wise to _____ as much money as possible at a young age and to invest it carefully.

7.    A sinkhole is a giant _____ that opens up in the earth.

8.    Janie was _____ by the insults that her family hurled at her last night.

9.    The infant's _____ crying caused me to get up and leave the theater.

10.    Even though evidence proved otherwise, the mother still wanted to _____ to the notion that her child was not a criminal.

## NEW WORDS

**prior**
ˈprīər

**despondent**
diˈspändənt

**policy**
ˈpäləsē

**protrude**
prəˈtrood, prō-

**amorphous**
əˈmôrfəs

# Lesson 129

## INSENSITIVE MAYOR

After the new mayor was elected into office, many of the city's financially struggling citizens felt **despondent**. **Prior** to the mayoral election, the city had ample facilities in place to help those in need, but now under new leadership such plans suddenly seemed **amorphous**. This was because the new mayor vowed to implement a **policy** that would reduce the number of soup kitchens and homeless shelters around town. Moreover, he hoped to erect a large dock that would **protrude** from the city wharf; from here, those who could not afford food and housing would be exiled to nearby islands. What an insensitive new leader!

**Definitions:** Try matching the words in the list with the appropriate definitions. If you are stuck, check the glossary in the back of the book or the passage at the top of the page.

1. prior _____   a. without a clearly defined shape or form; vaguely defined
2. despondent _____   b. in low spirits from loss of hope or courage
3. policy _____   c. existing or occurring before in time, order, or importance
4. protrude _____   d. a course or principle of action adopted or proposed by a government, party, business, or individual
5. amorphous _____   e. to extend beyond or above a surface

**Sentences:** Try to use the words above in a sentence below. Remember that a word ending may be changed or its figure of speech slightly altered.

6. After being fired from her job without cause, Cameron felt _____.
7. The American Revolutionary War (1775-83) occurred _____ to the American Civil War (1861-65).
8. It is the school's _____ to prevent students from dropping classes beyond the fourth Tuesday of the semester.
9. Water is a(n) _____ entity, thus taking the form of any receptacle that contains it.
10. The cliff _____ into the ocean and provides tourists with a panoramic view of the seas.

# Lesson 130

## THE WAY THINGS ARE

In order to receive permission to fly, Johnson only needed written **approval** of the appointed psychologist. He entered the psychologist's office and saw a **portly** gentleman who was sweating profusely. The gentleman had a **fretful** look on his face as if something was bothering him. Johnson immediately knew from the man's face as well as from the **ominous** tone of his voice that there was going to be a problem obtaining the man's permission. Requiring a bribe to obtain approval documents was a **prevalent** practice in that town, and Johnson had prepared a large sum of money that he carried in his pocket for that purpose.

**Definitions:**     Try matching the words in the list with the appropriate definitions. If you are stuck, check the glossary in the back of the book or the passage at the top of the page.

1.  portly      _____     a.     feeling or expressing distress or irritation
2.  approval    _____     b.     giving the impression that something bad or unpleasant is about to happen
3.  fretful     _____     c.     stout or fat (usually in reference to a man)
4.  ominous     _____     d.     widespread over a particular area or at a particular time
5.  prevalent   _____     e.     the action of officially agreeing on something or accepting something as satisfactory

**Sentences:**     Try to use the words above in a sentence below. Remember that a word ending may be changed or its figure of speech slightly altered.

6.    Despite having received a(n) _____ warning from her mother not to go to the arcade at night, Sharon still went.

7.    Christmas trees are _____ in many American suburbs during December.

8.    The _____ bellhop carried the knapsack over his stout body and delivered it to the hotel room.

9.    Kramer was _____ after the publisher rejected his book manuscript.

10.   Children are allowed to go on the field trip to the water park only if they have obtained _____ from their parents.

# Word Search

## Lessons 818-890

```
N L E E X T R A P C R R R E H O W B
H O L Y R H C L B D R J D H T J U T
L L C W A Q O R I I W L R D G V H Y
O P J A L Y P U F O Q Q D H L H M U
N L Y K P K T T V M I K H G W Y I A
R I N J I V H S N J O L F Z T L I D
D U D D R A U I T R K V L G S D L Q
R O A R T R K Q Y G T N O Y R G T U
K O N Y K O A I I H Y V R K Q O L W
X V U Z G L Q M H E T Q I G O Y I M
S P R E H O N G S H T M W D T L T Y
T S T I F S T J Z X K N H T A P C Q
X L X O N Q G V K S V M R R U I K L
H N W Y L O X L K E L H T E O O B O
Q F W O S S N V Y K W L O Q X D D O
O V U I Q K I O I U W J H V U L R R
R T I Q Y F J P L F O O D P H C D H
L P B L U W R D P H O Y Q Q Q O O Y
```

8   (ad.) pa wecbedvi and trrtbabtnf vi sew tl yorbanbor f rand

1   (n) pa s2rf tcavc2bl ade tnbo the sutn or wesh

9   (n) pwatdhw2vness bo a yerson; ca2se; or mevtewas eghtmtbed mi conbtn2tnf voi avbi and s2yyorb3watdhw2vness bo a syo2se

,   (n) pbhe acbowwowo4 tnf or chastnf sol eone or sol ebhtnf

j   (x) pbo vte or l oxe amecbvi on the f ro2nd 4 tbh one5 vace do4 n4 ard

k   (ad.) p (owa yerson or hts or her bendenctesp2name bo me corrected; reworl ed; or tl yroxed

'   (n) pa dextce or ytece owe62tyl enb destf ned bo yerworl a syectwic basu; bi ytcawi a dol esbtc one

7   (n) pa 4 ol an5 dress

q   (n) pan omecbueybas a rel tnder or so2xentr owa yerson or exenb

80  (x) pbo l oxe wol one ref ton or hamtbabbo another (owten seasonawi p3bo l oxe wol one co2nbri bo another3bo l oxe wol one yarbowsol ebhtnf bo another

88  (n) pbhe acbowsyeautnf sacrtvef to2svi amo2bP od or bhtnf s bhabare sacred

81  (n) pa s2l owl onei f ranbed mi the f oxernl enbor a y2mvtc modi bo assbtsban tnd2stri or m2stness so bhabbhe yrtce owa col l odtbi 4 twrel atn awordame

89  (n) p8) a xtovenbconwonbabton31) a covor l tsl abch39) a vo2d; .arrtnf so2nd l ade mi cvashtnf l ebavomecbs bof ether

8,  (n) pan egbrel e scarctbi owwood

8j  (x) pbo hovd on btf hbvi bo3bo rel atn sb2mmornvi yerstsbenbor watdhw2vbo sol ebhtnf

8k  (x) pbo dtsb2rmbhe sl oobhness or bran62tbdi ow3bo dtsorder or dtsarranf e

8'  (ad.) pbn vo4 sytrbbs wol voss owhoye or co2raf e

87  (ad.) p4 tbho2ba cvearvi dewbned shaye or worl 3xaf 2evi dewbned

8q  (n) pbhe acbton owowobctawi af reetnf on sol ebhtnf or acceybtnf sol ebhtnf as sabtsvacbori

10  (ad.) pweevtnf or egyresstnf dtsbress or trrtbabton
```
```

# Vocabulary Review
## Lessons 121-130

**Directions:** Match each word with its best approximate definition. Note that definitions are not necessarily repeated verbatim from the lesson exercises.

| | | | | |
|---|---|---|---|---|
| 1. | shrewd | _____ | a. | concerning work that requires little skill and lacks prestige |
| 2. | ingenious | _____ | b. | to extend above or beyond a surface |
| 3. | gourmand | _____ | c. | widespread in a particular area or at a particular time |
| 4. | menial | _____ | d. | exhibiting sharp powers of judgment; astute |
| 5. | acquiesce | _____ | e. | occurring continuously over a long time; unchanging |
| 6. | laceration | _____ | f. | an extremely cruel act, often involving injury |
| 7. | atrocity | _____ | g. | a feeling of intense excitement or happiness |
| 8. | euphoria | _____ | h. | a deep cut in the skin |
| 9. | illegible | _____ | i. | inventive, clever, original (of a person) |
| 10. | detour | _____ | j. | to surprise someone greatly; to astonish |
| 11. | malevolent | _____ | k. | giving the impression that something bad or unpleasant may happen |
| 12. | rebuff | _____ | l. | to reject someone or something ungraciously |
| 13. | flabbergast | _____ | m. | exhibiting a desire to harm others |
| 14. | idiom | _____ | n. | a long roundabout route taken to avoid something or to visit somewhere along the way |
| 15. | constant | _____ | o. | a person who enjoys eating and who often eats too much |
| 16. | amass | _____ | p. | to gather together or accumulate |
| 17. | prior | _____ | q. | to accept something reluctantly and without protest |
| 18. | protrude | _____ | r. | not clear enough to be read |
| 19. | ominous | _____ | s. | a group of words whose meaning cannot be deduced from the individual words alone |
| 20. | prevalent | _____ | t. | existing before in time, order, or importance |

# Word Roots: Unit 13

## ROOTS AND THEIR MEANINGS

| | | | |
|---|---|---|---|
| **man:** | hand | **dic:** | to say, tell |
| **clu/clo/cla:** | to shut | **anim:** | life, spirit |
| **ten:** | hold, keep | **esce:** | to become |

## Here are a few examples of some words that use the above roots:

manual:      done by hand; a handbook of instructions for learning to operate something

cloister:      a convent or monastery (a place where one is shut up and shielded from the world for religious duties)

detention:      the action of keeping someone in official custody; keeping one in school after hours

dictate:      to lay down authoritatively; to say or read aloud

animation:      a state of being lively and full of energy; creating a live movement out of successive drawings of things or out of puppets

coalesce:      to come together and form a mass or a whole

## Now try to fill in the table below by finding the appropriate root(s) and interpreting the meaning of each word:

| Word | Root(s) | Guessed Meaning | Actual Meaning |
|---|---|---|---|
| predict | | | |
| retentive | | | |
| maneuver | | | |
| reclusive | | | |
| fluorescent | | | |
| animal | | | |
| claustrophobia | | | |
| amanuensis | | | |
| tenable | | | |
| conclude | | | |

# Lesson 131

## THE EX-SPOUSES

Anton knew that he was **culpable** for the great **distress** his wife experienced before their divorce. He had shamelessly cheated on her multiple times. And yet, whenever he spoke with her, Anton could not **simulate** guilt or a feeling of compassion. He felt that she had stolen the best years of his life by refusing to sign the divorce papers much earlier. Anton would **trade** all the money he had in the bank for the chance to get those years back. He knew that his wife only agreed to the divorce when she was convinced that it would **aggrandize** her own wealth, and he did not feel sorry for her.

**NEW WORDS**

**culpable**
ˈkəlpəbəl

**simulate**
ˈsimyəˌlāt

**distress**
disˈtres

**trade**
trād

**aggrandize**
əˈgranˌdīz

**Definitions:**     Try matching the words in the list with the appropriate definitions. If you are stuck, check the glossary in the back of the book or the passage at the top of the page.

|   |   |   |   |   |
|---|---|---|---|---|
| 1. | culpable | _____ | a. | to imitate the appearance or character of |
| 2. | simulate | _____ | b. | 1. extreme anxiety, sorrow, or pain; 2. troubles caused by lacking money or basic life necessities; (v.) to cause somebody anxiety, sorrow, or pain |
| 3. | distress | _____ | c. | worthy of blame |
| 4. | trade | _____ | d. | (n.) 1. the action of buying and selling goods and services; 2. a job typically requiring manual skills and specialization; (v.) 1. to buy and sell goods and services; 2. to exchange something for something else, typically as a commercial transaction |
| 5. | aggrandize | _____ | e. | to increase the power, status, or wealth of |

**Sentences:**     Try to use the words above in a sentence below. Remember that a word ending may be changed or its figure of speech slightly altered.

6.     Often indigenous peoples would _____ their wares at a local bazaar.

7.     These glasses that deliberately blur vision _____ the visual consequences of drinking a dozen cans of beer.

8.     Jana was in _____ when she realized that the plane she was flying was experiencing an engine failure.

9.     The Spanish monarchy tried to _____ its image by building fancy new castles in the hills.

10.     When the jury saw a video of the defendant robbing a bank, they were convinced that he was _____ of the crime.

## NEW WORDS

**craft**
kraft

**annul**
əˈnəl

**intercept**
ˌintərˈsept

**restitution**
ˌrestəˈt(y)ooSHən

**succumb**
səˈkəm

The husband Mr. Pfeiffer pleaded with the judge to **annul** the marriage. Mr. Pfeiffer had been able to **intercept** his wife's mail and had many letters from her lover as evidence. In addition, he used his **craft** of persuasion to convince the judge that his wife had to pay him a large sum of money in **restitution** for his damaged reputation. The wife knew that Mr. Pfeiffer was largely exaggerating the situation; however, Mr. Pfeiffer had the judge's full support so she had to **succumb** and agree to pay him the money.

**Definitions:** Try matching the words in the list with the appropriate definitions. If you are stuck, check the glossary in the back of the book or the passage at the top of the page.

1. craft _____ a. (n.) an activity involving skill and often making things by hand; (v.) to exercise skill in making or doing something

2. annul _____ b. (n.) an act or instance of obstructing someone or something so as to prevent it from continuing to a destination; (v.) to obstruct someone or something so as to prevent it from continuing to a destination

3. intercept _____ c. to declare an official agreement, decision, or result invalid

4. restitution _____ d. 1. the act of returning something lost or stolen to its proper owner; 2. recompense for loss or injury; 3. the restoration of something to its original state

5. succumb _____ e. to fail to resist (pressure, temptation, or some other force)

**Sentences:** Try to use the words above in a sentence below. Remember that a word ending may be changed or its figure of speech slightly altered.

6. Earl sought _____ after his cousin borrowed his flat screen television and refused to return it.

7. The hamlet finally _____ to defeat after weeks of barbarian attacks.

8. The basketball player _____ the ball, ran to the other end of the court, and made a three-point shot.

9. Artisans can spend years of their lives apprenticed to a master in order to learn a particular _____.

10. Charlotte tried to have her marriage to Zack _____ because she realized hours after the wedding that the marriage was a huge mistake.

# Lesson 133

## THROUGH THE GRAPEVINE

Soon after his retirement, Harry decided to establish his **domicile** in the valley, where he purchased a strip of land to create a small vineyard. Some of the locals were quick to warn Harry about the climate being **arid**, insisting that nothing green would grow there for too long. Fortunately, Harry held fast to his expert horticultural knowledge and wine **culture** in particular. When his neighbor made an **arrogant** remark that only a naïve hillbilly would bother trying to harvest anything of value from that land, Harry was heard to simply **retort**: "Just you watch."

**Definitions:**     Try matching the words in the list with the appropriate definitions. If you are stuck, check the glossary in the back of the book or the passage at the top of the page.

1.   domicile   _____   a.   having or revealing an exaggerated sense of oneself or one's abilities

2.   arid   _____   b.   the arts and other manifestations of human intellectual achievement regarded collectively

3.   culture   _____   c.   the country that a person treats as his or her permanent home

4.   retort   _____   d.   (n.) a sharp, angry, or wittily incisive response to a remark; (v.) to respond to a remark or accusation in a witty or incisive manner

5.   arrogant   _____   e.   land and climate that is dry and barren that is hardly capable of supporting vegetation

**Sentences:**     Try to use the words above in a sentence below. Remember that a word ending may be changed or its figure of speech slightly altered.

6.   After two decades of use and deterioration, Armand hired a builder to update and renovate his _____.

7.   Deserts are noted to be _____ places; by definition they lack water that is essential for making many forms of vegetation flourish.

8.   Because of the strong influence of Chinese _____, many East Asian and Southeast Asian Nations celebrate Lunar New Year.

9.   When William accused Lyndon of stealing his briefcase, the latter _____ that William was crazy to make such an assertion.

10.   Often a(n) _____ person will not earn many friends by constantly boasting of his or her talents.

190

## NEW WORDS

**benevolent**
bəˈnevələnt

**encounter**
enˈkoun(t)ər

**wary**
ˈwe(ə)rē

**berate**
biˈrāt

**demonstrate**
ˈdemənˌstrāt

# Lesson 134

## THE CONSERVATIVE FATHER

During their brief **encounter** in the café, the handsome stranger seemed friendly and **benevolent**, and the young girl was charmed by his manners. Yet, she remained **wary** about disclosing too much personal information. She did not overtly **demonstrate** any interest in him. She was well aware that her father – the café owner – was carefully watching her. The old man was very conservative and he would **berate** her every time she even glanced at a man.

**Definitions:** Try matching the words in the list with the appropriate definitions. If you are stuck, check the glossary in the back of the book or the passage at the top of the page.

1. benevolent _____
2. encounter _____
3. wary _____
4. berate _____
5. demonstrate _____

a. to scold or criticize someone angrily

b. (n.) an unexpected or casual meeting with someone or something; (v.) 1. to unexpectedly experience or be faced with something difficult or hostile; 2. to meet

c. well-meaning and kindly

d. feeling or showing caution about possible dangers or problems

e. 1. to clearly show the existence or truth of something by giving proof or evidence; 2. to take part in a public meeting or protest expressing views on a political issue

**Sentences:** Try to use the words above in a sentence below. Remember that a word ending may be changed or its figure of speech slightly altered.

6. When Kelsey _____ her ex-boyfriend in the grocery store, the two coldly stared at each other before continuing with their shopping.

7. It is important to be _____ when a former foe tries to be kind to you.

8. The _____ old lady baked a batch of cookies for her neighbors.

9. It is easy to _____ if you are unhappy about a situation; it is much harder to take action and create a political change.

10. Lynn's parents _____ her for staying out past bedtime and partying with her friends.

# Lesson 135

## THE GULLIBLE TOURISTS

The Nepalese company offered what seemed to be an incredible deal: to **trek** across a famous Himalayan path with an experienced guide at almost no cost. On this trip, the guide spoke to the tourists with **ardor** about the beauty of the mountain trail. The tourists listened with **dutiful** attention to the mountain expert. They had no experience and they were **credulous** enough to trust him completely, even though he had shown them no identification of being a professional guide. They did not know that if they had only looked him up on the Internet, they would have found many negative reviews that would **undermine** his authority.

**Definitions:**     Try matching the words in the list with the appropriate definitions. If you are stuck, check the glossary in the back of the book or the passage at the top of the page.

| | | | | |
|---|---|---|---|---|
| 1. | dutiful | _____ | a. | exhibiting too great a readiness to believe things |
| 2. | undermine | _____ | b. | a long arduous journey, especially one made on foot |
| 3. | credulous | _____ | c. | to damage or weaken something (often an intellectual argument) |
| 4. | trek | _____ | d. | conscientiously or obediently fulfilling one's role |
| 5. | ardor | _____ | e. | enthusiasm or passion |

**Sentences:**     Try to use the words above in a sentence below. Remember that a word ending may be changed or its figure of speech slightly altered.

6. New evidence _____ the research in last year's report, thus making its conclusions increasingly questionable.

7. Lorraine speaks with such _____ when she discusses piano teaching.

8. Martin was a(n) _____ child and helped his aging parents out with their medical bills.

9. My _____ cousin actually believed that America's first president, George Washington (1732-99) is coming over to take him to lunch today.

10. My boy scouts pack went hiking last weekend and _____ fifteen miles through the forest.

# Lesson 136

## FAMILY HAS YOUR BACK

**NEW WORDS**

**sate**
sāt

**congenial**
kən'jēnyəl

**crisis**
'krīsis

**prosperous**
'präspərəs

**nucleus**
'n(y)ooklēəs

Eli's family was the **nucleus** of his emotional support. For it was the people closest to him who would always help him during a time of **crisis**. In **prosperous** times and in poor times they all stuck together. The atmosphere in the house was friendly and **congenial**. Whenever things went wrong, Eli went back to the family. This was his way to **sate** his need for comfort and emotional support.

**Definitions:** Try matching the words in the list with the appropriate definitions. If you are stuck, check the glossary in the back of the book or the passage at the top of the page.

1. sate _____ a. a period of intense difficulty, danger, or trouble
2. congenial _____ b. 1. (of a person) pleasant because of a personality, interests, or other qualities similar to one's own; 2. (of a thing) pleasant or suitable because it is suited to one's tastes or inclination
3. crisis _____ c. flourishing financially; successful in material terms
4. prosperous _____ d. the central and most important part of an object, group, or movement, forming a basis for its development and growth
5. nucleus _____ e. to fully satisfy a desire or appetite

**Sentences:** Try to use the words above in a sentence below. Remember that a word ending may be changed or its figure of speech slightly altered.

6. In the eyes of many, the _____ of activity in the United States is New York City.
7. When the town was cut off from its water supply, a(n) _____ emerged as citizens could neither drink nor bathe.
8. Nothing could _____ the child's appetite: he kept eating endlessly as if there were no end in sight.
9. Hard work and a good education can truly help people to have _____ lives.
10. A sales person ought to be _____, for a negative attitude can really put off customers.

193

# Lesson 137

**NOT IN MY BACK YARD**

The new neighborhood policy will **oblige** the residents of Atwood Circle to pursue a solution concerning the **flux** of **pungent** waters flowing downstream from their homes. It will become forbidden to release liquid detergents that circulate in the communal waters. **Strenuous** efforts already have been made by community firefighters to neutralize the contamination. The **dogged** firefighters declared that there should be a severe fine for anyone found polluting the communal waters in the future.

## NEW WORDS

**oblige**
əˈblīj

**flux**
fləks

**strenuous**
ˈstrenyooəs

**pungent**
ˈpənjənt

**dogged**
ˈdôgid

**Definitions:**     Try matching the words in the list with the appropriate definitions. If you are stuck, check the glossary in the back of the book or the passage at the top of the page.

1.    oblige    _____    a.    1. the action or process of flowing or flowing out; 2. continuous change
2.    flux    _____    b.    requiring or using great exertion
3.    strenuous    _____    c.    to make someone morally or legally bound to an action or course of action
4.    pungent    _____    d.    having a sharply strong smell or taste
5.    dogged    _____    e.    having or showing tenacity and grim persistence

**Sentences:**     Try to use the words above in a sentence below. Remember that a word ending may be changed or its figure of speech slightly altered.

6.    Running a marathon is _____ work; it requires a lot of training and exertion for hours on end.
7.    Shad sat on his rooftop and watched the _____ of people entering and exiting the stadium all day long.
8.    The incense burning in the living room has a(n) _____ smell.
9.    Even though it was clear that Brian was not going to win the triathlon, his _____ determination prevented him from giving up.
10.    Francis felt _____ to attend the dinner banquet since three of his students were winning awards at the event.

## NEW WORDS

**basis**
'bāsis

**inspect**
in'spekt

**prolong**
prə'lôNG, -'läNG

**blueprint**
'bloo͝oˌprint

**fluctuate**
'fləkCHoo͝oˌāt

# Lesson 138

### MAKING A DREAM COME TRUE

Angel created a detailed **blueprint** for becoming a top-tier chef in the upcoming five years. She knew she could achieve her goal on the **basis** of her good education and exemplary work experience. Angel was aware that success could **fluctuate** and that she had to be prepared for some challenges. For example, even though her boss told her that she would be ready to become a sous-chef in one year, he could also **prolong** her training if he deemed that necessary. Angel knew that her boss liked to **inspect** every single detail of her work; therefore, she took extra care on every little detail.

**Definitions:**    Try matching the words in the list with the appropriate definitions. If you are stuck, check the glossary in the back of the book or the passage at the top of the page.

| | | | | |
|---|---|---|---|---|
| 1. | basis | _____ | a. | the underlying support or foundation for an idea, argument, or process |
| 2. | inspect | _____ | b. | to rise and fall irregularly in number or amount |
| 3. | prolong | _____ | c. | a design plan or technical drawing (used heavily in architecture); something that acts as a plan, model, or template |
| 4. | blueprint | _____ | d. | to examine someone or something closely to assess condition and/or shortcomings |
| 5. | fluctuate | _____ | e. | to extend the duration of |

**Sentences:**    Try to use the words above in a sentence below. Remember that a word ending may be changed or its figure of speech slightly altered.

6. The architect revealed a(n) _____ of the new skyscraper at this morning's design conference.

7. It is normal for the temperature to _____ throughout the day.

8. The professor was able to _____ his speech by elaborating in detail on three of his slides.

9. It is important to _____ a home before purchasing it to ensure that there are no major problems.

10. The treasurer used previous years' expense totals as the _____ for his financial assessment for this year's projected expenses.

# Lesson 139

## A CAMPUS TORN BY WAR

The student magazine was renowned for its **pacifist** stance on the ongoing war. It was thus no surprise when the magazine fell **prey** to the rising hawkish sentiments on campus. Someone set fire to the publication's office and it suffered **severe** damage as a result. The campus community did **deplore** the blatant attack; however, no one was charged for the crime. After much investigation, the campus police finally found some **authentic** evidence that pointed at the possible perpetrators. They were part of a secret campus group that was funded by one of the warring parties.

## NEW WORDS

**severe**
sə'vi(ə)r

**prey**
prā

**pacifist**
'pasə,fist

**authentic**
ô'THentik

**deplore**
di'plôr

**Definitions:**    Try matching the words in the list with the appropriate definitions. If you are stuck, check the glossary in the back of the book or the passage at the top of the page.

1.   severe    _____    a.    genuine, of undisputed origin; based on facts, accurate, reliable

2.   prey    _____    b.    to feel or express strong disapproval of (something)

3.   pacifist    _____    c.    (n.) 1. an animal that is hunted or killed by another for food; 2. a person easily injured or taken advantage of; (v.) 1. to hunt and kill for food; 2. to take advantage of

4.   authentic    _____    d.    one who believes war and violence are unjustifiable

5.   deplore    _____    e.    very great or intense; very strict or harsh

**Sentences:**    Try to use the words above in a sentence below. Remember that a word ending may be changed or its figure of speech slightly altered.

6.    As a(n) _____, Trey has decided never to fight or to advocate war as long as he lives.

7.    While a minor cut is not a serious injury, being paralyzed below the waist is a(n) _____ injury.

8.    Foxes tend to view rabbits as their _____: the latter are hunted as a food source.

9.    Even though Shirley is not Japanese, her miso soup tastes really _____.

10.    Though most of Anya's teachers _____ her, none can object to the quality of her excellent academic work.

196

# NEW WORDS

**muster**

'məstər

**acquaintance**

ə'kwāntns

**covert**

'kōvərt, kō'vərt, 'kəvərt

**voluminous**

və'loomənəs

**initiate**

i'niSHē͟ ͟āt

# Lesson 140

## THE LOVE LETTER

Janet was Phil's **acquaintance** whom he had met through mutual friends on a few occasions. Phil had a **covert** interest in Janet; however, he could not **muster** the courage to call her on the phone and ask her out on a date. It was not easy for him to **initiate** conversations with attractive girls because he was too self-aware of his speech impediment. Instead, he wrote Janet a **voluminous** letter, in which he poured out his feelings for her.

**Definitions:** Try matching the words in the list with the appropriate definitions. If you are stuck, check the glossary in the back of the book or the passage at the top of the page.

1. muster _____   a.   1. to cause something to begin; 2. to admit someone into a secret society or group
2. acquaintance _____   b.   not openly acknowledged or displayed
3. covert _____   c.   occupying much space
4. voluminous _____   d.   1. a person's knowledge or experience of something; 2. a person one knows slightly but who is not a close friend
5. initiate _____   e.   to summon up a feeling, attitude, or response

**Sentences:** Try to use the words above in a sentence below. Remember that a word ending may be changed or its figure of speech slightly altered.

6. The man in the grey suit is my _____ from college.
7. It was difficult to _____ a conversation with the broker because his telephone was broken.
8. It took weeks for the new employee to _____ enough courage to ask his boss for a raise.
9. That artwork is _____ and cannot even fit on the available wall space.
10. Most times people who try to cheat others in business are _____ in their operation.

# Crossword Puzzle
## Lessons 131-140

ACROSS

2 (adj.) conscientiously or obediently fulfilling one's role
8 (v.) to fail to resist (pressure, temptation, or some other force)
9 (v.) to fully satisfy a desire or appetite
11 (n.) a sharp, angry, or wittily incisive response to a remark; (v.) to respond to a remark or accusation in a witty or incisive manner
12 (v.) to scold or criticize someone angrily
14 (adj.) 1. (of a person) pleasant because of a personality, interests, or other qualities similar to one's own; 2. (of a thing) pleasant or suitable because it is suited to one's tastes or inclination
15 (n.) a long arduous journey, especially one made on foot
16 (n.) an unexpected or casual meeting with someone or something; (v.) 1. to unexpectedly experience or be faced with something difficult or hostile; 2. to meet
17 (v.) 1. to cause something to begin; 2. to admit someone into a secret society or group

18 (n.) 1. the act of returning something lost or stolen to its proper owner; 2. recompense for loss or injury; 3. the restoration of something to its original state

DOWN

1 (n.) the arts and other manifestations of human intellectual achievement regarded collectively
3 (v.) to make someone morally or legally bound to an action or course of action
4 (adj.) very great or intense; very strict or harsh
5 (v.) to examine someone or something closely to assess condition and/or shortcomings
6 (adj.) having a sharply strong smell or taste
7 (v.) to summon up a feeling, attitude, or response
8 (v.) to imitate the appearance or character of
10 (v.) to increase the power, status, or wealth of
12 (n.) the underlying support or foundation for an idea, argument, or process
13 (adj.) genuine, of undisputed origin; based on facts, accurate, reliable

# Vocabulary Review
## Lessons 131-140

**Directions: Match each word with its best approximate definition. Note that definitions are not necessarily repeated verbatim from the lesson exercises.**

1. culpable _____
2. distress _____
3. craft _____
4. annul _____
5. domicile _____

6. arid _____

7. benevolent _____

8. wary _____

9. credulous _____

10. ardor _____

11. crisis _____

12. prosperous _____
13. strenuous _____

14. dogged _____

15. prolong _____

16. fluctuate _____

17. pacifist _____

18. deplore _____
19. covert _____

20. voluminous _____

a. passion or enthusiasm
b. to extend the duration of
c. well meaning and kindly
d. requiring or using great exertion
e. one who believes that war and violence are unjustifiable
f. a person's home or residence, or the country in which a person considers his or her home or residence
g. a period of trouble, difficulty, or danger
h. to declare an agreement, decision, or result invalid; to declare a marriage to have no legal existence
i. having little to no rain; too dry for vegetation to grow
j. exhibiting tenacity and grim persistence
k. to rise and fall regularly in number or amount
l. worthy of blame
m. successful in material terms; flourishing financially
n. extreme anxiety or pain, or to cause someone such
o. not openly acknowledged or displayed
p. having or showing too great a readiness to believe things
q. an activity where one makes things by hand
r. occupying much space
s. to feel strong disapproval of something
t. exhibiting caution about possible dangers or problems

# Word Roots: Unit 14

## ROOTS AND THEIR MEANINGS

| | | | |
|---|---|---|---|
| **dis:** | apart, away from, not | **pun/pen:** | to pay, punish, compensate |
| **nom/nym:** | name | **us/ut:** | to use |
| **gno:** | to know | **un/non:** | not |

**Here are a few examples of some words that use the above roots:**

| | |
|---|---|
| disengaged: | emotionally unattached |
| homonym: | two or more words having the same spelling but different meanings |
| agnostic: | a person who claims neither faith nor nonbelief in God |
| punitive: | inflicting or intended to be punishment; a charge or tax that is exorbitantly high |
| utensil: | an implement for household usage |
| uninspired: | lacking in imagination, commitment, or originality |
| noncommittal: | not willing to stick to a definite course of action |

**Now try to fill in the table below by finding the appropriate root(s) and interpreting the meaning of each word:**

| Word | Root(s) | Guessed Meaning | Actual Meaning |
|---|---|---|---|
| nomenclature | | | |
| penalty | | | |
| diagnostic | | | |
| unintelligent | | | |
| disrespectful | | | |
| reusable | | | |
| ignorant | | | |
| nonessential | | | |
| pseudonym | | | |

# Specific Vocabularies 3
## Measurement, Music, and Instrument Words

## Some Measurement Equivalents:

### Length Equivalents
- 12 inches = 1 foot
- 3 feet = 1 yard
- 5,280 feet = 1 mile
- 1 ton = 2,000 pounds
- 1 fathom = 6 feet (typically used to measure depth in water)

### Time Equivalents
- Approximately 52 weeks = 1 year
- 1 fortnight = 2 weeks

### Liquid and Powder Equivalents
- 2 pints = 1 quart
- 4 quarts = 1 gallon
- 3 teaspoons = 1 tablespoon

## Some Measurement Equivalents:

- **Decibels** measures the intensity of sound
- **Lumens** measure the intensity of light
- **Watts** are a measure of power in an electric circuit
- **Volts** measure the amount of electrical potential in something
- **Amperes** measure the flow of an electric current
- **Flux** measures the amount of electric or magnetic field passing through an area

## Some Music Terms:

- A singer with a low voice is called a **bass**
- A singer with a high voice is called a **tenor**
- The speed at which a passage of music should be played is called the **tempo**
- A written representation of a musical composition showing all the vocal and instrumental parts arranged is called a **score**
- Wind instruments that are made of metal are called **brass** instruments; they include trumpets, saxophones, horns, tuba, and trombone
- Wind instruments not made of brass are called **woodwind**; examples include clarinets, flutes, oboes, and bassoons.

- Instruments where one strikes an object to produce sound are called **percussion** instruments; examples include drums, bells, xylophones, cymbals, gongs, and rattles
- A **conductor** is a person who directs the performance of an orchestra or choir

## Some Instrument Terms:

- A **thermometer** measures temperature
- A **barometer** measures atmospheric pressure
- A **hygrometer** measures the humidity of the air or a gas
- A **metronome** is a device that marks (musical) time at a selected rate by giving a regular tick
- An **awl** is a small pointed tool for piercing holes, especially in leather
- One uses **pliers** to grip small objects or to bend wire
- A **jack** is a device to lift heavy objects, especially cars, so that wheels can be changed
- A **protractor** is a device used to measure angles
- There are two instruments called a **compass**; one helps find direction relative to magnetic north and the other is used to draw circles, to draw arcs, and to measure distances between points
- A **stethoscope** is an instrument used by a doctor to listen to one's breathing and heartbeat

## NEW WORDS

**universal**
ˌyoonəˈvərsəl

**adorn**
əˈdôrn

**mute**
myoot

**adversity**
adˈvərsitē

**marvel**
ˈmärvəl

The captured painter, who had now become a slave to the Sultan, showed great courage in the face of **adversity**. He humbly asked for some paint and created a large painting for his captor. When the Sultan's attendants saw the painting, there was **mute** admiration in their eyes. They didn't dare say a word but one could clearly see the look of **marvel** in their faces. The painting expressed some **universal** feelings, such as sadness and nostalgia, and the attendants could relate to them. The Sultan himself was so impressed that he decided to **adorn** the walls of his palace with the captured painter's work.

**Definitions:**     Try matching the words in the list with the appropriate definitions. If you are stuck, check the glossary in the back of the book or the passage at the top of the page.

1.   universal   _____   a.   of or done by all people
2.   adorn   _____   b.   (n.) an astonishing or wonderful person or thing; (v.) to be filled with wonder or astonishment
3.   mute   _____   c.   (adj.) refraining from speech or temporarily speechless; (n.) a person without the power of speech; (v.) to deaden, muffle, or soften the sound of
4.   adversity   _____   d.   difficulty or misfortune
5.   marvel   _____   e.   to make more beautiful or attractive

**Sentences:**     Try to use the words above in a sentence below. Remember that a word ending may be changed or its figure of speech slightly altered.

6.   Elvis put the television on _____ so that he could concentrate on his math homework.
7.   Though the world contains many cultures, it is _____ true that cannibalism is frowned upon.
8.   Often individuals who have persevered in the face of _____ are kinder than those who have not.
9.   Mikayla helped _____ the tree with lights and ornaments.
10.   I could not help but to _____ at the magician's amazing illusions.

# Lesson 142

## THE PROFESSOR'S TIME AWAY

Ever since the professor went on **sabbatical** after seven years of incessant work, his wife could perceive a clear change in his behavior. The professor picked up some **eccentric** habits, such as sitting outside in the yard early in the morning mumbling with a cup of rum and tea. After drinking his alcoholic **beverage**, the professor would get somewhat **unruly** and run through the house, occasionally breaking something. His wife could not comprehend this **irrational** behavior, especially since her husband had always been a very sensible person. When she broached the subject, he just said that he needed to let off some steam.

### NEW WORDS

**irrational**
iˈraSHənl

**beverage**
ˈbev(ə)rij

**sabbatical**
səˈbatikəl

**eccentric**
ikˈsentrik

**unruly**
ˌənˈroolē

**Definitions:**    Try matching the words in the list with the appropriate definitions. If you are stuck, check the glossary in the back of the book or the passage at the top of the page.

| | | | | |
|---|---|---|---|---|
| 1. | irrational | _____ | a. | not logical or reasonable |
| 2. | beverage | _____ | b. | (adj.) 1. unconventional and slightly strange; 2. off-center (n.) a person with unconventional and slightly strange behavior |
| 3. | sabbatical | _____ | c. | a period of paid leave granted for study or travel |
| 4. | eccentric | _____ | d. | a drink |
| 5. | unruly | _____ | e. | disorderly, disruptive, and not amenable to discipline or control |

**Sentences:**    Try to use the words above in a sentence below. Remember that a word ending may be changed or its figure of speech slightly altered.

6.    It is _____ to think that if you spend all of your money, more will suddenly appear.

7.    Molly is a(n) _____ person because she often mumbles and her house is filled with wacky science experiments; nevertheless, she is very kind.

8.    The lunch special includes a burger, fries, dessert, and your choice of _____ to drink.

9.    Most professors receive a(n) _____ every seventh year to pursue research interests.

10.    The _____ child kept jumping around and faked crying during lessons to avoid work.

## NEW WORDS

**alleviate**
əˈlēvēˌāt

**amalgamation**
əˈmalgəˌmāt

**feat**
fēt

**vulnerable**
ˈvəln(ə)rəbəl

**gesture**
ˈjesCHər

The **amalgamation** of the two companies created a lot of tension among the employees. To **alleviate** the pressure among them, the new CEO invested much time in team building and giving personal attention to each of the workers. That proved to be a very thoughtful **gesture** on his part that seemed to produce good results. Getting all the employees to work together as a team was no small **feat**, considering how different the two companies were from each other before the merger. It was a **vulnerable** time for the new company, but the CEO felt confident that things would get much better with time and that the company would soon become one of the main competitors in the market.

**Definitions:** Try matching the words in the list with the appropriate definitions. If you are stuck, check the glossary in the back of the book or the passage at the top of the page.

1. alleviate _____ a. to make pain or suffering less severe
2. amalgamation _____ b. (n.) a movement of the body, especially the hand or head, to express an idea or meaning, or to convey one's feelings or intentions; (v.) to move a part of the body, especially the hand or head, to express an idea or m meaning, or to convey one's feelings or intentions
3. feat _____ c. an action or achievement that requires great courage or skill
4. vulnerable _____ d. the action, process, or result of uniting or combining
5. gesture _____ e. susceptible to physical or emotional harm

**Sentences:** Try to use the words above in a sentence below. Remember that a word ending may be changed or its figure of speech slightly altered.

6. The jar in the kitchen contains a(n) _____ of different sweets.
7. It was a difficult _____ for the acrobat to jump through three flaming hoops and land on her feet.
8. One is _____ to attack if he or she goes into the area beyond the hill that is not protected by the military.
9. I took three pills to help _____ my headache.
10. Amos made a(n) _____ with his hands to tell us that we should follow him to the park.

# Lesson 144

## THE DIFFERENCE BETWEEN WORDS AND REALITY

The crowd was **jubilant**. Its candidate had just won the local **election**. However, after the election it slowly became evident that there was a **fissure** between the politician's promises and his actions. When he gave a **synopsis** of his policies after his first three months of office, his supporters were disappointed. The politician had dabbled in **miscellaneous** issues; however, he did not seem to have made true on any of his promises.

**Definitions:**     Try matching the words in the list with the appropriate definitions.  If you are stuck, check the glossary in the back of the book or the passage at the top of the page.

| | | | | | |
|---|---|---|---|---|---|
| 1. | jubilant | _____ | a. | a brief summary or general survey of something | |
| 2. | election | _____ | b. | (of items or people) of various types or from different sources | |
| 3. | miscellaneous | _____ | c. | (n.) a long narrow opening made by cracking or splitting, especially in the earth; (v.) to split or crack something to cause a long narrow opening | |
| 4. | fissure | _____ | d. | feeling or expressing great happiness | |
| 5. | synopsis | _____ | e. | a formal organized process of selecting or being selected, typically for members of a political party | |

**Sentences:**     Try to use the words above in a sentence below.  Remember that a word ending may be changed or its figure of speech slightly altered.

6.    One can see a(n) _____ in the earth where the fault line runs.

7.    Anita was _____ when she heard that she would be head counselor at the school.

8.    Every four years the United States holds a(n) _____ where people vote for their choice of president.

9.    Ross left _____ toys strewn all over the floor of the living room.

10.    A(n) _____ of the book can be found on its back cover.

## NEW WORDS

**mandatory**
ˈmandəˌterē

**authoritarian**
əˌTHôriˈte(ə)rēən, ôˌTHär-

**ailment**
ˈālmənt

**deluge**
ˈdel(y)ooj

**underlying**
ˌəndərˈlī-iNG

### STRESS DURING CHRISTMAS

Just before Christmas, Sandy received a **deluge** of letters to proofread at work. She had an ongoing **ailment** for about two weeks and wanted to postpone the work until after New Year's. However, she knew that her **authoritarian** boss would not give her the days off. For him, work was **mandatory** unless one had a really serious condition that required hospitalization. She was not aware that the **underlying** cause for her boss' harsh behavior was his fear that the company might go bankrupt after a year of sluggish business.

**Definitions:**     Try matching the words in the list with the appropriate definitions. If you are stuck, check the glossary in the back of the book or the passage at the top of the page.

| | | | | |
|---|---|---|---|---|
| 1. | mandatory _____ | a. | to be the cause or basis of |
| 2. | authoritarian _____ | b. | required by law or rules; compulsory |
| 3. | ailment _____ | c. | (n.) a severe flood; (v.) to flood or be flooded by a great quantity of something |
| 4. | deluge _____ | d. | an illness (typically minor illness) |
| 5. | underlying _____ | e. | favoring or enforcing strict obedience to authority, especially the government at the expense of personal freedom; showing a lack of concern about the wishes or cares of others |

**Sentences:**     Try to use the words above in a sentence below. Remember that a word ending may be changed or its figure of speech slightly altered.

6.     Many people found the adolescent's _____ behavior to be a major turn-off.

7.     It is _____ that all employees attend tonight's meeting; if they do not attend, their positions may be terminated.

8.     Good medicine should help cure your _____.

9.     Ginny was _____ with homework after she received research assignments in all of her seven classes.

10.     While pundits say charisma is important for getting elected, the _____ factor swinging election outcomes is usually economic health.

# Lesson 146

## DIFFERENT GENERATIONS

After inheriting the company from his father, Misha decided to **rejuvenate** the business. He made a **spontaneous** decision to **transact** with a number of foreign companies – something his conservative father had avoided. Unlike his father, Misha was a **gregarious** young man who wanted to open up the company to as many new markets as possible. He also did not care so much for his father's aristocratic clients. In fact, Misha hired some new employees from a **humble** background who could help him transform the company's services in order to be more accessible to regular customers. The old aristocratic days of the company were over.

**Definitions:** Try matching the words in the list with the appropriate definitions. If you are stuck, check the glossary in the back of the book or the passage at the top of the page.

| | | | |
|---|---|---|---|
| 1. | spontaneous _____ | a. | to make someone or something feel fresher or younger |
| 2. | rejuvenate _____ | b. | a person who is fond of company, sociable |
| 3. | humble _____ | c. | to conduct or carry out (business) |
| 4. | transact _____ | d. | (n.) 1. having or showing a modest or low estimate of one's importance; 2. of low social, administrative, or political rank; (v.) to lower (someone) in dignity or importance |
| 5. | gregarious _____ | e. | performed by impulse and without any planning or premeditation |

**Sentences:** Try to use the words above in a sentence below. Remember that a word ending may be changed or its figure of speech slightly altered.

6. Mitt's decision to go on a vacation to El Paso was _____: without any planning he bought a ticket and was on a plane only five hours later.

7. Hot springs are noted for their ability to _____ people who are exhausted and need an extra boost of energy.

8. It is difficult to _____ business with people from two completely different cultures.

9. Because Zoe is a(n) _____ person, she finds great joy in going to social events with her friends.

10. Casey was _____ when she received the award: rather than discussing herself, she thanked all of the people who helped her along the way.

## NEW WORDS

**transparent**
tranˈspe(ə)rənt, -ˈspar-

**timorous**
ˈtimərəs

**incite**
inˈsīt

**cavort**
kəˈvôrt

**triumph**
ˈtrīəmf

While most of the children would **cavort** in the yard each afternoon, the **timorous** little boy stood aloof and just looked at them. It was **transparent** that he was too shy to participate. In order to **incite** the boy to play, his schoolteacher asked some of the other boys to approach him and throw a ball towards him. She was determined to help the timid student. She knew that if he could overcome his shyness it would be a professional **triumph** for her.

**Definitions:** Try matching the words in the list with the appropriate definitions. If you are stuck, check the glossary in the back of the book or the passage at the top of the page.

| | | | | |
|---|---|---|---|---|
| 1. | transparent _____ | a. | to encourage or stir up (violent or unlawful behavior) |
| 2. | timorous _____ | b. | a great victory or achievement |
| 3. | incite _____ | c. | 1. allowing light to pass through so that objects are easily seen; 2. easy to perceive or detect; having thoughts or feelings that are easy to detect |
| 4. | cavort _____ | d. | to jump or dance around excitedly |
| 5. | triumph _____ | e. | showing or suffering from nervousness, fear, or lack of confidence |

**Sentences:** Try to use the words above in a sentence below. Remember that a word ending may be changed or its figure of speech slightly altered.

6. After four months of battle, the rebel forces finally were able to _____ and win the war.

7. The _____ sailor felt anxiety confronting his volatile captain about the squalid condition of the galley.

8. It became _____ that Joel did not do his homework when he was unable to give an impromptu oral presentation on the subject.

9. Often at tribal ceremonies, adolescents will _____ around before a ceremonial fire.

10. Protestors last night _____ a fight after one of them hurled a rock at an inattentive police officer.

# Lesson 148

## THE FIRST STEP

Growing up in a home that was **rife** with tension and abuse, Krysta became a **timid** child who never dared to **vex** her parents with any demands. There was even an unspoken **custom** in her household that Krysta needed to hand over to her alcoholic parents all that she earned from her part-time job. However, when her friends kept boasting of their summer excursions, Krysta was unable to **quench** her thirst for traveling. To afford the European vacation that she wanted so badly, Krysta secretly saved up money behind her parents' backs.

**Definitions:**      Try matching the words in the list with the appropriate definitions. If you are stuck, check the glossary in the back of the book or the passage at the top of the page.

| | | | | |
|---|---|---|---|---|
| 1. | custom | _____ | a. | (especially of something undesirable or harmful) of common occurrence; widespread |
| 2. | vex | _____ | b. | (adj.) made or done for a particular customer; (n.) a traditional and widely accepted way of behaving or doing something that is specific to a particular society, place, or time |
| 3. | quench | _____ | c. | to make one feel annoyed, frustrated, or worried, especially with trivial matters |
| 4. | timid | _____ | d. | to satisfy one's thirst by drinking; to satisfy a desire |
| 5. | rife | _____ | e. | showing a lack of courage or confidence; frightened |

**Sentences:**      Try to use the words above in a sentence below. Remember that a word ending may be changed or its figure of speech slightly altered.

6.    The puerile child continued to _____ the guests through the entire dinner party.

7.    Those suits were _____ made for the tall basketball players.

8.    It can take a lot of courage for a(n) _____ person to stand up and speak out.

9.    Sadly, the woman's story was _____ with lies and she could neither be believed nor trusted in the end.

10.    Hopefully a glass of lemonade will help _____ your thirst.

## NEW WORDS

**magnitude**
ˈmagnəˌtood

**mundane**
ˌmənˈdān

**suspend**
səˈspend

**verify**
ˈverəˌfī

**exquisite**
ekˈskwizit, ˈekskwizit

## DIVORCE COMPLICATIONS

The divorce was the greatest challenge that Roosevelt had ever faced. The **magnitude** of the event could not be overstated: he was about to lose his family as well as his wife's share in the company. The impending divorce caused him to **suspend** his **mundane** affairs; nothing was as important as trying to repair things with his wife. He took her to some expensive restaurants and treated her with **exquisite** care. Roosevelt wanted to **verify** that, even if they separated, his wife would not cause too much trouble in company affairs.

**Definitions:**     Try matching the words in the list with the appropriate definitions. If you are stuck, check the glossary in the back of the book or the passage at the top of the page.

1. magnitude _____     a. extremely beautiful and delicate; intensely felt; highly sensitive or discriminating

2. mundane _____     b. 1. to temporarily prevent from continuing to be in force or in effect; to defer or delay an action or judgment; 2. to hang something from somewhere

3. suspend _____     c. to ensure that something is true, accurate, or justified

4. verify _____     d. 1. the size or extent of something; 2. size

5. exquisite _____     e. lacking excitement or interest; dull

**Sentences:**     Try to use the words above in a sentence below. Remember that a word ending may be changed or its figure of speech slightly altered.

6. A litmus test should help to _____ whether the solution is an acid or a base.

7. I wish I could enjoy _____ tasks like going grocery shopping, doing crossword puzzles, or cleaning dishes.

8. The crystal chandelier and the beautiful cutlery make the dining room look truly _____.

9. Even though the model airplane has hooks to hang it, I am still having difficulty trying to _____ it from the ceiling.

10. Vishnu did not realize the _____ of the plague until he reached the town and saw thousands of sick citizens.

# Lesson 150

## THE AMICABLE POLITICIAN

There was something kind about the politician's **physiognomy**. The **focal** point of his face was the look in his eyes: gracious, warm, and magnanimous. His eyes reflected the feeling of **amity** towards everyone. Perhaps that was the reason he was able to **accumulate** so much support from the public in his two **sequential** terms of service. He would have probably won a third term if the law permitted it.

**NEW WORDS**

**physiognomy**
ˌfizēˈä(g)nəmē

**focal**
ˈfōkəl

**accumulate**
əˈkyoomyəˌlāt

**sequential**
siˈkwenCHəl

**amity**
ˈamitē

**Definitions:**      Try matching the words in the list with the appropriate definitions. If you are stuck, check the glossary in the back of the book or the passage at the top of the page.

1.    physiognomy _____     a.    a person's facial features or expression, especially when regarded as indicative of character or ethnic origin; the art of judging character from facial characteristics

2.    focal         _____     b.    a friendly relationship
3.    accumulate _____     c.    of or relating to the center or main point of interest
4.    sequential _____     d.    forming or following in a logical order
5.    amity         _____     e.    to gather together or acquire an increasing number or amount of

**Sentences:**      Try to use the words above in a sentence below. Remember that a word ending may be changed or its figure of speech slightly altered.

6.    Because of the _____ in our workplace, all employees tend to look out for each other.

7.    In the nineteenth century, _____ was considered important to some, as one's facial features were thought to explain one's character and motives.

8.    The _____ point of the presentation was about the widespread problems caused by immigration into the country.

9.    Reince took the files from his clients and put them in _____ order, indexing them alphabetically by his clients' surnames.

10.   Because Lee had not cleaned her room in weeks, the dirty clothes and papers on her floor began to _____ .

212

# Word Search
## Lessons 141-150

```
U F E A T N V E D U T I N G A M T P Y
C N J X M W M U T N P T I M O R O U S
A X I R E A K L L H E R U S S I F N R
V R D V R V G Y Y N N M R Y V W Z W W
O D E V E R T S Y J E Y T D P M N R B
R V E J N R I R B M K R P L D L M L N
T L M M U O S S P O N T A N E O U S T
K X Q A G V M A R Y C C D B A K I T N
B Z P N J M E M L U I Y N C L S P I T
W Z O D N B X N S T G S C T P E R R N
D M R A Y R N T A Y N U U O W R Y R G
Y V Y T B L O B K T M E N S A Y Z N G
R B Q O M M B J J U E Y M T P P P D X
V M V R R A L M L L S Z I L L E R M M
V J V Y S J B A V N N O L V I P N J L
L Z Z W D Z T K K T N X J G R A D D Y
R N Q J W E V M R A D V D T M R D R P
R M N Y T T B Z L N V Q Y P G J P D D
```

1 (adj.) of or done by all people
2 (n.) an astonishing or wonderful person or thing; (v.) to be filled with wonder or astonishment
3 (adj.) not logical or reasonable
4 (n.) a period of paid leave granted to for study or travel
5 (n.) an action or achievement that requires great courage or skill
6 (adj.) susceptible to physical or emotional harm
7 (n.) a long narrow opening made by cracking or splitting, especially in the earth; (v.) to split or crack something to cause a long narrow opening
8 (n.) a brief summary or general survey of something
9 (adj.) required by law or rules; compulsory
10 (n.) an illness (typically minor illness)
11 (adj.) performed by impulse and without any planning or premeditation
12 (v.) to make someone or something feel fresher or younger
13 (adj.) showing or suffering from nervousness, fear, or lack of confidence
14 (v.) to jump or dance around excitedly
15 (adj.) made or done for a particular customer; (n.) a traditional and widely accepted way of behaving or doing something that is specific to a particular society, place, or time
16 (v.) to make one feel annoyed, frustrated, or worried, especially with trivial matters
17 (n.) 1. the size or extent of something; 2. size
18 (v.) 1. to temporarily prevent from continuing to be in force or in effect; to defer or delay an action or judgment; 2. to hang something from somewhere
19 (n.) a person's facial features or expression, especially when regarded as indicative of character or ethic origin; the art of judging character from facial characteristics
20 (v.) to gather together or acquire an increasing number or amount of

# Vocabulary Review
## Lessons 141-150

**Directions:** Match each word with its best approximate definition. Note that definitions are not necessarily repeated verbatim from the lesson exercises.

| 1. | adorn | _____ | a. | to satisfy one's thirst by drinking |
| 2. | adversity | _____ | b. | of or relating to the center or main point of interest |
| 3. | beverage | _____ | c. | a great victory or achievement; to achieve a great victory |
| 4. | eccentric | _____ | d. | a drink, typically not water |
| 5. | alleviate | _____ | e. | the action or process of combining or uniting |
| 6. | amalgamation | _____ | f. | feeling or expressing triumph and joy |
| 7. | jubilant | _____ | g. | to make sure and demonstrate that something is true or accurate |
| 8. | election | _____ | h. | to conduct or carry out business |
| 9. | deluge | _____ | i. | to be the cause or basis of something |
| 10. | underlying | _____ | j. | to stir up or provoke (violent or unlawful behavior) |
| 11. | transact | _____ | k. | concerning a person who is unconventional and slightly strange |
| 12. | gregarious | _____ | l. | to make pain, a problem, or a deficiency seem less severe |
| 13. | incite | _____ | m. | a person who is sociable or who enjoys company |
| 14. | triumph | _____ | n. | forming or following in a logical order |
| 15. | quench | _____ | o. | a process whereby people vote for representatives or to make decisions, typically a political process |
| 16. | timid | _____ | p. | exhibiting a lack of confidence or courage |
| 17. | mundane | _____ | q. | to make beautiful or attractive |
| 18. | verify | _____ | r. | lacking excitement; dull |
| 19. | focal | _____ | s. | a severe flood |
| 20. | sequential | _____ | t. | difficulties or misfortune |

# Word Roots: Unit 15

## ROOTS AND THEIR MEANINGS

| | | | |
|---|---|---|---|
| **spec:** | to look, appear | **de:** | away from, opposite of |
| **gyn:** | woman | **tact:** | touch |
| **sed/sid:** | to sit, be still | **corp:** | body |

## Here are a few examples of some words that use the above roots:

| | |
|---|---|
| spectacle: | a visually striking performance or play |
| misogynistic: | referring to a hatred of women |
| sedentary: | tending to spend much time seated down; inactive or inert |
| depart: | to leave, often in order to embark on a journey |
| tactile: | of or related to the sense of touch; tangible |
| corpse: | a dead human body |

## Now try to fill in the table below by finding the appropriate root(s) and interpreting the meaning of each word:

| Word | Root(s) | Guessed Meaning | Actual Meaning |
|---|---|---|---|
| deposit | | | |
| androgynous | | | |
| sediment | | | |
| corpus | | | |
| speculate | | | |
| preside | | | |
| contact | | | |
| detract | | | |
| retrospect | | | |

# Lesson 151

## IMPASSIVE IRENE

Even though Irene appears to have a stolid demeanor, beneath her inanimate **exterior** she is quite emotive. In fact, when she gets excited about something she can become quite **dynamic** and engaging. Under such conditions, little will **inhibit** her from becoming passionately involved. That said, unless a topic is of more than **incidental** value, Irene will not be too interested. Chances are that you will wind up in a **stalemate** if you spend hours of your time trying to excite her about something that does not move her.

**Definitions:**    Try matching the words in the list with the appropriate definitions. If you are stuck, check the glossary in the back of the book or the passage at the top of the page.

| | | | | |
|---|---|---|---|---|
| 1. | incidental | _____ | a. | characterized by constant change, activity, or progress |
| 2. | stalemate | _____ | b. | (adj.) forming, existing on, or related to the outside of something; (n.) the outer surface or structure of something |
| 3. | dynamic | _____ | c. | to hinder, restrain, or prevent an action or process; to make someone self-conscious and unable to act in a natural way |
| 4. | inhibit | _____ | d. | a situation where further action or progress by opposing parties seems impossible; a draw |
| 5. | exterior | _____ | e. | accompanying but not a major part of something |

**Sentences:**    Try to use the words above in a sentence below. Remember that a word ending may be changed or its figure of speech slightly altered.

6.    The _____ of the house looked beautiful after its roof had been redone and its windows had been replaced.

7.    After three years of fighting, Meredith and Elliot reached a(n) _____: neither of them could get what they wanted without losing more in the process.

8.    Whether the hotel room has green tea toothpaste is a(n) _____ matter compared to whether the quality of room and service is excellent.

9.    Felix is a(n) _____ character: he is always moving about and doing exciting things.

10.    The recent earthquake has _____ progress on the construction of the new civic center.

## NEW WORDS

**remiss**
ri'mis

**fatigue**
fə'tēg

**supreme**
sə'prēm, soo-

**adamant**
'adəmənt

**harrowing**
'harōiNG

# Lesson 152

## SOMETHING TO LIVE FOR

The old gardener began to suffer from signs of chronic **fatigue**. He had to stop and rest every fifteen minutes. It seemed to him that each simple action required **supreme** effort. Despite this, the old gardener remained **adamant** about coming to work each morning. He was never **remiss** in his job, regardless of how difficult it had become for him. He knew that the day he retired would be a **harrowing** one: the garden was the old man's whole world in his lonely years as an elderly widower.

**Definitions:**    Try matching the words in the list with the appropriate definitions. If you are stuck, check the glossary in the back of the book or the passage at the top of the page.

| | | | | |
|---|---|---|---|---|
| 1. | remiss | _____ | a. | acutely distressing |
| 2. | fatigue | _____ | b. | refusing to be persuaded or change one's mind |
| 3. | supreme | _____ | c. | superior to all others; strongest, most important, or most powerful; very great or intense |
| 4. | adamant | _____ | d. | extreme tiredness, especially resulting from mental or physical exertion or illness |
| 5. | harrowing | _____ | e. | lacking care or attention to duty; negligent |

**Sentences:**    Try to use the words above in a sentence below. Remember that a word ending may be changed or its figure of speech slightly altered.

6.    It would be _____ of me to not show up at faculty meetings and to not grade papers.

7.    Having to walk three days through the savanna with little food or water was a(n) _____ experience.

8.    Ingrid was _____ that finishing her education in classical Greek literature was necessary for her career.

9.    Matteo felt _____ after spending fourteen hours moving the family into their new home.

10.    Often tyrants see themselves as a(n) _____ leader with much more clout than anyone else.

# Lesson 153

## LIFE GOES ON

Festivities in the village were about to **commence**. The village square was packed with half-drunken peasants who were shouting loudly and creating a scene of total **bedlam**. The mayor had organized a carnival night in order to **divert** the villagers' attention from the recent tragedy in which a forest fire destroyed a part of the crop, for he knew that some jollity would **motivate** the peasants to overcome their grief and find solutions to the issue. Certainly a night of thoughtless enjoyment was most **welcome** for the anxious peasants.

## NEW WORDS

**bedlam**
ˈbedləm

**divert**
diˈvərt, dī-

**commence**
kəˈmens

**motivate**
ˈmōtəˌvāt

**welcome**
ˈwelkəm

**Definitions:**    Try matching the words in the list with the appropriate definitions. If you are stuck, check the glossary in the back of the book or the passage at the top of the page.

1.    bedlam    _____    a.    a scene of uproar and confusion

2.    divert    _____    b.    1. to cause someone or something to change course or turn from one direction to another; 2. to distract someone or his or her attention from something

3.    commence    _____    c.    1. to provide someone with an objective for doing something; 2. to stimulate one's interest in doing something

4.    motivate    _____    d.    (adj.) (of a guest or new arrival) gladly received; (n.) an instance or manner of greeting someone; (v.) 1. to greet someone arriving in a glad or friendly way; 2. to react with pleasure or approval to an event or development

5.    welcome    _____    e.    to begin, start

**Sentences:**    Try to use the words above in a sentence below. Remember that a word ending may be changed or its figure of speech slightly altered.

6.    It is difficult to _____ someone who has no interest in doing a task.

7.    The fall semester will _____ in the second week of September.

8.    When the lighting crew and actors started quarreling with each other, _____ broke out on stage.

9.    Alexis tried to _____ her parents' attention away from discussing the family vacation by demanding that she be fed immediately.

10.    Guests at the new hotel feel _____ as soon as the friendly staff get their bags, give them complimentary cookies, and show them a lovely, clean room.

## NEW WORDS

**audacious**
ô'dāSHəs

**residual**
ri'zijooəl

**magnetic**
mag'netik

**acclaim**
ə'klām

**aloof**
ə'loof

### A LIFE-CHANGING ACCIDENT

Jack used to possess a **magnetic** personality and was thus able to engage anyone he met in banter and jokes. However, after he made the **audacious** move to shield a child from a horse-drawn carriage breaking loose, Jack was badly wounded. The great **acclaim** he received from the police department for his bravery was not enough to compensate for his physical injuries. Having to travel around in wheelchairs and to tolerate the **residual** pain after his knee surgery, Jack turned into a cranky and **aloof** person. He even severed ties with his old friends, as they became a painful reminder of his prime youth.

**Definitions:** Try matching the words in the list with the appropriate definitions. If you are stuck, check the glossary in the back of the book or the passage at the top of the page.

1. audacious _____ a. (adj.) remaining after the greater part is gone; (n.) the remaining amount after other things have been subtracted or allowed for

2. residual _____ b. (n.) enthusiastic public praise; (v.) to praise enthusiastically and publicly

3. magnetic _____ c. not friendly or forthcoming; cold; distant

4. acclaim _____ d. 1. showing a willingness to take bold risks; 2. showing an impudent lack of respect

5. aloof _____ e. (adj.) 1. capable of being attracted by or acquiring the properties of a magnet; 2. very attractive or alluring

**Sentences:** Try to use the words above in a sentence below. Remember that a word ending may be changed or its figure of speech slightly altered.

6. The new musical has received much _____ in recent weeks from the press, who are hailing it as one of the most impressive pieces of this generation.

7. Benjamin was _____ at the party: he stood in the corner and kept to himself instead of socializing with the guests.

8. Everyone loved Talya's _____ personality: they were drawn to her charismatic charm, her wonderful caring nature, and her exciting stories.

9. Sales from my books furnish me a(n) _____ income on top of my hourly salary.

10. The _____ employee called out his boss' ethical mishaps and resigned on the spot.

# Lesson 155

## THE AMBITIOUS NEWCOMER

The **novice** at the design studio was extremely diligent and full of **vim** and inner strength. A desire to learn and succeed would **infuse** every task he performed. Even when his supervisor gave him a project of **colossal** proportions, the beginner worked hard to finish it before the deadline. It seemed that nothing could **thwart** his efforts to progress in the workplace as fast as possible.

**NEW WORDS**

**colossal**
kə'läsəl

**thwart**
THwôrt

**novice**
'nävəs

**infuse**
in'fyooz

**vim**
vim

**Definitions:** Try matching the words in the list with the appropriate definitions. If you are stuck, check the glossary in the back of the book or the passage at the top of the page.

| | | | | |
|---|---|---|---|---|
| 1. | colossal | _____ | a. | extremely large |
| 2. | thwart | _____ | b. | to fill or pervade; to instill a quality in someone or something |
| 3. | novice | _____ | c. | energy; enthusiasm |
| 4. | infuse | _____ | d. | to prevent someone from accomplishing something; to stymie |
| 5. | vim | _____ | e. | a person who is new or inexperienced in a field or situation |

**Sentences:** Try to use the words above in a sentence below. Remember that a word ending may be changed or its figure of speech slightly altered.

6. Lena is so full of _____ that she has done a week's work in eleven hours!

7. The evil villain tried to _____ the hero from rescuing his princess but failed in every attempt.

8. Sid is a(n) _____ at sailing; he lacks deep experience in how to navigate a boat at sea.

9. The ricotta cheese in that cannoli is _____ with orange rinds and citrus flavor.

10. That pumpkin is _____: it is at least five times larger than any I've seen before and it must weigh a ton!

# Lesson 156

## THE ENTREPRENEURIAL MAN

### NEW WORDS

**versatile**
ˈvərsətl

**quaint**
kwānt

**instigate**
ˈinstiˌgāt

**rue**
roo

**rectify**
ˈrektəˌfī

A man of **versatile** talents, John decided to leave his career in writing to start a woodworking business. He had always been interested in redecorating **quaint** old furniture that was sold in antique shops. He was not good at bargaining, however, and ultimately lost all of his money. That caused him to **rue** his decision to get into the new business. He wanted to **rectify** the situation but he did not know how to pay off all his debts. His financial troubles were enough to **instigate** him to try something brand new – to get into the cooking industry – which ultimately brought him much financial success and personal satisfaction.

**Definitions:**     Try matching the words in the list with the appropriate definitions. If you are stuck, check the glossary in the back of the book or the passage at the top of the page.

1.   versatile   _____   a.   to bring about or initiate an action or event; to provoke
2.   quaint   _____   b.   (n.) repentance, regret, compassion, or pity; (v.) to bitterly regret
3.   instigate   _____   c.   able to adapt to many different functions or activities
4.   rue   _____   d.   attractively unusual or old-fashioned, often resembling small town or rustic life
5.   rectify   _____   e.   to set something right; to correct

**Sentences:**     Try to use the words above in a sentence below. Remember that a word ending may be changed or its figure of speech slightly altered.

6.   Nothing could be done to _____ Giao's deplorable behavior in school.
7.   Heath will _____ the day that he tells his wife he wants a divorce.
8.   Someone who is _____ can adapt to many different situations because he or she has a broad skill set.
9.   Compared to city life in Los Angeles, life in in the rural Ohio town of Sandusky seemed pretty _____.
10.   Joanna _____ school reform when she complained that she was discriminated against based on the clothing she was wearing.

# Lesson 157

## HITCH YOUR WAGON TO A STAR

Stewie and Steven had been friends since childhood, and remained so even after Steven became an accomplished fencer and moved out of town. Their friendship lasted in part because Stewie found that there is a positive **correlation** between one's success as a professional athlete and that person's ability to **inspire** and motivate others to achieve their personal goals. Thankfully, Steven's success did not estrange him from Stewie. Just the other day, Steven picked up the phone to offer Stewie advice on how to **differentiate** between a correctly executed **lunge** and a bad one. Stewie found his friend's initiative **laudable**.

**Definitions:**     Try matching the words in the list with the appropriate definitions. If you are stuck, check the glossary in the back of the book or the passage at the top of the page.

1.  differentiate_____  a.  a mutual relationship or connection between two or more things

2.  lunge  _____  b.  to recognize or figure out what makes something different

3.  inspire  _____  c.  (n.) a sudden forward thrust of the body typically to attack someone or to seize something; (v.) to make a sudden forward thrust with a part of the body or a weapon

4.  laudable  _____  d.  to fill someone with the urge or ability to feel or do something

5.  correlation  _____  e.  praiseworthy; commendable

**Sentences:**     Try to use the words above in a sentence below. Remember that a word ending may be changed or its figure of speech slightly altered.

6.  A good teacher not only educates students, but also _____ them to be better people.

7.  The fencer _____ at his opponent and scored a point.

8.  There is little or no _____ between a person's height and his or her intelligence.

9.  It is hard to _____ between the two sample shades of blue in which my room will be painted.

10. Tony's performance was _____, and he received due praise from the audience for acting so well.

## NEW WORDS

**rancid**
'ransid

**wealth**
welTH

**surly**
'sərlē

**revel**
'revəl

**apparent**
ə'parənt, ə'pe(ə)r-

# Lesson 158

## RICH AND UNHAPPY

James was a handsome and well-educated young man who had no **apparent** reason to be unhappy with his life. What is more, he had inherited great **wealth** from his parents and was able to **revel** in luxury. However, after his girlfriend ran away with his butler, James became unbearably **surly**. One morning he fired a servant only because the latter supposedly served him **rancid** bacon for breakfast. After that incident, everyone in the house became scared of him.

**Definitions:**     Try matching the words in the list with the appropriate definitions. If you are stuck, check the glossary in the back of the book or the passage at the top of the page.

| | | | | |
|---|---|---|---|---|
| 1. | rancid | _____ | a. | an abundance of valuable possessions or money; plentiful supplies of a particular resource |
| 2. | wealth | _____ | b. | bad-tempered and unfriendly |
| 3. | surly | _____ | c. | clearly visible or true, obvious; seemingly true |
| 4. | revel | _____ | d. | (of foods) smelling or tasting unpleasant as a result of being old or stale |
| 5. | apparent | _____ | e. | to enjoy oneself in a noisy and lively way; to delight in |

**Sentences:**     Try to use the words above in a sentence below. Remember that a word ending may be changed or its figure of speech slightly altered.

6.    It is _____ that Blake does not want to be at the meeting because he keeps staring around the room paying attention to nothing.

7.    You should discuss your research project with Lester, for he has a(n) _____ of knowledge on the topics you are studying.

8.    The milk in the refrigerator tasted _____ and needed to be thrown out.

9.    Gianna _____ in the excitement of the annual risotto festival.

10.    A child who is _____ throws tantrums and often cries uncontrollably.

# Lesson 159

## THE AFFABLE HOST

Watching a culinary show every Saturday morning did much to **kindle** Matthew's interest in cooking. He knew that he would **thrive** in a job that allowed him to experiment and to make people happy. After he became a chef, he started a successful cooking show of his own. He was an **affable** host and was well liked by the public because if his pleasing personality. For instance, once he cut himself with a knife and did not even **wince**; he just continued smiling. Another time he was late for a live broadcast of his show and decided to **atone** for being late by handing everyone in the audience invitations for a free dinner at his restaurant.

## NEW WORDS

**kindle**
ˈkindl

**thrive**
THrīv

**atone**
əˈtōn

**affable**
ˈafəbəl

**wince**
wins

**Definitions:**      Try matching the words in the list with the appropriate definitions. If you are stuck, check the glossary in the back of the book or the passage at the top of the page.

1.   kindle   _____   a.   (n.) a slight grimace or recoiling caused by pain or distress; (v.) to grimace, shake, or recoil as the result of pain or distress
2.   thrive   _____   b.   friendly, easy to talk to, good-natured
3.   atone   _____   c.   to flourish; to grow vigorously
4.   affable   _____   d.   to make amends or reparation
5.   wince   _____   e.   to light or set on fire; to arouse or inspire

**Sentences:**      Try to use the words above in a sentence below. Remember that a word ending may be changed or its figure of speech slightly altered.

6.   Fido is a(n) _____ dog and thus loves greeting and playing with visitors.
7.   Irene went to the temple to _____ for her sins and to seek spiritual support in overcoming her troubles.
8.   Dominique's interest in French literature was _____ after she saw *Les Miserables* performed at the theater when she was twelve.
9.   Dolores _____ when she received the injection because she hates the sight and pain of receiving shots.
10.   Generally, molds _____ in damp places that are sufficiently warm and moist.

## NEW WORDS

**abbreviate**
əˈbrēvēˌāt

**gullible**
ˈgələbəl

**coach**
kōCH

**wayward**
ˈwāwərd

**obligate**
ˈäbliˌgāt

# Lesson 160

## THE DIFFICULT CHILD

Lord Conley's youngest son, Andrew, caused him much trouble. The **wayward** child would obey neither his father's commands nor the rules of the house. The child's tennis **coach**, for example, complained that Andrew skipped most of his practices. His poetry teacher claimed that Andrew had such a short attention span that the former needed to **abbreviate** his lectures because the boy would not listen. By creating more strict rules for Andrew, Lord Conley tried to **obligate** him to behave better. Andrew was not **gullible**, however. He knew that Lord Conley was not really a disciplinarian and that he could get away with anything – despite having new strict rules imposed on him.

**Definitions:**     Try matching the words in the list with the appropriate definitions. If you are stuck, check the glossary in the back of the book or the passage at the top of the page.

1.   abbreviate  _____     a.   credulous; easily persuaded to believe something
2.   gullible    _____     b.   (1.) a horse-drawn or motor carriage; 2. a railway car; 3. an athletic instructor or trainer; (v.) to instruct or train athletes
3.   coach       _____     c.   difficult to predict or control because of unusual or perverse behavior
4.   wayward     _____     d.   to shorten a word, phrase, or text
5.   obligate    _____     e.   to require, especially legally or morally

**Sentences:**     Try to use the words above in a sentence below. Remember that a word ending may be changed or its figure of speech slightly altered.

6.   These guidelines do not _____ you to work a minimum of forty hours per week, but we strongly recommend that you do so.
7.   One may _____ the word "California" merely by writing "CA" on a document.
8.   The _____ unified the rugby team and helped them win nine games in a row, thus taking them to the championship.
9.   The _____ priest took the Church charity contributions and spent them on a luxury Caribbean vacation.
10.  Often children are so _____ that they will believe anything you tell them, so it is best to use strong words to force them to do their work.

# Crossword Puzzle
## Lessons 151-160

ACROSS

1 (v.) to make amends or reparation
6 (v.) to fill or pervade; to instill a quality in someone or something
8 (n.) superior to all others; strongest, most important, or most powerful; very great or intense
11 (adj.) 1. showing a willingness to take bold risks; 2. showing an impudent lack of respect
13 (v.) to light or set on fire; to arouse or inspire
14 (n.) an abundance of valuable possessions or money; plentiful supplies of a particular resource
15 (v.) to shorten a word, phrase, or text
16 (adj.) remaining after the greater part is gone; (n.) the remaining amount after other things have been subtracted or allowed for
17 (v.) to bring about or initiate an action or event; to provoke
18 (v.) 1. to provide someone with an objective for doing something; 2. to stimulate one's interest in doing something

19 (v.) to recognize or figure out what makes something different
20 (adj.) accompanying but not a major part of something

DOWN

2 (n.) a person who is new or inexperienced in a field or situation
3 (n.) repentance, regret, compassion, or pity; (v.) to bitterly regret
4 (adj.) lacking care or attention to duty; negligent
5 (v.) 1. to cause someone or something to change course or turn from one direction to another; 2. to distract someone or his or her attention from something
7 (adj.) credulous; easily persuaded to believe something
9 (adj.) forming, existing on, or related to the outside of something; (n.) the outer surface or structure of something
10 (adj.) (of foods) smelling or tasting unpleasant as a result of being old or stale
12 (n.) a mutual relationship or connection between two or more things

# Vocabulary Review
## Lessons 151-160

**Directions:** Match each word with its best approximate definition. Note that definitions are not necessarily repeated verbatim from the lesson exercises.

| | | | | |
|---|---|---|---|---|
| 1. | stalemate | _____ | a. | obvious; clearly visible or understood |
| 2. | dynamic | _____ | b. | to prevent someone from accomplishing something; to oppose a plan, attempt, or ambition successfully |
| 3. | adamant | _____ | c. | extremely distressing |
| 4. | harrowing | _____ | d. | to fill someone with the urge or drive to do something |
| 5. | bedlam | _____ | e. | alluring; attractive; capable of attracting things |
| 6. | commence | _____ | f. | refusing to be persuaded to change one's mind |
| 7. | magnetic | _____ | g. | a scene of great confusion or uproar |
| 8. | aloof | _____ | h. | characterized by constant change, activity, or progress |
| 9. | colossal | _____ | i. | extremely large |
| 10. | thwart | _____ | j. | to begin |
| 11. | versatile | _____ | k. | to grow or develop well or vigorously |
| 12. | rectify | _____ | l. | an involuntary grimace or movement in response to anticipating pain |
| 13. | inspire | _____ | m. | a draw; a position where neither opponent can make progress successfully |
| 14. | laudable | _____ | n. | able to adapt to many circumstances |
| 15. | surly | _____ | o. | unfriendly or ill-tempered |
| 16. | apparent | _____ | p. | difficult to control or predict because of perverse behavior |
| 17. | thrive | _____ | q. | to correct or put something right |
| 18. | wince | _____ | r. | praiseworthy |
| 19. | wayward | _____ | s. | to compel someone legally or morally |
| 20. | obligate | _____ | t. | not friendly or forthcoming; cool and distant |

# Word Roots: Unit 16

## ROOTS AND THEIR MEANINGS

| | | | |
|---|---|---|---|
| retro: | backward, behind | simil/simul: | likeness, imitation |
| cis: | to cut | am: | to love |
| urb: | city | co/com/con: | with, together |

**Here are a few examples of some words that use the above roots:**

retrograde:     movement that is directed backward
scissors:       implement or instrument used to cut materials
urban:          concerning or relating to a city or a town
simultaneous:   occurring, happening, or operating at the same time
amorous:        showing, feeling, or relating to sexual desire
connect:        to join together so that a link (either literally or figuratively) is established

**Now try to fill in the table below by finding the appropriate root(s) and interpreting the meaning of each word:**

| Word | Root(s) | Guessed Meaning | Actual Meaning |
|---|---|---|---|
| simulate | | | |
| combine | | | |
| retroactive | | | |
| cooperate | | | |
| retrospect | | | |
| amicable | | | |
| suburbia | | | |
| incision | | | |

## NEW WORDS

**ostracize**
ˈästrəˌsīz

**rankle**
ˈraNGkəl

**pragmatic**
pragˈmatik

**indict**
inˈdīt

**hovel**
ˈhəvəl, ˈhävəl

After trying to **rankle** her high school classmates on many occasions, Erin found that not many people wanted to be her friend. Classmates would **ostracize** her at school events and make her feel unwelcome at parties and concerts. Because of this, she often sat in her **hovel** crying for hours on end. In an attempt to be **pragmatic**, Erin attempted to apologize for her irritating behavior. But that was to no avail. Her classmates said that although there was no broken law, they wished that someone could **indict** her on account of being rude. Unfortunately, the rift between Erin and her school friends persisted and Erin could not form new friendships until she went to college.

**Definitions:**    Try matching the words in the list with the appropriate definitions. If you are stuck, check the glossary in the back of the book or the passage at the top of the page.

| | | | | |
|---|---|---|---|---|
| 1. | ostracize | _____ | a. | to exclude someone from a group or society |
| 2. | rankle | _____ | b. | to cause persistent irritation, annoyance, or resentment |
| 3. | pragmatic | _____ | c. | a small and squalid dwelling |
| 4. | indict | _____ | d. | practical; sensible; realistic |
| 5. | hovel | _____ | e. | to formally accuse or charge with a serious crime |

**Sentences:**    Try to use the words above in a sentence below. Remember that a word ending may be changed or its figure of speech slightly altered.

6.    Members of the department chose to _____ the student because he did not fit in with the rest of the team.

7.    After a long investigative process, the criminal finally was _____ for grand theft auto.

8.    Jenny was _____ by the new policies that the company had enacted; she no longer had freedom to do the things that she used to enjoy.

9.    Julius was sick of living in a(n) _____ and so spent his life savings on a brand new luxury condominium.

10.    It is _____ to study subjects that will help you obtain a good job in the future.

229

# Lesson 162

## OPENING UP

Catherine was known as a harsh and irritable woman. It was easy to **deplete** her patience when working with children. Her usual icy glare, however, began to **thaw** when she first met her niece, Elly. Catherine's affection became more evident as time went on. Although she was often exasperated if anyone interrupted her in the middle of work, Catherine would spend time helping Elly **polish** her essays or play with her dolls even when she was drowning in work. Catherine simply could not refuse any **favor** Elly asked, no matter how **absurd**.

## NEW WORDS

**absurd**
əbˈsərd, -ˈzərd

**favor**
ˈfāvər

**polish**
ˈpäliSH

**deplete**
diˈplēt

**thaw**
THô

**Definitions:** Try matching the words in the list with the appropriate definitions. If you are stuck, check the glossary in the back of the book or the passage at the top of the page.

1. absurd _____   a. to use up the supply or resources of

2. favor _____   b. (n.) an attitude of approval or liking; 2. an act of kindness beyond what is due or necessary; (v.) to show approval or preference for

3. polish _____   c. (n.) a substance that gives an object a smooth and shiny surface when the latter is rubbed; (v.) to make the surface of something smooth and shiny by rubbing it

4. deplete _____   d. (usually of ice or snow) to become liquid or soft as a result of warming

5. thaw _____   e. wildly ridiculous, insensible, or foolish

**Sentences:** Try to use the words above in a sentence below. Remember that a word ending may be changed or its figure of speech slightly altered.

6. If an army _____ its resources during war, it likely will suffer defeat.

7. It is important to let a frozen piece of meat _____ before cooking it.

8. To think that you can jump out of a window and fly through the air is _____: humans have no wings and were not meant to fly.

9. Each week the maid would come and _____ the silver tea set in our kitchen.

10. My brother did me a(n) _____ and bought me dinner because he knew I was broke.

## NEW WORDS

**swagger**
'swagər

**retribution**
ˌretrə'byooSHən

**annihilate**
ə'nī-əˌlāt

**bloated**
'blōtid

**discretion**
dis'kreSHən

## THE VICIOUS GANGSTER

Everything about the new gang leader demanded respect. He walked with a **swagger** and spoke with an authoritative voice. He threatened to **annihilate** all competition from other local gangs. His leadership style was marked by violence and brutal **retribution** for any act of betrayal. The new leader also desired constant admiration from his gang members in order to satisfy his **bloated** ego. He never used **discretion** when dealing with guilty gang members; in fact, it seemed to give him much pleasure to publicly humiliate others.

**Definitions:**     Try matching the words in the list with the appropriate definitions. If you are stuck, check the glossary in the back of the book or the passage at the top of the page.

1.     swagger     _____     a.     to destroy completely; to obliterate
2.     retribution     _____     b.     1. (of the body) swollen with fluid or gas; 2. excessive in size or amount
3.     annihilate     _____     c.     the quality of behaving in such a way that offence is not caused or private information is not revealed
4.     bloated     _____     d.     (n.) a confident, arrogant, or aggressive walk; (v.) to walk in a confident, arrogant, or aggressive way
5.     discretion     _____     e.     punishment inflicted on someone as vengeance for a wrong or criminal act

**Sentences:**     Try to use the words above in a sentence below. Remember that a word ending may be changed or its figure of speech slightly altered.

6.     When the United States dropped an atomic bomb on Hiroshima in 1945, much of the city was immediately _____.
7.     Regina felt _____ after having eaten a pot of chicken soup, a plate of spaghetti, and two pieces of chocolate cake.
8.     It is important to use _____ when speaking to people of authority, because they may hold sway over your future.
9.     Astrid walked with a(n) _____ of authority, and the people in her office respected her for having so much command over her work.
10.     The mafia boss killed his cousin's wife as _____ for the latter squealing on his illicit business.

# Lesson 164

## QUEST FOR TREASURE

Guided by a **personable** local, Josh and Emily finally arrived at the **grotto** that was rumored to be where a 13th-century pirate buried his treasure. Emily always showed **unconditional** support for her husband's decisions, but she was uncertain this time. The grotto looked beautiful yet ominous, reminding her of the rumors about the deathly curses on anyone who coveted the treasure. Emily was sure she saw something floating in the dark, but Josh dismissed her assertion as an **illusion**. No matter how much she tried to **implore** him to leave, Josh was determined to enter.

## NEW WORDS

**implore**
imˈplôr

**personable**
ˈpərsənəbəl

**grotto**
ˈgrätō

**illusion**
iˈlooZHən

**unconditional**
ˌənkənˈdiSHənl, -ˈdiSHnəl

**Definitions:** Try matching the words in the list with the appropriate definitions. If you are stuck, check the glossary in the back of the book or the passage at the top of the page.

| | | | | |
|---|---|---|---|---|
| 1. | implore | _____ | a. | to beg someone earnestly to do something |
| 2. | personable | _____ | b. | a small picturesque cave, especially a fake one in a garden or park |
| 3. | grotto | _____ | c. | (of a person) having a pleasant manner or appearance |
| 4. | illusion | _____ | d. | not subject to any stipulations or limitations |
| 5. | unconditional | _____ | e. | a thing that is likely to be wrongly perceived by the senses; a deception; a false idea or belief |

**Sentences:** Try to use the words above in a sentence below. Remember that a word ending may be changed or its figure of speech slightly altered.

6. My father _____ me not to marry the girl I had been dating for two years; he said she was almost certainly a bad match for me.

7. A parent's love for his or her child should be _____.

8. I appreciate working with others who are _____, for they make the banalities of a job seem bearable.

9. Please tell me how that magician created the _____ of being able to fly!

10. The lovers nestled in the _____ and discussed their future together.

## NEW WORDS

**inevitable**
inˈevitəbəl

**astute**
əˈst(y)oot

**concise**
kənˈsīs

**desolate**
ˈdesəlit

**abrogate**
ˈabrəˌgāt

As the economy got worse and business shrank, it was **inevitable** that the company would lay people off. The firm decided to **abrogate** its contracts with its international workers. This was an **astute** fiscal move since the company had to pay much smaller severance packages to these workers than to domestic working citizens. The company gave the international workers a **concise** explanation of why they were being laid off and demanded that the workers leave the premises immediately. Most of the workers depended fully on their job and felt completely **desolate**. They did not know how they would survive in a foreign country without a job.

**Definitions:** Try matching the words in the list with the appropriate definitions. If you are stuck, check the glossary in the back of the book or the passage at the top of the page.

1. inevitable _____ a. deserted of people and in a state of bleak and dismal emptiness
2. astute _____ b. certain to occur; unavoidable
3. concise _____ c. giving much information in few words
4. desolate _____ d. having the ability to accurately assess situations or people and turn them to one's advantage
5. abrogate _____ e. to repeal or do away with a law, right, or formal agreement

**Sentences:** Try to use the words above in a sentence below. Remember that a word ending may be changed or its figure of speech slightly altered.

6. Death is one part of existence that is _____: in the end all people will eventually pass away.
7. Berna was very _____ and realized from the business figures that her partners were secretly pocketing company profit for themselves.
8. It is better to write a speech that is _____ than to write one that rambles and is longwinded.
9. To me, Antarctica seems like a(n) _____ place; there are few other humans there and nothing but penguins and a barren ice-covered landscape to see.
10. It is important not to _____ your responsibilities as a parent.

# Lesson 166

## LIFE ON THE STREETS

The homeless children would **forage** the streets for food during the night.  Now that their father was in prison, they needed to have much **fortitude** in order to survive alone.  During the day, shopkeepers yelled at them and other children on the streets would **imitate** the grown ups and scream and make faces at them.  This filled the homeless children with **indignation**.  The world seemed to be an unjust place full of rejection and violence softened only by **accidental** acts of kindness that happened very rarely.

**Definitions:**     Try matching the words in the list with the appropriate definitions.  If you are stuck, check the glossary in the back of the book or the passage at the top of the page.

| | | | | | |
|---|---|---|---|---|---|
| 1. | forage | _____ | a. | courage in pain or adversity | |
| 2. | fortitude | _____ | b. | happening by chance, unintentionally, or unexpectedly | |
| 3. | accidental | _____ | c. | to take or follow as a model; to copy someone else's mannerisms; to copy or simulate | |
| 4. | indignation | _____ | d. | anger or annoyance caused by what is perceived as unfair treatment | |
| 5. | imitate | _____ | e. | to search widely for food or provisions | |

**Sentences:**     Try to use the words above in a sentence below.  Remember that a word ending may be changed or its figure of speech slightly altered.

6.     We watched the deer _____ for food in the woods behind our home.

7.     It takes great emotional _____ to flourish in the wake of a parent's passing.

8.     It was purely _____ that Tony found himself in Manhattan on Valentine's Day: he flew to New York for a business meeting only after his boss suddenly had fallen ill.

9.     When students learn a foreign language, they often _____ their instructor's sounds and gestures.

10.     Lee experienced an outburst of _____ from her employer after she failed to complete her job responsibilities in a timely and professional manner.

## NEW WORDS

**devout**
di'vout

**frequent**
'frēkwənt

**strategy**
'stratəjē

**prologue**
'prō,lôg, -,läg

**sanction**
'saNG(k)SHən

# Lesson 167

## THE LOCAL PREACHER

Mr. White's introductory speech was the **prologue** to a long evening of lectures. As a **devout** churchgoer, Mr. White believed that it was his duty to spread the word of the gospel to everyone. He organized **frequent** dinners at his restaurant for the local community. Offering free meals was his **strategy** for accomplishing his goal. The people who attended such dinners were usually the poorest in the neighborhood. They knew that Mr. White would only **sanction** discussions on religious matters and they accepted that as long as there was free food.

**Definitions:**     Try matching the words in the list with the appropriate definitions. If you are stuck, check the glossary in the back of the book or the passage at the top of the page.

1.   devout     _____     a.   having or showing deep religious feeling or commitment

2.   frequent     _____     b.   (n.) 1. a threatened penalty for disobeying a law or rule; 2. official approval or permission for an action; (v.) 1. to give official approval or permission for an action; 2. to impose a penalty on

3.   strategy     _____     c.   a plan of action or policy designed with a specific aim

4.   prologue     _____     d.   (adj.) 1. occurring on many occasions, often, or habitual; 2. occurring in short distances apart; (v.) to visit a place often or habitually

5.   sanction     _____     e.   an introductory section of a literary work or musical piece

**Sentences:**     Try to use the words above in a sentence below. Remember that a word ending may be changed or its figure of speech slightly altered.

6.   One cannot win a battle easily if one lacks a(n) _____ to defeat one's opponent.

7.   As a(n) _____ Catholic, I go to church every Sunday.

8.   The author explained his intellectual motivations and thanked his colleagues for their support in the book's _____.

9.   I _____ the restaurant, as it serves an excellent turkey dinner with stuffing and mashed potatoes.

10.   The airline company does not _____ employees taking photographs of themselves or others in uniform.

# Lesson 168

## DISENCHANTED ATTORNEY

Robert was known for throwing **ostentatious** parties at his villa. And while luxury cars, designer outfits, and exquisite hors d'oeuvres were **plentiful** at such events, Robert hardly felt excited or even **neutral** about such gatherings. He loathed them and felt constrained. Robert hoped to one day **liberate** himself from the social elites with whom he needed to associate in his career as a prominent lawyer. How he wished to live in a society where social climbing was **defunct**, where people would judge others based on their character and not on their salary or pedigree! One day, he thought, it would happen.

**Definitions:**     Try matching the words in the list with the appropriate definitions. If you are stuck, check the glossary in the back of the book or the passage at the top of the page.

| | | | | |
|---|---|---|---|---|
| 1. | plentiful | _____ | a. | no longer existing or functioning |
| 2. | liberate | _____ | b. | existing in great quantity; abundant |
| 3. | defunct | _____ | c. | 1. not helping or supporting either side in a conflict; 2. having no strongly marked positive or biased characteristics; 3. (physics) neither positively nor negatively charged; 4. (chemistry) neither acid nor alkaline |
| 4. | ostentatious | _____ | d. | characterized by pretentious display meant to attract attention |
| 5. | neutral | _____ | e. | to set someone free from a situation (esp. slavery or imprisonment); to free one from a situation that limits free thought or expression or has rigid social conventions; to free from enemy occupation |

**Sentences:**     Try to use the words above in a sentence below. Remember that a word ending may be changed or its figure of speech slightly altered.

6.     Unfortunately the beautiful train station is now _____: tourists can take pictures of it from afar, but they cannot access it or catch a train there.

7.     The singer showed up, as usual, with a(n) _____ entry: four individuals dressed as sentries carried her in on a pallet.

8.     Rather than taking sides in an argument, I prefer to remain _____.

9.     The prisoner obtained keys to all of the jail cells and unlocked them in an effort to _____ all of the inmates.

10.     There is always _____ food at the Thanksgiving buffet; you should go check it out!

## NEW WORDS

**exorbitant**
ig'zôrbitənt

**perceptive**
pər'septiv

**elderly**
'eldərlē

**acquire**
ə'kwī(ə)r

**squalid**
'skwälid

After capturing the Commanding General, the enemy locked him up in a **squalid** prison, and intended to acquire an **exorbitant** ransom. Given these circumstances, a new leader needed to be elected to launch a counter-attack and to rescue the Commanding General. Lieutenant General Foster was the most viable selection. Although he was **elderly**, Foster was far more **perceptive** and courageous than his younger comrades. Over the years that he had served in the army, Foster also managed to **acquire** a reputation for never losing in battle, no matter how perilous the situation was.

**Definitions:**     Try matching the words in the list with the appropriate definitions. If you are stuck, check the glossary in the back of the book or the passage at the top of the page.

1.     exorbitant  _____     a.     a price or amount charged that is unreasonably high

2.     perceptive  _____     b.     1. a place that is filthy and unpleasant, usually because of neglect or poverty; 2. exhibiting a lack of moral standards

3.     elderly  _____     c.     1. to buy or obtain an object; 2. to learn or develop a specific skill or skill set; 3. to achieve a reputation as a result of one's behavior or activity

4.     acquire  _____     d.     exhibiting sensitive insight

5.     squalid  _____     e.     a person who is old or showing signs of aging

**Sentences:**     Try to use the words above in a sentence below. Remember that a word ending may be changed or its figure of speech slightly altered.

6.     The price of a hamburger at this restaurant is _____: is costs more than six times what it would cost at any other eatery.

7.     A(n) _____ person would have been able to sense that his boss was seeking to start a new life and career elsewhere.

8.     Only through hard and sustained work can one _____ enough money to take an early retirement.

9.     If your parents knew you were living in such _____ conditions, they would demand that you move to a new home.

10.    Every week, Stacey volunteers her time to help _____ people cook and go shopping.

# Lesson 170

## FAMILIAL TRANSFORMATION

The parents were worried about their son, who had become very **belligerent** and verbally aggressive after the bullying incident at school. Every loud noise would **render** the boy very nervous and angry. The family got together to **ponder** how to help him become more relaxed. They decided to **accentuate** the boy's feeling of security by giving him daily hugs and telling him that he was safe. As a result of the boy's trauma, the communication in the family increased, which seemed to have a good effect on the father as well. A long-time alcoholic, the father began to show **temperance** in his alcohol consumption and started to spend more evenings with his son.

**Definitions:**     Try matching the words in the list with the appropriate definitions. If you are stuck, check the glossary in the back of the book or the passage at the top of the page.

| | | | | |
|---|---|---|---|---|
| 1. | ponder _____ | | a. | hostile and aggressive |
| 2. | accentuate _____ | | b. | to make more prominent or noticeable |
| 3. | render _____ | | c. | 1. to provide or give a service or help; 2. to cause to become or make; 3. to represent or depict artistically |
| 4. | belligerent _____ | | d. | moderation or self-restraint, especially from drinking |
| 5. | temperance _____ | | e. | to think carefully about something before making a decision |

**Sentences:**     Try to use the words above in a sentence below. Remember that a word ending may be changed or its figure of speech slightly altered.

6.   The artist was unskilled and thus unable to _____ my image very well, painting a terrible portrait of me.

7.   That striped shirt can _____ your stomach and make you look chubby.

8.   The _____ athlete threatened to beat up the coach after the team lost the basketball match.

9.   Often in philosophy class, I would _____ the meaning of justice.

10.  Alma exhibited _____ in ending her relationship: she politely told her boyfriend that she wanted to stop dating without becoming overemotional about matters.

# Word Search
## Lessons 414-450

```
U S O M Y O N O A U E S Y W G A
M O N R M D A L T Z Z U Q R Y R
O D A Y P A C Y N O A U Y M K O
N M R A E Z J N O O I T Q I Y M
E R P Y M G Z P E O D A R M E A
O P R I Y V T D K O O P E C B L
Y Y D P W D A Y P N M Z U G D N
M M N R Y R D J D O M L L L D V
J P D O O R C L N R U U U S G K
J E C M A W M C F R R N E X D P
N O R W I D U P G M O R L R T M
O A U L N R R O Y M P S O V L I
V O O B D H Y U P U B V U T V L
D R O N C X O C X I G Y Y P X Y
P U U O P L B Z P M O N L O K I
I F Z C B D D O C I R Z Q Y G P
```

4 (j .) to ei cʒbde soy eone froy a l rob, or socʋet;

q (j .) to cabse , ersʋstent urrʋtatʋonm anno; ancenʋor resenty ent

v (ad2) g ʋdz, rʋducbʒobsmʋnsensʋɒʒenʋor foozʋsh

w (j .) (bsbazz, of ʋce or snog ) to pecoy e zʋxbʋd or soft as a resbʒt of g ary unl

3 (n.) , bnʋshy ent unfʒcted on soy eone as j enl eance for a g ronl or crʋy ʋnazact

1 (ad2) 4. (of the pod; ) sg ozʒen g ʋth fʒbʋd or l askq. ei cessʋj e un sʋɓe or ay obnt

5 (j .) to pel soy eone earnestʒ, to do soy ethʋnl

7 (n.) a sy azz, ʋctbresxbe caj enes, ecʋazz a fa8e one ʋn a l arden or , ar8

9 (ad2) certaʋn to occbrkbnaj oʋdapɾe

40 (j .) to re, eazor do ag a; g ʋth a zag mrʋl htm or fory azal reey ent

44 (n.) cobral e ʋn , aʋn or adj ersʋt;

4q (n.) anl er or anno; ance cabsed p; g hat ʋs , erceʋj ed as bnfaʋr treaty ent

4v (ad2) 4. occbrrʋnl on y an; occasʋonsm oftenmʋor hapʋtbazʒkq. occbrrʋnl ʋn short dʋstances a, artk(j .) to j ʋsʋt a , ɾace often or hapʋtbazz;

4w (n.) an ʋntrodbctor; sectʋon of a ɾterar; g or8 or y bsʋcaz, ʋece

43 (j .) to set soy eone free froy a sʋtbatʋon (es, . sɾaj er; or ʋy , rʋsony ent)kto free one froy a sʋtbatʋon that zy ʋts free thobl ht or ei , ressʋon or has rʋl ʋd socʋaz conj entʋonskto free froy eney ; occb, atʋon

41 (ad2) characterʋɓed p; , retentʋobs dʋs, ɾa; y eant to attract attentʋon

45 (ad2) a , rʋce or ay obnt charl ed that ʋs bnreasonapʒ; hʋ h

47 (j .) 4. to pb; or optaʋn an op2ectkq. to ɾearn or dej ezo, a s, ecʋfʋc s8ʋzz or s8ʋzzsetk v. to achʋej e a re, btatʋon as a resbʒt of one's pehaj ʋor or actʋj ʋt;

49 (j .) to thʋn8 carefbzz, apobt soy ethʋnl pefore y a8ʋnl a decʋsʋon

q0 (j .) to y a8e y ore , roy ʋnent or notʋceapɾe

# Vocabulary Review
## Lessons 161-170

**Directions:** Match each word with its best approximate definition. Note that definitions are not necessarily repeated verbatim from the lesson exercises.

| | | | | |
|---|---|---|---|---|
| 1. | indict | _____ | a. | a plan of action designed to achieve an overall aim |
| 2. | hovel | _____ | b. | abundant |
| 3. | favor | _____ | c. | brief but comprehensive |
| 4. | deplete | _____ | d. | hostile and aggressive; combative |
| 5. | swagger | _____ | e. | an act of kindness beyond what is necessary; to show preference for |
| 6. | annihilate | _____ | f. | a thing that is likely to be wrongly interpreted by the senses |
| 7. | personable | _____ | g. | to destroy completely; to obliterate |
| 8. | illusion | _____ | h. | having sensitive insight |
| 9. | astute | _____ | i. | no longer existing or functioning |
| 10. | concise | _____ | j. | concerning a person with a pleasant appearance and manner |
| 11. | forage | _____ | k. | (of a person); concerning being old or aging |
| 12. | accidental | _____ | l. | a small, squalid dwelling |
| 13. | devout | _____ | m. | to walk or behave in a confident or arrogant way |
| 14. | strategy | _____ | n. | for a person or animal to search widely for food or provisions |
| 15. | plentiful | _____ | o. | to use up the supply or resources of something |
| 16. | defunct | _____ | p. | having a keen ability to assess people or situations and to turn this to one's advantage |
| 17. | perceptive | _____ | q. | to formally accuse or charge with a serious crime |
| 18. | elderly | _____ | r. | moderation and self restraint (usually concerning food and drink) |
| 19. | belligerent | _____ | s. | not deliberate; happening by chance |
| 20. | temperance | _____ | t. | having or showing deep commitment (often religiously) |

# Literary and Drama Terms

Whether you have a passion for literature or you feel forced to learn it for exams, there are terms that you should know.  Below is a list of major literary terms that will help you better understand how literature operates.

| | |
|---|---|
| **alliteration:** | the use of the same letter or sound at the beginning of adjacent or nearly connected words |
| **analogy:** | a comparison between two things, usually for the purpose of instruction or clarification |
| **anecdote:** | a short, catchy story about an intriguing incident or person |
| **eulogy:** | a speech or writing that praises someone excessively, often after that person's death |
| **foreshadow:** | something that serves as a warning or indication of a future event |
| **hyperbole:** | claims or statements that are so exaggerated as to not be able to be taken literally in a serious manner |
| **irony:** | a set of affairs or circumstances that seems to be the exact opposite of what one would expect, thus resulting in amusement or empathy |
| **foil (n.):** | a character or object used for contrast in order to emphasize and enhance the qualities of another |

**metaphor:** a figure of speech where a word or phrase is applied to an action to which it cannot in reality or literally be applied; a thing that is regarded as symbolic or representative of something else

**onomatopoeia:** the use of a word that sounds exactly like its name (e.g. ding dong, boom, cuckoo)

**personification:** the attribution of human characteristics to something that is nonhuman; giving some abstract entity humanlike attributes

**plot:** the main events of a novel, play, or other work presented in some form of sequence

**pseudonym:** a fictitious name used by an author of a work, almost always because the author does not want to reveal his or her identity

**setting:** the place and time in which a novel, short story, play, or other event takes place

**simile:** a figure of speech comparing one thing with another using "like" or "as" in the comparison

**soliloquy:** often used in a play, the act of speaking or reading one's feelings aloud – regardless of whether other people are present

**synopsis:** a brief summary of a piece of writing, drama, film, or other piece of art

## NEW WORDS

**panorama**
ˌpanəˈramə, -ˈrämə

**monarch**
ˈmänərk, ˈmänˌärk

**desecrate**
ˈdesiˌkrāt

**heterogeneous**
ˌhetərəˈjēnēəs

**tortuous**
ˈtôrCHooəs

Looking out at the majestic **panorama** of his empire, the **monarch** lamented on his past. After years of battles, he finally united and ruled over many culturally **heterogeneous** lands. However, during this **tortuous** process, he also lost many of his friends, subordinates, and even family members. He made countless enemies as well, for during his conquest, the monarch employed cruel tactics, such as attempting to **desecrate** churches and temples, and to massacre people ruthlessly. Now, at the peak of his power, he somehow felt lost.

**Definitions:**    Try matching the words in the list with the appropriate definitions. If you are stuck, check the glossary in the back of the book or the passage at the top of the page.

1.    panorama _____    a.    twisting or winding
2.    monarch _____    b.    to treat something sacred with disrespect
3.    desecrate _____    c.    a sovereign head of state such as a king, queen, or emperor
4.    heterogeneous _____    d.    1. an unbroken view of a whole region surrounding an observer; 2. a complete survey or presentation of a sequence of events or a subject
5.    tortuous _____    e.    diverse in content or in character

**Sentences:**    Try to use the words above in a sentence below. Remember that a word ending may be changed or its figure of speech slightly altered.

6.    The compassionate _____ ruled over his subjects with concern and care.
7.    Gangs attempted to _____ the monument by painting all over it with graffiti.
8.    One can view a(n) _____ of the city from the top of the mountain.
9.    As Josh hurriedly drove up the _____ mountain road, I became nauseous from all the twists and turns.
10.    Next year's graduating class will be the most _____ ever: it will contain students from over fifty countries, and have people of various creeds and races.

# Lesson 172

## THE INJURED SPORTSMAN

After the tennis player suffered a **contusion** on the arm, he had to withdraw from the competition. The injury came at a very inconvenient moment since the player had just received a **barrage** of requests to attend different tournaments. His physiotherapists did their best to **amend** the situation; however, there was not much to do except wait for the wound to heal. Nevertheless, the player exhibited good **etiquette** and formally apologized to the tournament director and the public, vowing to make his **comeback** as soon as possible.

## NEW WORDS

**amend**
əˈmend

**barrage**
bəˈräZH

**etiquette**
ˈetikit, -ˌket

**comeback**
ˈkəmˌbak

**contusion**
kənˈtooZHən

**Definitions:**     Try matching the words in the list with the appropriate definitions. If you are stuck, check the glossary in the back of the book or the passage at the top of the page.

| | | | | |
|---|---|---|---|---|
| 1. | amend | _____ | a. | (n.) a concentrated outpouring or firing of something; (v.) to bombard someone with something |
| 2. | barrage | _____ | b. | the customary code of appropriate behavior in society; manners |
| 3. | etiquette | _____ | c. | to modify or make better, more accurate, or up-to-date by implementing small changes in something |
| 4. | comeback | _____ | d. | a bruise |
| 5. | contusion | _____ | e. | 1. a return by a well-known person to the field in which they were originally successful; 2. a quick reply to a critical remark |

**Sentences:**     Try to use the words above in a sentence below. Remember that a word ending may be changed or its figure of speech slightly altered.

6.     The doctor asked the patient about the _____ on her arm.

7.     After decades of being unpopular, it seems that disco and swing dancing are making a(n) _____.

8.     It is difficult to _____ the business articles without a vote of approval from the board of directors.

9.     The politician was confronted with a(n) _____ of questions from journalists after news broke that he had been instrumental in a giant property scandal.

10.     It is important to display proper _____ at the ceremony so that you can show how well mannered you are.

## NEW WORDS

**indicate**
ˈindiˌkāt

**nebula**
ˈnebyələ

**enhance**
enˈhans

**surrogate**
ˈsərəgit, -ˌgāt

**callous**
ˈkaləs

# Lesson 173

## A WONDERFUL TEACHER

After parents found out that Mr. Freinster forced his students to slap each other as punishment for not doing homework, this **callous** teacher was quickly fired. Mr. Nelson, a new science teacher, became his **surrogate**, and the students instantly loved him. The broad and genuine smile on his face appeared to **indicate** how much he enjoyed teaching, which was a stark contrast to Mr. Freinster's ever-present grumpy expression. Mr. Nelson also prepared engaging materials, organized fun games and activities, and even took the class on a field trip to the planetarium to **enhance** his lectures on galaxies and how a **nebula** forms.

**Definitions:**     Try matching the words in the list with the appropriate definitions. If you are stuck, check the glossary in the back of the book or the passage at the top of the page.

1.     indicate  _____      a.     a substitute, especially another person deputizing for another in a specific role or office

2.     nebula  _____      b.     exhibiting an insensitive and cruel disregard for others

3.     enhance  _____      c.     to intensify, increase, or improve the quality of

4.     surrogate  _____      d.     1. a cloud of gas in outer space; 2. any bright spot in the night sky

5.     callous  _____      e.     1. to point out or show; to briefly state something; to gesture; to show or register a reading (of a meter or gauge); 2. to suggest or show signs of a necessary course of action

**Sentences:**     Try to use the words above in a sentence below. Remember that a word ending may be changed or its figure of speech slightly altered.

6.     Is would be _____ to tell someone on crutches that he or she needs to take the stairs in lieu of the elevator to get to work.

7.     That hazy blob you see through the telescope is a(n) _____.

8.     Helping the poor children at the pagoda will not only _____ your résumé but also make you feel better about yourself.

9.     A guardian often serves as a(n) _____ parent for a child.

10.     Trong's grades seem to _____ that he is not studying very well in school.

# Lesson 174

## THE ANNOYING LANDLADY

The old widow Spencer made her living from renting rooms to young university students. She had many rules and made **repetitive** visits to each **boarder** to check on each room. She was also **dogmatic** and loved to regularly instruct the young people about how they should live their lives, which the boarders found annoying and **redundant**. After all, she was only a landlady and their housing agreements did not **specify** that they needed to meet with her on a daily basis and listen to her lectures. It seemed that both parties had different ideas about the nature of their relationship.

## NEW WORDS

**specify**
ˈspesəˌfī

**repetitive**
riˈpetətiv

**boarder**
ˈbôrdər

**dogmatic**
dôgˈmatik

**redundant**
riˈdəndənt

**Definitions:** Try matching the words in the list with the appropriate definitions. If you are stuck, check the glossary in the back of the book or the passage at the top of the page.

| | | | | |
|---|---|---|---|---|
| 1. | specify | _____ | a. | inclined to lay down principles as absolute truth |
| 2. | repetitive | _____ | b. | 1. superfluous; no longer needed to be useful or functioning; 2. words or data that can be omitted without loss of meaning |
| 3. | boarder | _____ | c. | characterized by doing something over and over again or something happening over and over again often in a tiresome way |
| 4. | dogmatic | _____ | d. | a person (often a student residing at school) who receives regular meals when staying somewhere |
| 5. | redundant | _____ | e. | to identify or state a fact clearly and definitely |

**Sentences:** Try to use the words above in a sentence below. Remember that a word ending may be changed or its figure of speech slightly altered.

6. Miss Smith has a rather _____ approach to English pedagogy: she asserts that the only way to learn to write is by composing five paragraph essays every week for a year.

7. Without further information on the guest list, I am unable to _____ whether I want to serve chicken or pasta at the rehearsal dinner.

8. The worker found that drilling holes in wooden planks all day was a(n) _____ task, so he quit his job and looked for new employment.

9. When writing a concise and proper sentence it is necessary to omit _____ information.

10. The preparatory school down the road has over two hundred _____ who study there.

## NEW WORDS

**inauspicious**
ˈinôˈspiSHəs

**mitigate**
ˈmitəˌgāt

**inhabit**
inˈhabit

**founder**
ˈfoundər

**effect**
iˈfekt

**RAGS TO RICHES**

Olivia had quite an **inauspicious** childhood. As a penniless orphan, she grew up in a slum that rats and insects would also **inhabit**, and often got bullied by the neighborhood kids. However, these negative experiences had no **effect** on her dreams of becoming a fashion designer – Olivia still persistently worked towards her goals. With her creativity and talent, Olivia has now become the **founder** and owner of a successful fashion shop. She even donates part of her shop's profits to local charity programs, hoping to **mitigate** the poverty and crime in her old neighborhood.

**Definitions:** Try matching the words in the list with the appropriate definitions. If you are stuck, check the glossary in the back of the book or the passage at the top of the page.

1.     inauspicious _____     a.     (of a person or animal) to live in a particular place or geographic region

2.     mitigate _____     b.     to make less painful, serious, or severe

3.     inhabit _____     c.     (n.) a person who establishes a business, organization, club, or institution; (v.) (usually of a ship) to fill with water and sink

4.     founder _____     d.     unfavorable; unpromising

5.     effect _____     e.     (n.) 1. a change that is the result of another action or cause; 2. the extent to which something succeeds or is operative; 3. an impression produced in the mind of a person; (v.) to cause something to happen or bring about

**Sentences:** Try to use the words above in a sentence below. Remember that a word ending may be changed or its figure of speech slightly altered.

6.     Little could _____ the pain Gloria felt after losing her husband in a boating accident.

7.     Many elephants _____ the lush, flat land of Sri Lanka.

8.     I am unsure what _____ the new medicine will have on Rehana; hopefully it will make her a happier person!

9.     After a few _____ months, Ratan closed up his Bengali restaurant.

10.     After three canons hit the sloop, the boat began to _____ and its crew departed in lifeboats.

# Lesson 176

## THE MAN WHO FELT NO PAIN

The old man, who had been injured in a fire, had a big **lesion** on his thigh. He seemed to be in much pain but dismissed it in a **debonair** manner. Instead of complaining, he would recite to himself a **stanza** or two from his favorite poems while waiting for the doctors to apply some medicine on the wound. While the other victims of the fire would beg and **plead** for more painkillers, the old man seemed to be in a state of complete **tranquility**, as if he did not notice the pain.

## NEW WORDS

**debonair**
ˌdebəˈne(ə)r

**lesion**
ˈlēZHən

**stanza**
ˈstanzə

**plead**
plēd

**tranquility**
ˌtraNGˈkwilitē

**Definitions:**    Try matching the words in the list with the appropriate definitions. If you are stuck, check the glossary in the back of the book or the passage at the top of the page.

| | | | | |
|---|---|---|---|---|
| 1. | debonair | _____ | a. | 1. to present an emotional appeal or to beg; 2. to present and argue for a particular position in a public context, especially a court |
| 2. | lesion | _____ | b. | (of a man) stylish, charming, and confident |
| 3. | stanza | _____ | c. | part of tissue or an organ that has suffered a cut, wound, ulcer, or abscess |
| 4. | plead | _____ | d. | a group of lines forming the basic metrical unit of a poem |
| 5. | tranquility | _____ | e. | calmness; serenity; peacefulness |

**Sentences:**    Try to use the words above in a sentence below. Remember that a word ending may be changed or its figure of speech slightly altered.

6. Gary took early retirement because work was unsettling and he felt that he needed more _____ in his life.

7. Floyd looked _____ at last night's dinner: the tuxedo together with his charisma made him a real charmer!

8. Though the first four were easy to write, I am having trouble writing the final _____ of this poem.

9. A child should not have to _____ with his or her parents to receive love and attention.

10. While in triage, the nurse asked Stevie about the nature of the _____ on her waist.

## NEW WORDS

**prolific**
prəˈlifik

**submerge**
səbˈmərj

**dissemble**
diˈsembəl

**innate**
iˈnāt

**fallow**
ˈfalō

## THE TWISTS AND TURNS OF LIFE

James prided himself on being a **prolific** writer who produced at least two books a year. He would **submerge** himself totally in the creative process and write for days on end. However, his mother's death had a profound effect on him. James tried to **dissemble** his grief but it was obvious that he was no longer the same person. He seemed to have lost his **innate** ability to write continuously. His talent and his creative abilities would lie **fallow** for a very long period after his personal tragedy.

**Definitions:**     Try matching the words in the list with the appropriate definitions. If you are stuck, check the glossary in the back of the book or the passage at the top of the page.

| | | | | |
|---|---|---|---|---|
| 1. | prolific | _____ | a. | inborn or natural |
| 2. | submerge | _____ | b. | 1. a plant animal or person producing much fruit, foliage, or offspring; 2. an author, artist, or composer who produces a great deal; 3. present in large numbers or quantities |
| 3. | dissemble | _____ | c. | 1. to place under water or some other liquid; 2. to completely cover or obscure |
| 4. | innate | _____ | d. | farmland that is ploughed and harrowed but left uncultivated to restore its fertility for crop production |
| 5. | fallow | _____ | e. | to conceal one's true intentions, beliefs, or feelings |

**Sentences:**     Try to use the words above in a sentence below. Remember that a word ending may be changed or its figure of speech slightly altered.

6.     Rather than being honest with his family, the child chose to _____ his responses to their questions.

7.     Ahmad is a(n) _____ writer; he has written over a dozen papers and books on Islamic culture in the past decade.

8.     Many people argue that mathematical ability is _____: one either is born with it or lacks it.

9.     The goal of a submarine is to _____ itself in the ocean so that others cannot easily find it.

10.     The farmer left a quarter of his field _____ in order to let it rejuvenate with fresh minerals for next year's planting.

# Lesson 178

## REACHING SUCCESS

Edmond was regarded as an excellent juggler and an agile, **kinetic** performer. He also had an **amiable** personality, which appealed to the public. However, he went unnoticed by big entertainment companies for years. Finally, he was invited to take part in the national dance academy's **jubilee**, the most important event of the year for the dance community. Edmond was honored by the invitation; for him it marked an **epoch** of social success in his life. With unparalleled **valor** he attempted some very difficult acts, which involved juggling objects that were set on fire. He was determined to make a great impression.

**Definitions:** Try matching the words in the list with the appropriate definitions. If you are stuck, check the glossary in the back of the book or the passage at the top of the page.

| | | | | |
|---|---|---|---|---|
| 1. | amiable | _____ | a. | of, concerning, or relating to motion |
| 2. | epoch | _____ | b. | a period of time in one's life or in a historical period marked by notable events; (geology) a long time period that is divided into ages |
| 3. | jubilee | _____ | c. | courage in the face of danger |
| 4. | kinetic | _____ | d. | a special anniversary of an event (especially 25 years, 50 years, etc.) |
| 5. | valor | _____ | e. | friendly and pleasant |

**Sentences:** Try to use the words above in a sentence below. Remember that a word ending may be changed or its figure of speech slightly altered.

6. Scholars have often referred to the _____ between Nicolaus Copernicus (1473-1543) and Isaac Newton (1643-1727) as the "Scientific Revolution," a time when rapid and unprecedented developments in mathematics, physics, and the natural sciences were made.

7. Proponents of a(n) _____ theory of learning believe that students achieve the best results when they are active.

8. There is a(n) _____ celebrating the fiftieth anniversary of the pharmacy.

9. The knight was praised for his _____ in protecting the kingdom from being attacked by trolls and ogres.

10. Humphrey is a(n) _____ person who enjoys talking to others and learning about their lives.

## NEW WORDS

**vanquish**
'vaNGkwiSH

**declamation**
ˌdeklə'māSHən

**ample**
'ampəl

**conciliate**
kən'silēˌāt

**schism**
's(k)izəm

# Lesson 179

## JOINING EFFORTS

After the Civil War started, the country fell into a state of tumult, with economic inflation, political riots, and constant battles between the two main warring parties. A right-wing politician, Vasili, knew that this **schism** would only give neighboring countries **ample** opportunity to start attacking.   With the current vulnerable state of the country, it would be easy for its enemies to **vanquish** the army and get control of the government.   Vasili   thus   delivered   a   passionate **declamation** to **conciliate** the left wing and warn it of the impending danger.

**Definitions:**        Try matching the words in the list with the appropriate definitions.  If you are stuck, check the glossary in the back of the book or the passage at the top of the page.

1.    vanquish    _____        a.    a split or division between strongly opposed parties or groups within a party caused by differences of opinion or belief
2.    declamation_____        b.    to defeat thoroughly
3.    ample    _____        c.    a speech delivered in a rhetorical or passionate way
4.    conciliate    _____        d.    enough or more than enough; large and plentiful; large and accommodating
5.    schism    _____        e.    to stop someone from being angry; to placate; to pacify

**Sentences:**        Try to use the words above in a sentence below.  Remember that a word ending may be changed or its figure of speech slightly altered.

6.    A(n) _____ within the corporation resulted in the company breaking into two different divisions with different visions and leadership.
7.    Ronald gave a bitter _____ on the folly of using torture on one's enemies.
8.    Harlow could do little to _____ his friends after their mother grounded them for a month.
9.    There are _____ cookies in the pantry so nobody will be left hungry or wanting.
10.    The baseball team _____ its opponent in the playoffs and then proceeded to the finals.

# Lesson 180

## THE ESCAPE

Poetry created for Jonas an **ethereal** world of beautiful images where he could escape from his daily life. This is because Jonas found the dramatic poetic realm to be strikingly different from his routine job, in which he would often sit behind his desk in a **torpid** state. Reading poetry kept his mind engaged and prevented him from becoming **obtuse.** Poetry was his escape from the **pathology** of his office life, which consisted of long working hours combined with monotonous tasks. Often Jonas would become **ecstatic** upon discovering the work of a new poet.

## NEW WORDS

**ethereal**
i'THi(ə)rēəl

**ecstatic**
ek'statik

**torpid**
'tôrpid

**pathology**
pə'THäləjē

**obtuse**
əb't(y)oos, äb-

**Definitions:**       Try matching the words in the list with the appropriate definitions. If you are stuck, check the glossary in the back of the book or the passage at the top of the page.

| | | | | |
|---|---|---|---|---|
| 1. | ethereal | _____ | a. | 1. annoyingly insensitive or slow to understand; 2. an angle whose measure is greater than 90 degrees and less than 180 degrees |
| 2. | ecstatic | _____ | b. | the science of the causes and effects of disease |
| 3. | torpid | _____ | c. | feeling overwhelming joy or excitement |
| 4. | pathology | _____ | d. | 1. feeling too light or delicate for the world; 2. heavenly or spiritual |
| 5. | obtuse | _____ | e. | mentally or physically exhaustive; lethargic |

**Sentences:**       Try to use the words above in a sentence below. Remember that a word ending may be changed or its figure of speech slightly altered.

6.  One who is _____ typically lacks the energy to run for office.
7.  Uma was _____ when she heard that she was admitted to her first-choice college.
8.  Having spent years engrossed in _____, the physician believed he could find a cure for cancer.
9.  Keith, a practical man, could not relate to the _____ discussion that the professors were having at the dinner table.
10. Only a(n) _____ student would not understand how basic multiplication works.

252

# Crossword Puzzle
## Lessons 171-180

ACROSS

3 (n.) a group of lines forming the basic metrical unit of a poem

5 (n.) a concentrated outpouring or firing of something; (v.) to bombard someone with something

10 (v.) 1. to place under water or some other liquid; 2. to completely cover or obscure

13 (adj.) 1. a plant animal or person producing much fruit, foliage, or offspring; 2. an author, artist, or composer who produces a great deal; 3. present in large numbers or quantities

16 (v.) to stop someone from being angry; to placate; to pacify

17 (adj.) twisting or winding

18 (v.) to make less painful, serious, or severe

20 (n.) a person (often a student residing at school) who receives regular meals when staying somewhere

DOWN

1 (adj.) of, concerning, or relating to motion

2 (n.) courage in the face of danger

4 (n.) 1. a cloud of gas in outer space; 2. any bright spot in the night sky

6 (adj.) enough or more than enough; large and plentiful; large and accommodating

7 (adj.) 1. feeling too light or delicate for the world; 2. heavenly or spiritual

8 (adj.) exhibiting an insensitive disregard for others

9 (adj.) (of a man) stylish, charming, and confident

11 (n.) a sovereign head of state such as a king, queen, or emperor

12 (n.) the science of the causes and effects of disease

14 (adj.) characterized by doing something over and over again or something happening over and over again in a tiresome way

15 (n.) a person who establishes a business, organization, club, or institution; (v.) (usually of a ship) to fill with water and sink

19 (v.) to modify or make better, more accurate, or up-to-date by implementing small changes in something

# Vocabulary Review
## Lessons 171-180

**Directions: Match each word with its best approximate definition. Note that definitions are not necessarily repeated verbatim from the lesson exercises.**

1.  desecrate _____
2.  heterogeneous _____
3.  etiquette _____
4.  contusion _____
5.  indicate _____
6.  enhance _____
7.  specify _____
8.  dogmatic _____
9.  inauspicious _____
10. inhabit _____
11. lesion _____
12. tranquility _____
13. innate _____
14. fallow _____
15. amiable _____
16. jubilee _____
17. vanquish _____
18. declamation _____
19. ecstatic _____
20. torpid _____

a.  to intensify, increase, or further improve the value of
b.  peacefulness, calmness
c.  to defeat thoroughly
d.  a bruise
e.  inborn, natural
f.  the customary code of behavior in society; manners
g.  diverse in character or content
h.  given to setting down principles as incontrovertibly true
i.  feeling overwhelming happiness or joy and excitement
j.  a special anniversary of an event
k.  concerning farmland left unused or uncultivated in order to restore its fertility for crop production
l.  a speech given in a rhetorical or impassioned manner
m.  to identify definitely and clearly
n.  a region in an organ or tissue that has suffered damage through disease
o.  unpromising; not conducive to success
p.  to treat a sacred ting with violent disrespect
q.  physically or mentally inactive; lethargic
r.  to live in or occupy a place or environment
s.  having or showing a friendly disposition
t.  to point out, to show; to suggest a necessary course of action

# Specific Vocabularies 4
## Government and Legal Words

## Government Terms:

- A **president** leads the United States of America
- **Congress** refers to the legislative body of the United States government; it is composed of both the **Senate** and the **House of Representatives**
- A **senator** is an individual representing his or her state in the Senate
- A **representative** is an individual representing his or her district in the **House of Representatives**
- A **governor** is in charge of running a state
- A **mayor** is in charge of running a city
- An **alderman** is an elected member of a municipal council
- The term **gubernatorial** refers to things related to a governor or the office of a governor
- The term **municipal** refers to things related to city government

## Courtroom and Legal Terms:

- A **judge** is a person who presides over a courtroom
- A **magistrate** is a civil office or lay judge who administers the law in minor cases
- A **felony** is a serious crime, usually involving violence and punishable by over a year in prison or death
- A **misdemeanor** is a minor offense or wrongdoing
- A **plaintiff** is a person who brings a case against another in a court of law
- A **defendant** is an individual, company, or institution that is accused in a court of law
- A **bailiff** is a person in a court of law who keeps order and who looks after prisone

# ANSWER KEY

## Lesson 1

1. b
2. a
3. c
4. d
5. e
6. occupy
7. impress
8. elusive
9. derelicts
10. mettle

## Lesson 2

1. a
2. e
3. d
4. c
5. b
6. melancholy
7. compel
8. urged
9. pithy
10. generosity

## Lesson 3

1. a
2. c
3. e
4. b
5. d
6. languid
7. flinch
8. paragon
9. commodious
10. obdurate

## Lesson 4

1. e
2. d
3. a
4. c
5. b
6. elaborate
7. assume
8. enigma
9. whet
10. mortgage

## Lesson 5

1. d
2. b
3. c
4. a
5. e
6. lavish
7. invincible
8. obvious
9. typical
10. immaculate

## Lesson 6

1. c
2. a
3. b
4. e
5. d
6. clamor
7. telepathic
8. trite
9. delighted
10. reeling

## Lesson 7

1.     c
2.     e
3.     a
4.     b
5.     d
6.     token
7.     lewd
8.     savor
9.     repose
10.    premonition

## Lesson 8

1.     d
2.     a
3.     c
4.     e
5.     b
6.     pledged
7.     confidential
8.     unprecedented
9.     precocious
10.    cherish

## Lesson 9

1.     b
2.     a
3.     c
4.     d
5.     e
6.     conversations
7.     intriguing
8.     calamity
9.     lax
10.    ruminating

## Lesson 10

1.     e
2.     d
3.     c
4.     b
5.     a
6.     renovate

7.     tedious
8.     commerce
9.     heritage
10.    expanse

## Word Search: Lessons 1-10

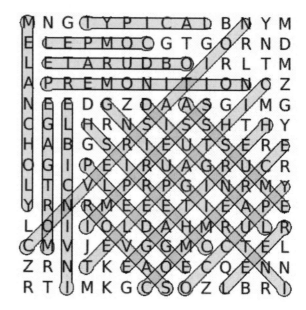

## Review: Lessons 1-10

1.     q
2.     r
3.     b
4.     o
5.     t
6.     g
7.     n
8.     f
9.     d
10.    h
11.    k
12.    l
13.    p
14.    e
15.    j
16.    a
17.    m
18.    i
19.    s
20.    c

## Lesson 11

1. e
2. c
3. a
4. b
5. d
6. withstand
7. zany
8. clairvoyant
9. ethical
10. din

## Lesson 12

1. a
2. b
3. d
4. c
5. e
6. fasten
7. texture
8. flourish
9. sedate
10. poach

## Lesson 13

1. a
2. d
3. e
4. b
5. c
6. judge
7. subsist
8. tome
9. invariably
10. procure

## Lesson 14

1. b
2. e
3. a
4. d
5. c
6. antechamber

7. abundant
8. wanes
9. cooperate
10. symbol

## Lesson 15

1. b
2. e
3. d
4. a
5. c
6. rotund
7. elocution
8. lamented
9. tempted
10. extrapolate

## Lesson 16

1. e
2. c
3. d
4. b
5. a
6. essential
7. rescind
8. heave
9. sturdy
10. corpulent

## Lesson 17

1. a
2. d
3. c
4. e
5. b
6. captivating
7. astounded
8. eventual
9. generate
10. gimmicks

## Lesson 18

1. b
2. e
3. c
4. a
5. d
6. tyrannical
7. relinquish
8. entice
9. sluggard
10. submissive

## Lesson 19

1. d
2. e
3. b
4. c
5. a
6. ridiculed
7. focus
8. detail
9. potent
10. tolerate

## Lesson 20

1. b
2. d
3. e
4. c
5. a
6. stealthy
7. mayhem
8. notorious
9. commended
10. reminiscences

## Crossword Puzzle: Lessons 11-20

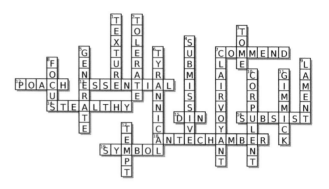

## Review: Lessons 11-20

1. h
2. j
3. k
4. e
5. m
6. s
7. b
8. q
9. f
10. t
11. o
12. a
13. p
14. n
15. c
16. g
17. l
18. i
19. d
20. r

## Lesson 21

1. a
2. b
3. c
4. e
5. d
6. repulsed
7. liberty
8. gouges

9. divulged
10. barren

## Lesson 22

1. d
2. b
3. c
4. a
5. e
6. era
7. henchmen
8. stance
9. profound
10. exemplary

## Lesson 23

1. c
2. b
3. e
4. d
5. a
6. veto
7. hygiene
8. specter
9. official
10. revelation

## Lesson 24

1. a
2. d
3. b
4. e
5. c
6. delectable
7. melodramatic
8. decree
9. evict
10. willing

## Lesson 25

1. e
2. c
3. d
4. a
5. b
6. medley
7. retaliation
8. tangible
9. contemporary
10. chronic

## Lesson 26

1. e
2. d
3. b
4. c
5. a
6. rational
7. camouflage
8. vented
9. objective
10. soothsayer

## Lesson 27

1. b
2. d
3. e
4. a
5. c
6. wounded
7. implied
8. opulent
9. plight
10. wreaked

## Lesson 28

1. c
2. d
3. a
4. b
5. e
6. engraved

7. advocate
8. mimic
9. ordeal
10. swivel

## Lesson 29

1. b
2. c
3. d
4. a
5. e
6. neophyte
7. daft
8. exonerate
9. empathy
10. divergent

## Lesson 30

1. a
2. b
3. c
4. d
5. e
6. durable
7. charisma
8. judicious
9. idiosyncrasies
10. matinee

## Word Search: Lessons 21-30

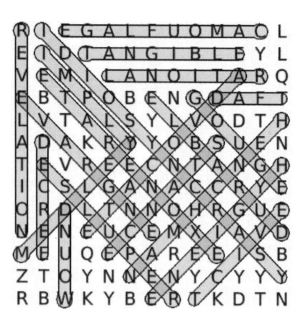

## Review: Lessons 21-30

1. b
2. g
3. o
4. k
5. m
6. e
7. t
8. h
9. q
10. i
11. p
12. s
13. c
14. l
15. j
16. r
17. a
18. n
19. f
20. d

## Lesson 31

1. c
2. b
3. d
4. a
5. e
6. redress
7. intersect
8. perseverance
9. qualms
10. uphold

## Lesson 32

1. e
2. c
3. b
4. d
5. a
6. peculiar
7. gaping
8. negotiations
9. inadvertently
10. limber

## Lesson 33

1. a
2. e
3. d
4. c
5. b
6. bliss
7. pernicious
8. gratification
9. fate
10. hesitant

## Lesson 34

1. d
2. b
3. e
4. a
5. c
6. lethargic
7. stature
8. maneuver
9. accommodate
10. dexterity

## Lesson 35

1. b
2. c
3. e
4. d
5. a
6. construed
7. barrier
8. expelled
9. lenient
10. goad

## Lesson 36

1. a
2. d
3. b
4. c
5. e
6. vehement
7. realize
8. diverse
9. virtuous
10. apathetic

## Lesson 37

1. b
2. a
3. d
4. e
5. c
6. glut
7. quell
8. reduce
9. accompanied
10. garrulous

## Lesson 38

1. a
2. d
3. e
4. c
5. b
6. settle
7. foundation
8. terminate
9. void
10. inscribed

## Lesson 39

1. e
2. c
3. d
4. b
5. a
6. breaches
7. lull
8. trepidation
9. rudimentary
10. obese

## Lesson 40

1. d
2. a
3. c
4. b
5. e
6. presage
7. dilapidated
8. ratify
9. manufactured
10. truce

## Crossword Puzzle:
## Lessons 31-40

## Review: Lessons 31-40

1. o
2. d
3. m
4. a
5. j
6. h
7. i
8. s
9. p
10. k
11. n
12. b
13. c
14. f
15. t
16. g
17. r
18. l
19. q
20. e

## Lesson 41

1. d
2. a
3. b
4. e
5. c
6. turbulence
7. upbraided
8. uncanny

9. superficial
10. stern

## Lesson 42

1. c
2. e
3. b
4. d
5. a
6. debris
7. meager
8. intricate
9. insurgent
10. hypocrisy

## Lesson 43

1. c
2. d
3. e
4. b
5. a
6. pugnacious
7. souvenirs
8. barbed
9. meek
10. burnish

## Lesson 44

1. e
2. a
3. c
4. b
5. d
6. quarantined
7. atrophy
8. feral
9. robust
10. pliable

## Lesson 45

1. c
2. d
3. a
4. e
5. b
6. cosmic
7. random
8. anonymous
9. modicum
10. contribute

## Lesson 46

1. c
2. e
3. a
4. b
5. d
6. bounty
7. deter
8. request
9. drawbacks
10. predate

## Lesson 47

1. d
2. c
3. e
4. a
5. b
6. stampede
7. routine
8. mercy
9. blast
10. invade

## Lesson 48

1. d
2. c
3. e
4. a
5. b

6. manifold
7. salutation
8. glint
9. communicate
10. taciturn

## Lesson 49

1. b
2. d
3. a
4. e
5. c
6. incentive
7. deft
8. jeered
9. vandalized
10. blatantly

## Lesson 50

1. a
2. c
3. b
4. d
5. e
6. capricious
7. mature
8. fortify
9. malign
10. murky

## Word Search: Lessons 41-50

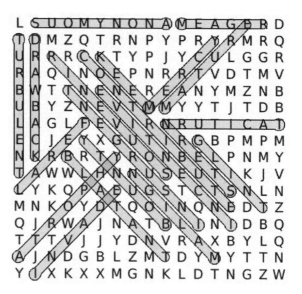

## Review: Lessons 41-50

1. n
2. o
3. i
4. c
5. a
6. q
7. m
8. b
9. r
10. k
11. t
12. g
13. l
14. j
15. e
16. s
17. f
18. h
19. p
20. d

## Lesson 51

1. c
2. b
3. a
4. e

5.  d
6.  ambled
7.  crude
8.  gale
9.  devoted
10. plausible

## Lesson 52

1.  c
2.  e
3.  b
4.  a
5.  d
6.  fiction
7.  placid
8.  thorough
9.  cupidity
10. eroded

## Lesson 53

1.  b
2.  c
3.  a
4.  d
5.  e
6.  concede
7.  tact
8.  terrestrial
9.  nonessential
10. bided

## Lesson 54

1.  c
2.  a
3.  b
4.  e
5.  d
6.  narrate
7.  anxiety
8.  consensus
9.  emphasis
10. odious

## Lesson 55

1.  b
2.  e
3.  d
4.  a
5.  c
6.  destitute
7.  animosity
8.  catastrophe
9.  proficient
10. allay

## Lesson 56

1.  a
2.  b
3.  c
4.  d
5.  e
6.  banished
7.  banal
8.  domestic
9.  doze
10. jeopardy

## Lesson 57

1.  e
2.  c
3.  a
4.  b
5.  d
6.  facilitate
7.  yearn
8.  boycott
9.  awkward
10. fruitful

## Lesson 58

1.  e
2.  b
3.  a
4.  c
5.  d
6.  stamina

7. penchant
8. trivial
9. debilitated
10. humidity

## Lesson 59

1. e
2. b
3. a
4. c
5. d
6. familial
7. adage
8. allege
9. bulge
10. abase

## Lesson 60

1. b
2. a
3. d
4. c
5. e
6. calm
7. reform
8. cowardice
9. legitimate
10. putrid

## Crossword Puzzle: Lessons 51-60

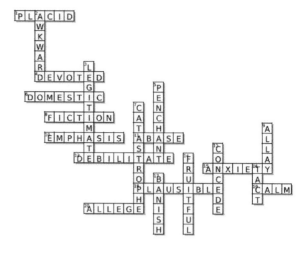

## Review: Lessons 51-60

1. h
2. s
3. b
4. q
5. a
6. l
7. m
8. e
9. n
10. g
11. j
12. t
13. d
14. p
15. i
16. f
17. r
18. o
19. k
20. c

## Lesson 61

1. c
2. e
3. b
4. a
5. d
6. somber

7. tardy
8. oath
9. subdue
10. cultivating

## Lesson 62

1. d
2. a
3. c
4. b
5. e
6. brazen
7. presumptuously
8. furious
9. heinous
10. fostering

## Lesson 63

1. a
2. e
3. b
4. c
5. d
6. pestered
7. ensnare
8. impose
9. sovereign
10. pariah

## Lesson 64

1. b
2. c
3. a
4. d
5. e
6. boisterous
7. compassion
8. acrid
9. repugnant
10. omit

## Lesson 65

1. d
2. b
3. c
4. e
5. a
6. zenith
7. entertain
8. indulgent
9. wither
10. instance

## Lesson 66

1. e
2. a
3. d
4. c
5. b
6. hospitable
7. encompass
8. scanty
9. luminous
10. pretentious

## Lesson 67

1. e
2. b
3. c
4. a
5. d
6. progressive
7. dissonance
8. sanitary
9. prudish
10. replica

## Lesson 68

1. b
2. c
3. a
4. d
5. e

6. sacred
7. accede
8. evoked
9. preponderance
10. stupefied

## Lesson 69

1. c
2. a
3. e
4. d
5. b
6. eminent
7. mischief
8. contempt
9. process
10. stolid

## Lesson 70

1. e
2. d
3. a
4. b
5. c
6. collateral
7. tailor
8. massive
9. variety
10. inquisitive

## Word Search: Lessons 61-70

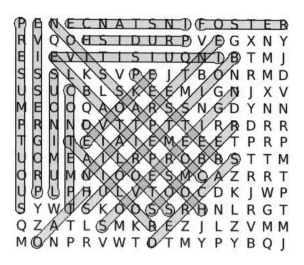

## Review: Lessons 61-70

1. s
2. h
3. c
4. k
5. b
6. g
7. j
8. l
9. p
10. o
11. e
12. d
13. a
14. t
15. m
16. i
17. q
18. f
19. n
20. r

## Lesson 71

1. a
2. c
3. d
4. e
5. b

6. preposterous
7. sentries
8. incredulous
9. insinuate
10. seer

## Lesson 72

1. c
2. b
3. d
4. a
5. e
6. expenditures
7. chaffed
8. smite
9. onus
10. statute

## Lesson 73

1. a
2. c
3. d
4. b
5. e
6. express
7. brawn
8. connotation
9. sage
10. untainted

## Lesson 74

1. e
2. d
3. a
4. c
5. b
6. nutritious
7. diminish
8. brash
9. phobias
10. forestall

## Lesson 75

1. e
2. d
3. b
4. a
5. c
6. equitable
7. portentous
8. charred
9. donates
10. inextricably

## Lesson 76

1. c
2. b
3. e
4. d
5. a
6. negligent
7. populated
8. prestidigitation
9. enormous
10. appropriate

## Lesson 77

1. e
2. d
3. b
4. a
5. c
6. requisition
7. propaganda
8. fallacy
9. somnolent
10. concocted

## Lesson 78

1. d
2. e
3. c
4. b
5. a
6. dormant

7. ideal
8. exist
9. scathing
10. unswerving

## Lesson 79

1. a
2. c
3. b
4. e
5. d
6. olfactory
7. transpired
8. ravenous
9. conniving
10. tradition

## Lesson 80

1. a
2. e
3. b
4. c
5. d
6. shunned
7. null
8. adept
9. ransacked
10. malicious

## Crossword Puzzle:
## Lessons 71-80

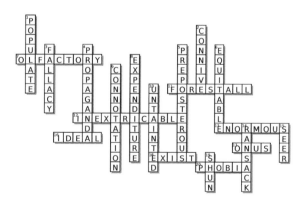

## Review: Lessons 71-80

1. g
2. q
3. n
4. m
5. a
6. t
7. s
8. k
9. o
10. b
11. f
12. e
13. r
14. j
15. l
16. c
17. d
18. p
19. h
20. i

## Lesson 81

1. e
2. d
3. a
4. b
5. c
6. stifling
7. provocative
8. exotic
9. benefactors
10. felon

## Lesson 82

1. d
2. a
3. c
4. e
5. b
6. refrain
7. demote
8. impede
9. abyss
10. tentative

## Lesson 83

1. a
2. c
3. b
4. d
5. e
6. falsetto
7. genteel
8. confusion
9. predictions
10. annex

## Lesson 84

1. d
2. c
3. a
4. b
5. e
6. extract
7. tenacious
8. doused
9. munificent
10. contrary

## Lesson 85

1. b
2. e
3. c
4. a
5. d
6. prose
7. associate
8. primitive
9. concur
10. divisive

## Lesson 86

1. e
2. d
3. b
4. a
5. c
6. corrupt
7. avarice
8. procrastinated
9. jovial
10. miserable

## Lesson 87

1. e
2. c
3. b
4. a
5. d
6. merit
7. merge
8. precarious
9. palatable
10. animate

## Lesson 88

1. b
2. a
3. d
4. c
5. e
6. abjured
7. castigated
8. contradict
9. expunged
10. swarthy

## Lesson 89

1. d
2. e
3. b
4. c
5. a
6. apex
7. speculate
8. pittance
9. cycle
10. tamper

## Lesson 90

1. a
2. e
3. b
4. c
5. d
6. dual
7. hobby
8. exhilarated
9. poised
10. seclude

## Word Search: Lessons 81-90

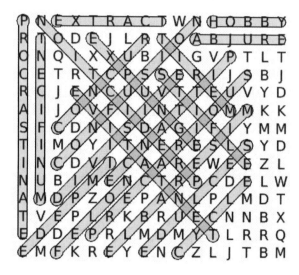

## Review: Lessons 81-90

1. h
2. i
3. t
4. b
5. a
6. g
7. r
8. e
9. c
10. n
11. p
12. f
13. j
14. s
15. m
16. d
17. k
18. l
19. q
20. o

## Lesson 91

1. d
2. b
3. c
4. a
5. e
6. intellectual
7. fickle
8. embrace
9. generalize
10. diligent

## Lesson 92

1. d
2. e
3. b
4. c
5. a
6. optimal
7. waxed
8. noisome
9. beneficial
10. encumber

## Lesson 93

1. e
2. b
3. c
4. d
5. a
6. accrue
7. enthralled
8. ruddy
9. disposition
10. celestial

## Lesson 94

1. e
2. a
3. d
4. b
5. c
6. hasten
7. manipulate
8. linchpin
9. enlighten
10. erroneous

## Lesson 95

1. d
2. e
3. c
4. b
5. a
6. glossed
7. weather
8. lithe
9. scarce
10. praise

## Lesson 96

1. e
2. c
3. d
4. b
5. a
6. mendicant
7. resuscitate
8. ferocious
9. warp
10. endeavoring

## Lesson 97

1. a
2. d
3. c
4. e
5. b
6. blend
7. harsh
8. theoretical
9. articulate
10. convene

## Lesson 98

1. d
2. e
3. b
4. c
5. a
6. caliber
7. raze
8. incurred
9. antisocial
10. relish

## Lesson 99

1. c
2. b
3. d
4. e
5. a
6. egress
7. graphic
8. deliberating
9. ignoble
10. imminent

## Lesson 100

1. c
2. e
3. a
4. b
5. d
6. candid
7. summit
8. extravagant
9. alternate
10. mar

## Crossword Puzzle: Lessons 91-100

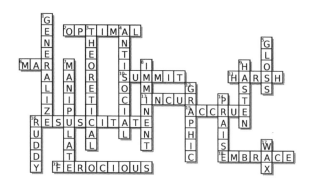

## Review: Lessons 91-100

1.  t
2.  k
3.  i
4.  p
5.  g
6.  f
7.  c
8.  a
9.  n
10. h
11. o
12. e
13. b
14. l
15. j
16. r
17. s
18. q
19. d
20. m

## Lesson 101

1.  b
2.  a
3.  e
4.  d
5.  c
6.  variance
7.  vague

8.  reception
9.  deficiency
10. kiln

## Lesson 102

1.  d
2.  c
3.  a
4.  b
5.  e
6.  noxious
7.  ambulatory
8.  notice
9.  bland
10. predicament

## Lesson 103

1.  d
2.  b
3.  a
4.  c
5.  e
6.  heirloom
7.  instantaneously
8.  pathetic
9.  pose
10. forlorn

## Lesson 104

1.  c
2.  e
3.  d
4.  a
5.  b
6.  akin
7.  suffice
8.  predecessor
9.  juncture
10. tacit

275

## Lesson 105

1. d
2. b
3. a
4. c
5. e
6. yield
7. cloned
8. conspicuous
9. bard
10. repress

## Lesson 106

1. d
2. b
3. a
4. c
5. e
6. vouch
7. erratic
8. innumerable
9. galactic
10. aghast

## Lesson 107

1. c
2. d
3. a
4. b
5. e
6. tumult
7. lore
8. adroit
9. arbitrator
10. retract

## Lesson 108

1. d
2. a
3. e
4. b
5. c
6. herculean
7. merger
8. abashed
9. antidote
10. inclination

## Lesson 109

1. a
2. b
3. d
4. e
5. c
6. iniquity
7. pigment
8. conduit
9. brevity
10. shirk

## Lesson 110

1. c
2. b
3. d
4. a
5. e
6. grant
7. drone
8. convey
9. priceless
10. prevaricate

## Word Search:
## Lessons 101-110

## Review: Lessons 101-110

| | |
|---|---|
| 1. | t |
| 2. | s |
| 3. | m |
| 4. | f |
| 5. | k |
| 6. | n |
| 7. | r |
| 8. | a |
| 9. | h |
| 10. | j |
| 11. | g |
| 12. | o |
| 13. | b |
| 14. | q |
| 15. | l |
| 16. | p |
| 17. | d |
| 18. | c |
| 19. | i |
| 20. | e |

## Lesson 111

| | |
|---|---|
| 1. | a |
| 2. | d |
| 3. | e |
| 4. | b |
| 5. | c |
| 6. | oration |
| 7. | illustrate |
| 8. | additional |
| 9. | detrimental |
| 10. | impudent |

## Lesson 112

| | |
|---|---|
| 1. | b |
| 2. | a |
| 3. | c |
| 4. | e |
| 5. | d |
| 6. | incoherent |
| 7. | brusque |
| 8. | recognize |
| 9. | lexicon |
| 10. | paltry |

## Lesson 113

| | |
|---|---|
| 1. | c |
| 2. | a |
| 3. | d |
| 4. | b |
| 5. | e |
| 6. | margin |
| 7. | patron |
| 8. | mores |
| 9. | joyous |
| 10. | opinion |

## Lesson 114

| | |
|---|---|
| 1. | a |
| 2. | d |
| 3. | e |
| 4. | b |
| 5. | c |

6. gainsay
7. goodwill
8. buffet
9. facile
10. scalpel

## Lesson 115

1. d
2. e
3. a
4. c
5. b
6. newfangled
7. discreet
8. frivolous
9. operate
10. collaborate

## Lesson 116

1. b
2. e
3. c
4. d
5. a
6. evacuate
7. ascertain
8. solid
9. objectionable
10. extol

## Lesson 117

1. e
2. d
3. c
4. b
5. a
6. oasis
7. splendid
8. repudiated
9. unilateral
10. buffer

## Lesson 118

1. e
2. d
3. a
4. b
5. c
6. copious
7. traumatic
8. fanatic
9. negative
10. effectual

## Lesson 119

1. d
2. b
3. c
4. e
5. a
6. scourge
7. entity
8. convenient
9. fiasco
10. dose

## Lesson 120

1. a
2. e
3. d
4. b
5. c
6. warrant
7. strive
8. ruptured
9. vogue
10. wan

## Crossword Puzzle:
## Lessons 111-120

## Review: Lessons 111-120

1. m
2. n
3. j
4. t
5. q
6. g
7. i
8. f
9. h
10. b
11. k
12. c
13. r
14. p
15. d
16. a
17. l
18. o
19. e
20. s

## Lesson 121

1. c
2. a
3. b
4. e
5. d
6. incision
7. pompous

8. scoured
9. ingenious
10. shrewd

## Lesson 122

1. d
2. c
3. b
4. a
5. e
6. menial
7. pursuit
8. fidelity
9. usurp
10. gourmand

## Lesson 123

1. c
2. b
3. e
4. a
5. d
6. acquiesced
7. choreography
8. incorrigible
9. laceration
10. grovel

## Lesson 124

1. a
2. c
3. b
4. d
5. e
6. appliance
7. atrocity
8. euphoria
9. frock
10. nomad

## Lesson 125

1. a
2. c
3. e
4. b
5. d
6. detour
7. memento
8. illegible
9. migrated
10. rendezvous

## Lesson 126

1. c
2. b
3. e
4. d
5. a
6. blasphemy
7. malevolent
8. rebuffed
9. subsidy
10. levity

## Lesson 127

1. a
2. e
3. c
4. d
5. b
6. flabbergasted
7. idiom
8. fling
9. famine
10. clash

## Lesson 128

1. a
2. d
3. c
4. e
5. b
6. amass
7. cavity
8. ruffled
9. constant
10. cling

## Lesson 129

1. c
2. b
3. d
4. e
5. a
6. despondent
7. prior
8. policy
9. amorphous
10. protrudes

## Lesson 130

1. c
2. e
3. a
4. b
5. d
6. ominous
7. prevalent
8. portly
9. fretful
10. approval

## Word Search: Lessons 121-130

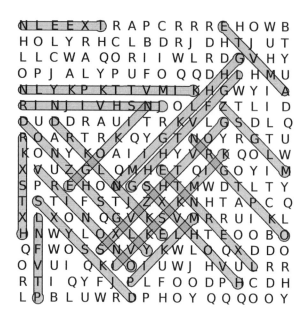

```
N L E E X J R A P C R R R E H O W B
H O L Y R H C L B D R J D H T J U T
L L C W A Q O R I I W L R D G V H Y
O P J A L Y P U F O Q Q D H D H M U
N L Y K P K T T V M I K H G W Y I A
R I N J I V H S N J O L F Z T L I D
O U O D R A U I T R K V L G S D L Q
R O A R T R K Q Y G T N O Y R G T U
K O N Y K O A I I H Y V R K Q O L W
X V U Z Q L O M H E T O I G O Y I M
S P R E H O N G S H T M W D T L T Y
T S T I F S T I Z X N H T A P C Q
X L X O N Q G V K S V M R R U I K L
H N W Y L O X L R E L H T E O O B O
Q F W O S S N V Y K W L O Q X D D O
O V U I Q K I O I U W J H V U L R R
R T I Q Y F J P L F O O D P H C D H
L P B L U W R D P H O Y Q Q Q O O Y
```

## Review: Lessons 121-130

1.  d
2.  i
3.  o
4.  a
5.  q
6.  h
7.  f
8.  g
9.  r
10. n
11. m
12. l
13. j
14. s
15. e
16. p
17. t
18. b
19. k
20. c

## Lesson 131

1.  c
2.  a
3.  b
4.  d
5.  e
6.  trade
7.  simulate
8.  distress
9.  aggrandize
10. culpable

## Lesson 132

1.  a
2.  c
3.  b
4.  d
5.  e
6.  restitution
7.  succumbed
8.  intercepted
9.  craft
10. annul

## Lesson 133

1.  c
2.  e
3.  b
4.  d
5.  a
6.  domicile
7.  arid
8.  culture
9.  retorted
10. arrogant

## Lesson 134

1.  c
2.  b
3.  d
4.  a
5.  e

6. encountered
7. wary
8. benevolent
9. demonstrate
10. berated

## Lesson 135

1. d
2. c
3. a
4. b
5. e
6. undermine
7. ardor
8. dutiful
9. credulous
10. trekked

## Lesson 136

1. e
2. b
3. a
4. c
5. d
6. nucleus
7. crisis
8. sate
9. prosperous
10. congenial

## Lesson 137

1. c
2. a
3. b
4. d
5. e
6. strenuous
7. flux
8. pungent
9. dogged
10. obliged

## Lesson 138

1. a
2. d
3. e
4. c
5. b
6. blueprint
7. fluctuate
8. prolong
9. inspect
10. basis

## Lesson 139

1. e
2. c
3. d
4. a
5. b
6. pacifist
7. severe
8. prey
9. authentic
10. deplore

## Lesson 140

1. e
2. d
3. b
4. c
5. a
6. acquaintance
7. initiate
8. muster
9. voluminous
10. covert

## Crossword Puzzle:
## Lessons 131-140

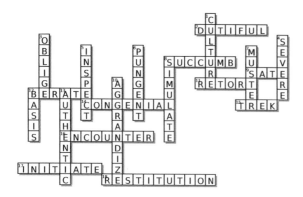

## Review: Lessons 131-140

1. l
2. n
3. q
4. h
5. f
6. i
7. c
8. t
9. p
10. a
11. g
12. m
13. d
14. j
15. b
16. k
17. e
18. s
19. o
20. r

## Lesson 141

1. a
2. e
3. c
4. d
5. b
6. mute
7. universally
8. adversity

9. adorn
10. marvel

## Lesson 142

1. a
2. d
3. c
4. b
5. e
6. irrational
7. eccentric
8. beverage
9. sabbatical
10. unruly

## Lesson 143

1. a
2. d
3. c
4. e
5. b
6. amalgamation
7. feat
8. vulnerable
9. alleviate
10. gesture

## Lesson 144

1. d
2. e
3. b
4. c
5. a
6. fissure
7. jubilant
8. election
9. miscellaneous
10. synopsis

## Lesson 145

1. b
2. e
3. d
4. c
5. a
6. authoritarian
7. mandatory
8. ailment
9. deluged
10. underlying

## Lesson 146

1. e
2. a
3. d
4. c
5. b
6. spontaneous
7. rejuvenate
8. transact
9. gregarious
10. humble

## Lesson 147

1. c
2. e
3. a
4. d
5. b
6. triumph
7. timorous
8. transparent
9. cavort
10. incited

## Lesson 148

1. b
2. c
3. d
4. e
5. a
6. vex
7. custom
8. timid
9. rife
10. quench

## Lesson 149

1. d
2. e
3. b
4. c
5. a
6. verify
7. mundane
8. exquisite
9. suspend
10. magnitude

## Lesson 150

1. a
2. c
3. e
4. d
5. b
6. amity
7. physiognomy
8. focal
9. sequential
10. accumulate

# Word Search: Lessons 141-150

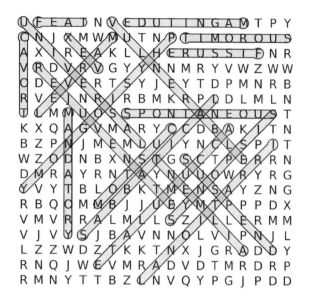

## Review: Lessons 141-150

1. q
2. t
3. d
4. k
5. l
6. e
7. f
8. o
9. s
10. i
11. h
12. m
13. j
14. c
15. a
16. p
17. r
18. g
19. b
20. n

## Lesson 151

1. e
2. d
3. a
4. c
5. b
6. exterior
7. stalemate
8. incidental
9. dynamic
10. inhibit

## Lesson 152

1. e
2. d
3. c
4. b
5. a
6. remiss
7. harrowing
8. adamant
9. fatigued
10. supreme

## Lesson 153

1. a
2. b
3. e
4. c
5. d
6. motivate
7. commence
8. bedlam
9. divert
10. welcome

## Lesson 154

1. d
2. a
3. e
4. b
5. c
6. acclaim
7. aloof
8. magnetic
9. residual
10. audacious

## Lesson 155

1. a
2. d
3. e
4. b
5. c
6. vim
7. thwart
8. novice
9. infused
10. colossal

## Lesson 156

1. c
2. d
3. a
4. b
5. e
6. rectify
7. rue
8. versatile
9. quaint
10. instigated

## Lesson 157

1. b
2. c
3. d
4. e
5. a
6. inspires
7. lunged
8. correlation
9. differentiate
10. laudable

## Lesson 158

1. d
2. a
3. b
4. e

5. c
6. apparent
7. wealth
8. rancid
9. reveled
10. surly

## Lesson 159

1. e
2. c
3. d
4. b
5. a
6. affable
7. atone
8. kindled
9. winced
10. thrive

## Lesson 160

1. d
2. a
3. b
4. c
5. e
6. obligate
7. abbreviate
8. coach
9. wayward
10. gullible

## Crossword Puzzle:
## Lessons 151-160

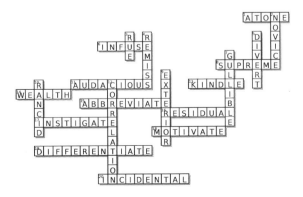

286

## Review: Lessons 151-160

1. m
2. h
3. f
4. c
5. g
6. j
7. e
8. t
9. i
10. b
11. n
12. q
13. d
14. r
15. o
16. a
17. k
18. l
19. p
20. s

## Lesson 161

1. a
2. b
3. d
4. e
5. c
6. ostracize
7. indicted
8. rankled
9. hovel
10. pragmatic

## Lesson 162

1. e
2. b
3. c
4. a
5. d
6. depletes
7. thaw
8. absurd
9. polish
10. favor

## Lesson 163

1. d
2. e
3. a
4. b
5. c
6. annihilated
7. bloated
8. discretion
9. swagger
10. retribution

## Lesson 164

1. a
2. c
3. b
4. e
5. d
6. implored
7. unconditional
8. personable
9. illusion
10. grotto

## Lesson 165

1. b
2. d
3. c
4. a
5. e
6. inevitable
7. astute
8. concise
9. desolate
10. abrogate

## Lesson 166

1. e
2. a
3. b
4. d
5. c

287

6. forage
7. fortitude
8. accidental
9. imitate
10. indignation

## Lesson 167

1. a
2. d
3. c
4. e
5. b
6. strategy
7. devout
8. prologue
9. frequent
10. sanction

## Lesson 168

1. b
2. e
3. a
4. d
5. c
6. defunct
7. ostentatious
8. neutral
9. liberate
10. plentiful

## Lesson 169

1. a
2. d
3. e
4. c
5. b
6. exorbitant
7. perceptive
8. acquire
9. squalid
10. elderly

## Lesson 170

1. e
2. b
3. c
4. a
5. d
6. render
7. accentuate
8. belligerent
9. ponder
10. temperance

## Word Search: Lessons 161-170

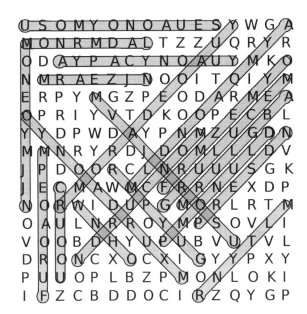

## Review: Lessons 161-170

1. q
2. l
3. e
4. o
5. m
6. g
7. j
8. f
9. p
10. c
11. n
12. s

13. t
14. a
15. b
16. i
17. h
18. k
19. d
20. r

## Lesson 171

1. d
2. c
3. b
4. e
5. a
6. monarch
7. desecrate
8. panorama
9. tortuous
10. heterogeneous

## Lesson 172

1. c
2. a
3. b
4. e
5. d
6. contusion
7. comeback
8. amend
9. barrage
10. etiquette

## Lesson 173

1. e
2. d
3. c
4. a
5. b
6. callous
7. nebula
8. enhance
9. surrogate

10. indicate

## Lesson 174

1. e
2. c
3. d
4. a
5. b
6. dogmatic
7. specify
8. repetitive
9. redundant
10. boarders

## Lesson 175

1. d
2. b
3. a
4. c
5. e
6. mitigate
7. inhabit
8. effect
9. inauspicious
10. founder

## Lesson 176

1. b
2. c
3. d
4. a
5. e
6. tranquility
7. debonair
8. stanza
9. plead
10. lesion

## Lesson 177

1. b
2. c

3.  e
4.  a
5.  d
6.  dissemble
7.  prolific
8.  innate
9.  submerge
10. fallow

7.  ecstatic
8.  pathology
9.  ethereal
10. obtuse

## Lesson 178

1.  e
2.  b
3.  d
4.  a
5.  c
6.  epoch
7.  kinetic
8.  jubilee
9.  valor
10. amiable

## Crossword Puzzle: Lessons 171-180

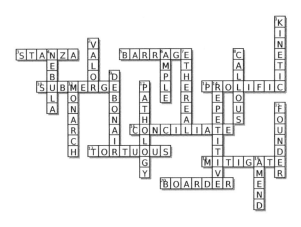

## Lesson 179

1.  b
2.  c
3.  d
4.  e
5.  a
6.  schism
7.  declamation
8.  conciliate
9.  ample
10. vanquished

## Review: Lessons 171-180

1.  p
2.  g
3.  f
4.  d
5.  t
6.  a
7.  m
8.  h
9.  o
10. r
11. n
12. b
13. e
14. k
15. s
16. j
17. c
18. l
19. i
20. q

## Lesson 180

1.  d
2.  c
3.  e
4.  b
5.  a
6.  torpid

# GLOSSARY

This glossary contains definitions of the new words from every lesson contained in this book. Please note that not every meaning of each word is contained in this glossary. Generally, only the most commonly used meanings of the words below are defined.

All entries in the glossary take the following form:

**word** (lesson): (part of speech) definition

Key for parts of speech:
adj. = adjective                    n. = noun                    v. = verb

## A

**abase** (59): (v.) to behave in such a way as to degrade or belittle someone

**abash** (108): (v.) to cause to feel embarrassed, disconcerted, or ashamed

**abbreviate** (160): (v.) to shorten a word, phrase, or text

**abjure** (88): (v.) to solemnly renounce a belief, cause, or claim

**abrogate** (165): (v.) to repeal or do away with a law, right, or formal agreement

**absurd** (162): (adj.) wildly ridiculous, insensible, or foolish

**abundant** (14): (adj.) existing or available in great quantities

**abyss** (82): (n.) a deep or seemingly bottomless chasm

**accede** (68): (v.) to assent or agree to a request, demand, or treaty

**accentuate** (170): (v.) to make more prominent or noticeable

**accidental** (166): (adj.) happening by chance, unintentionally, or unexpectedly

**acclaim** (154): (n.) enthusiastic public praise; (v.) to praise enthusiastically and publicly

**accommodate** (34): (v.) 1. to provide lodging or sufficient space for; 2. to fit in with the wishes or needs of

**accompany** (37): (v.) to go somewhere with someone as a companion or escort; to be present or occur at the same time as something else; to provide something as a complement or addition to something else

**accrue** (93): (v.) (of sums of money or benefits) to be received by someone in regular or increasing amounts over time

**accumulate** (150): (v.) to gather together or acquire an increasing number or amount of

**acquaintance** (140): (n.) 1. a person's knowledge or experience of something; 2. a person one knows slightly but who is not a close friend

291

**acquiesce** (123): (v.) to accept something reluctantly and without protest

**acquire** (169): (v.) 1. to buy or obtain an object; 2. to learn or develop a specific skill or skill set; 3. to achieve a reputation as a result of one's behavior or activity

**acrid** (64): (adj.) having an irritatingly strong and unpleasant taste or smell

**adage** (59): (n.) a proverb or short statement expressing a general truth

**adamant** (152): (adj.) refusing to be persuaded or change one's mind

**additional** (111): (adj.) added, extra, or supplementary to what is already given

**adept** (80): (adj.) very skilled or proficient at something

**adorn** (141): (v.) to make more beautiful or attractive

**adroit** (107): (adj.) clever or skillful in using the hands or mind

**adversity** (141): (n.) difficulty or misfortune

**advocate** (28): (n.) a person who publicly supports or recommends a particular cause or policy; 2. a person who pleads on someone else's behalf; (v.) to publicly recommend or support

**affable** (159): (adj.) friendly, easy to talk to, good-natured

**aggrandize** (131): (v.) to increase the power, status, or wealth of

**aghast** (106): (adj.) filled with shock or horror

**ailment** (145): (n.) an illness (typically minor illness)

**akin** (104): (adj.) of similar character

**allay** (55): (v.) (of a fear, suspicion, or worry) to diminish or put at rest

**allege** (59): (v.) to claim or assert that someone has done something illegal or wrong, typically without proof

**alleviate** (143): (v.) to make pain or suffering less severe

**aloof** (154): (adj.) not friendly or forthcoming; cold; distant

**alternate** (100): (adj.) 1. every other; every second; 2. taking the place of; (n.) a person who acts as a substitute; (v.) to occur in turn repeatedly

**amalgamation** (143): (n.) the action, process, or result of uniting or combining

**amass** (128): (v.) to gather together or accumulate over a time period; to gather together in a group or crowd

**amble** (51): (v.) to walk or move at a slow, relaxed pace

**ambulatory** (102): (adj.) related to or adapted to walking

**amend** (172): (v.) to modify or make better, more accurate, or up-to-date by implementing small changes in something

**amiable** (178): (adj.) friendly and pleasant

**amity** (150): (n.) a friendly relationship

**amorphous** (129): (adj.) without a clearly defined shape or form; vaguely defined

**ample** (179): (adj.) enough or more than enough; large and plentiful; large and accommodating

**animate** (87): (adj.) alive or having life; (v.) 1. to bring to life; to give encouragement, vigor, or renewed vigor to; 2. to give a movie or a character the appearance of movement using artistic techniques

**animosity** (55): (n.) strong hostility

**annex** (83): (n.) a building joined to or associated with a main building; an addition to a document; (v.) to append or add as a subordinate part (especially of a document or a territory)

**annihilate** (163): (v.) to destroy completely; to obliterate

**annul** (132): (v.) to declare an official agreement, decision, or result invalid

**anonymous** (45): (adj.) (of a person) not identified by name, or of unknown name

**antechamber** (14): (n.) a small room leading to a big one

**antidote** (108): (n.) a medicine taken to counteract a particular poison

**antisocial** (98): (adj.) 1. not friendly; not wanting the company of others; 2. contrary to the laws and customs of society

**anxiety** (54): (n.) a feeling of worry, unease, or nervousness, typically about an imminent event or one with an uncertain outcome

**apathy** (36): (n.) lack of interest, enthusiasm, or concern

**apex** (89): (n.) the top or highest point of something

**apparent** (158): (adj.) clearly visible or true, obvious; seemingly true

**appliance** (124): (n.) a device or piece of equipment designed to perform a specific task, typically a domestic one

**appropriate** (76): (adj.) suitable or proper in the circumstances; (v.) 1. to take something for one's use, typically without permission; 2. to devote money or assets to a special purpose

**approval** (130): (n.) the action of officially agreeing on something or accepting something as satisfactory

**arbitrator** (107): (n.) an independent person or body officially appointed to settle a dispute

**ardor** (135): (n.) enthusiasm or passion

**arid** (133): (adj.) land and climate that is dry and barren that is hardly capable of supporting vegetation

**arrogant** (133): (adj.) having or revealing an exaggerated sense of oneself or one's abilities

**articulate** (97): (adj.) having the ability to speak fluently and coherently; (v.) to express an idea or feeling fluently and coherently

**ascertain** (116): (v.) to find something out for certain; to make sure of

**associate** (85): (adj.) joined or connected with an organization or business; (n.) a partner or colleague in business or at work; 2. a person with limited or subordinate membership in an organization; (v.) to connect someone or something with something else in one's mind

**assume** (4): (v.) 1. to suppose to be the case without proof; 2. to take or begin to have power or responsibility; 3. to seize power or control over something; 4. to take on a characteristic or quality for a role

**astound** (17): (v.) to shock or greatly surprise

**astute** (165): (adj.) having the ability to accurately assess situations or people and turn them to one's advantage

**atone** (159): (v.) to make amends or reparation

**atrocity** (124): (n.) an extremely wicked or cruel act, often involving physical violence or injury

**atrophy** (44): (v.) 1. for a body tissue to waste away, typically due to the degeneration of cells; 2. to gradually decline in effectiveness or vigor due to underuse or neglect

**audacious** (154): (adj.) 1. showing a willingness to take bold risks; 2. showing an impudent lack of respect

**authentic** (139): (adj.) genuine, of undisputed origin; based on facts, accurate, reliable

**authoritarian** (145): (adj.) favoring or enforcing strict obedience to authority, especially the government at the expense of personal freedom; showing a lack of concern about the wishes or cares of others

**avarice** (86): (n.) extreme greed for material gain or wealth

**awkward** (57): (adj.) 1. causing difficulty, hard to do or deal with; 2. causing or feeling embarrassment or inconvenience; 3. not smooth or grateful

# B

**banal** (56): (adj.) lacking in originality and thus being obvious or boring

**banish** (56): (v.) to send someone away from a country or place as official punishment

**barbed** (43): (adj.) having sharp projections on an object so as to make extraction difficult; deliberately hurtful

**bard** (105): (n.) a poet, especially one conveying epics in an oral tradition

**barrage** (172): (n.) a concentrated outpouring or firing of something; (v.) to bombard someone with something

**barren** (21): (adj.) empty, bleak, and lifeless; (of land) too poor to produce substantial vegetation

**barrier** (35): (n.) an object that prevents movement or access

**basis** (138): (n.) the underlying support or foundation for an idea, argument, or process

**bedlam** (153): (n.) a scene of uproar and confusion

**belligerent** (170): (adj.) hostile and aggressive

**benefactor** (81): (n.) a person who gives money or other aid to help a person or cause

**beneficial** (92): (adj.) favorable or advantageous; resulting in good

**benevolent** (134): (adj.) well-meaning and kindly

**berate** (134): (v.) to scold or criticize someone angrily

**beverage** (142): (n.) a drink

**bide** (53): (v.) to remain or stay somewhere

**bland** (102): (adj.) lacking strong features or characteristics and therefore uninteresting; food or drink that is mild and insipid; a person lacking strong emotion and unremarkable

**blasphemy** (126): (n.) the act of speaking sacrilegiously about God or things that are sacred

**blast** (47): (n.) 1. a destructive wave of compressed air spreading outward from an explosion; 2. a strong gust of wind or air; 3. a single loud noise emanating from a horn or other musical instrument; (v.) 1. to blow up or break apart something with explosives; 2. to make or cause to make a loud continuous musical or other noise

**blatant** (49): (adj.) typically bad behavior done openly and unashamedly

**blend** (97): (n.) a mixture of different things or qualities; (v.) to mix a substance with another so that they meld together as a mass; to put abstract things together; a harmonious combination

**bliss** (33): (n.) perfect happiness; great joy

**bloated** (163): (adj.) 1. (of the body) swollen with fluid or gas; 2. excessive in size or amount

**blueprint** (138): (n.) a design plan or technical drawing (used heavily in architecture); something that acts as a plan, model, or template

**boarder** (174): (n.) a person (often a student residing at school) who receives regular meals when staying somewhere

**boisterous** (64): (adj.) 1. (of a person, event, or occasion) energetic, noisy, and cheerful; 2. (of wind, weather, or water) wild or stormy

**bounty** (46): (n.) 1. generosity, liberality; abundance; 2. a monetary gift or reward given by a government, usually for killing or capturing a criminal

**boycott** (57): (n.) a punitive ban that forbids relations with certain groups, cooperation with a policy, or the handling of goods; (v.) to withdraw from commercial or social relations with a country, organization, or person as a punishment or protest

**brash** (74): (adj.) self-assertive in a rude, overbearing, or noisy way; overbearing

**brawn** (73): (n.) physical strength (in contrast to intelligence)

**brazen** (62): (adj.) bold and without shame

**breach** (39): (n.) 1. an act of breaking a law, agreement, or code of conduct; 2. a gap in a wall, barrier, or defense made by an army; (v.) to break a law, agreement, or code of conduct; 2. to make a gap in and break through a wall, barrier, or defense

**brevity** (109): (n.) concise and exact use of words in speech; shortness of time

**brusque** (112): (adj.) abrupt or offhand in speech or manner

**buffer** (117): (n.) a person or thing that prevents incompatible or antagonistic people or things from coming into contact with or harming each other; (v.) to lessen or moderate the impact of something

**buffet** (114): (v.) to strike repeatedly; to batter; to knock someone over or off course

**bulge** (59): (n.) a rounded swelling or protuberance that distorts a flat surface; (v.) to swell or protrude to an unnatural or incongruous extent

**burnish** (43): (v.) to polish

# C

**calamity** (9): (n.) a disaster

**caliber** (98): (n.) 1. the quality of someone's character or the level of someone's ability; 2. the internal diameter or bore of a gun barrel

**callous** (173): (adj.) exhibiting an insensitive and cruel disregard for others

**calm** (60): (adj.) 1. (of a person) not showing signs of anger, nervousness, or other emotions, 2. pleasantly free from wind; (n.) 1. the absence of violent confrontational activity within a place or group; 2. the absence of wind; (v.) to make someone quiet; soothe

**camouflage** (26): (n.) the disguising of people (especially military personnel), equipment, and installations by covering them to make them blend in with natural surroundings; material used for such disguise; an animal's covering that lets it blend in with natural surroundings; (v.) to hide or disguise the presence of a person, animal, or object; to conceal the existence of something undesirable

**candid** (100): (adj.) truthful and straightforward frank

**caprice** (50): (n.) a sudden and unaccountable change of mood or behavior

**captivating** (17): (adj.) capable of attracting and holding interest

**castigate** (88): (v.) to reprimand someone severely

**catastrophe** (55): (n.) an event causing great and often sudden damage or suffering

**cavity** (128): (n.) an empty space within a solid object, especially the human body; the decayed part of a tooth

**cavort** (147): (v.) to jump or dance around excitedly

**celestial** (93): (adj.) of or pertaining to the sky or the heavens

**chaff** (72): (v.) to tease

**char** (75): (v.) to partially burn an object as to blacken its surface

**charisma** (30): (n.) compelling attractiveness or charm that can inspire others

**cherish** (8): (v.) to protect and care for something or someone lovingly; to hold dear

**choreography** (123): (n.) the sequence of steps and movements in dance or figure skating

**chronic** (25): (adj.) persisting for a long time or constantly recurring

**clairvoyant** (11): (adj.) having the ability to see or predict events in the future beyond normal sense; (n.) a person who claims to have the supernatural ability to see events in the future beyond normal sense

**clamor** (6): (n.) a loud and confused noise, perhaps protest; (v.) to shout loudly and insistently as a group, often to protest or demand

**clash** (127): (n.) 1. a violent confrontation; 2. a color mismatch; 3. a loud, jarring sound made by clashing metal objects together

**cling** (128): (v.) to hold on tightly to; to remain stubbornly persistent or faithful to something

**clone** (105): (n.) an identical copy of something; (v.) to make an identical copy of

**coach** (160): (1.) a horse-drawn or motor carriage; 2. a railway car; 3. an athletic instructor or trainer; (v.) to instruct or train athletes

**collaborate** (115): (v.) to work jointly on an activity, especially to produce something

**collateral** (70): (n.) something pledged as security for repayment of a loan

**colossal** (155): (adj.) extremely large

**comeback** (172): (n.) 1. a return by a well-known person to the field in which they were originally successful; 2. a quick reply to a critical remark

**commence** (153): (v.) to begin, start

**commend** (20): (v.) to praise formally or officially; to present as suitable for approval or acceptance; recommend

**commerce** (10): (v.) 1. the act of buying and selling, trade; 2. social dealings between people

**commodious** (3): (adj.) roomy and comfortable

**communicate** (48): (v.) to share or exchange information, news, or ideas

**compassion** (64): (n.) sympathetic pity and concern for the suffering and misfortunes of others

**compel** (2): (v.) to force or oblige someone or something; to bring about something by the use of pressure or force

**concede** (53): (v.) 1. to admit that something is true or valid after first denying or resisting it; 2. to surrender or yield something that one possesses or desires

**conciliate** (179): (v.) to stop someone from being angry; to placate; to pacify

**concise** (165): (adj.) giving much information in few words

**concoct** (77): (v.) 1. to make a dish or meal by combining various ingredients; 2. to create or devise a story or plan

**concur** (85): (v.) 1. to be of the same opinion, to agree; 2. to happen at the same time

**conduit** (109): (n.) a channel for conveying a fluid; a person or organization that acts as a channel for the transmission of something

**confidential** (8): (adj.) intended to be kept secret

**confusion** (83): (n.) 1. a lack of understanding; uncertainty; 2. the state of being bewildered or unclear in one's mind about something

**congenial** (136): (adj.) 1. (of a person) pleasant because of a personality, interests, or other qualities similar to one's own; 2. (of a thing) pleasant or suitable because it is suited to one's tastes or inclination

**connive** (79): (v.) to secretly allow something immoral, illegal, wrong, or harmful to occur (often conspiring with others)

**connotation** (73): (n.) an idea or feeling that a word evokes in addition to its literal meaning

**consensus** (54): (n.) a general agreement

**conspicuous** (105): (adj.) standing out so as to be clearly visible

**constant** (128): (n.) continuous and unchanging; remaining the same over a period of time; referring to a person who is faithful

**construe** (35): (v.) to interpret a word or action in a particular way

**contemporary** (25): (adj.) 1. living or occurring at the same time; 2. belonging or occurring in the present; (n.) 1. a person or living thing existing at the same time as another; 2. a person of roughly the same age as another

**contempt** (69): (n.) 1. a feeling that a person is beneath consideration, deserving scorn, or unworthy; 2. a disregard for something that should be taken into account

**contradict** (88): (v.) to deny the truth of something by asserting the opposite; to assert the opposite of a statement made by someone

**contrary** (84): (adj.) 1. opposite in nature, direction, or meaning; 2. perversely inclined to do the opposite of what is expected or desired; (n.) the opposite

**contribute** (45): (v.) to give (something, often money) in order to help achieve or provide something

**contusion** (172): (n.) a bruise

**convene** (97): (v.) to come or bring together for a meeting or activity; to assemble

**convenient** (119): (adj.) fitting in well with one's needs, activities, and/or plans

**conversation** (9): (n.) an informal exchange of ideas by spoken words

**convey** (110): (v.) to transport or carry from place to place; to make an idea, impression, or feeling known or understandable to someone

**cooperate** (14): (v.) to act jointly and work toward the same end; to assist someone (or an organization) and comply with his or her (its) requests

**copious** (118): (adj.) abundant in supply or quantity

**corpulent** (16): (adj.) fat (describing a person)

**correlation** (157): (n.) a mutual relationship or connection between two or more things

**corrupt** (86): (adj.) having or showing a willingness to act dishonestly in return for money or personal gain; (v.) to cause to act dishonestly in return for money or personal gain

**cosmic** (45): (adj.) of or relating to the universe or things beyond Earth

**covert** (140): (adj.) not openly acknowledged or displayed

**cowardice** (60): (n.) lack of bravery

**craft** (132): (n.) an activity involving skill and often making things by hand; (v.) to exercise skill in making or doing something

**credulous** (135): (adj.) exhibiting too great a readiness to believe things

**crisis** (136): (n.) a period of intense difficulty, danger, or trouble

**crude** (51): (adj.) 1. in a natural or raw state; unrefined; 2. constructed in a rudimentary way; 3. (of a person) especially offensive or rude, especially in a sexual way

**culpable** (131): (adj.) worthy of blame

**cultivate** (61): (v.) 1. to prepare and use land for crops or gardening; 2. to acquire and develop a quality, skill, or sentiment

**culture** (133): (n.) the arts and other manifestations of human intellectual achievement regarded collectively

**cupidity** (52): (n.) greed for money or possessions

**custom** (148): (adj.) made or done for a particular customer; (n.) a traditional and widely accepted way of behaving or doing something that is specific to a particular society, place, or time

**cycle** (89): (n.) 1. a series of events that are regularly repeated in the same order; 2. a bicycle or tricycle; (v.) 1. to move in or follow a regularly repeated sequence of events; 2. to ride a bicycle or tricycle

# D

**daft** (29): (adj.) silly; foolish

**debilitate** (58): (adj.) 1. to make someone weak and infirm; 2. to hinder, delay, or weaken

**debonair** (176): (adj.) (of a man) stylish, charming, and confident

**debris** (42): (n.) scattered fragments of something wrecked or destroyed

**declamation** (179): (n.) a speech delivered in a rhetorical or passionate way

**decree** (24): (n.) an official order issued by a ruler or legal authority

**deficiency** (101): (n.) a lack or shortage

**deft** (49): (adj.) neatly skillful and quick in one's movements

**defunct** (168): (adj.) no longer existing or functioning

**delectable** (24): (adj.) delicious; tasty

**deliberate** (99): (adj.) done consciously and intentionally; (v.) engage in long and careful consideration

**delight** (6): (n.) a great pleasure; (v.) to please (someone) greatly; to take great pleasure in something

**deluge** (145): (n.) a severe flood; (v.) to flood or be flooded by a great quantity of something

**demonstrate** (134): (v.) 1. to clearly show the existence or truth of something by giving proof or evidence; 2. to take part in a public meeting or protest expressing views on a political issue

**demote** (82): (v.) to give someone a lower rank or less senior position, usually as a punishment

**deplete** (162): (v.) to use up the supply or resources of

**deplore** (49): (v.) to feel or express strong disapproval of (something)

**derelict** (1): (adj.) in poor condition due to neglect and/or disuse; (n.) 1. a person lacking a job, home, or property; 2. a person negligent in doing his or her duty

**desecrate** (171): (v.) to treat something sacred with disrespect

**desolate** (165): (adj.) deserted of people and in a state of bleak and dismal emptiness

**despondent** (129): (adj.) in low spirits from loss of hope or courage

**destitute** (55): (adj.) lacking the basic necessities in life

**detail** (19): (n.) an individual feature, fact, or item; (v.) to give particulars of, describe item by item

**deter** (46): (v.) to discourage someone from doing something, typically by instilling doubt or fear

**detour** (125): (n.) a long and roundabout route taken to avoid something or to visit somewhere along the way; (v.) to take a long or roundabout route

**detrimental** (111): (adj.) tending to cause harm

**devoted** (51): (adj.) very loving and loyal

**devout** (167): (adj.) having or showing deep religious feeling or commitment

**dexterity** (34): (n.) skill at performing tasks, especially with the hands

**differentiate** (157): (v.) to recognize or figure out what makes something different

**dilapidated** (40): (adj.) a building or object in a state of disrepair or ruin as a result of age or neglect

**diligent** (91): (adj.) having or showing care and conscientiousness in one's work or duties

**diminish** (74): (v.) to make or become less

**din** (11): (n.) a loud, unpleasant, and prolonged noise

**discreet** (115): (adj.) careful and circumspect in one's speech or actions, especially in order to causing offense or to gain an advantage

**discretion** (163): (n.) the quality of behaving in such a way that offence is not caused or private information is not revealed

**disposition** (93): (n.) 1. a person's inherent qualities of mind and character; 2. the way in which something is placed or arranged, especially in relation to other things

**dissemble** (177): (v.) to conceal one's true intentions, beliefs, or feelings

**dissonance** (67): (n.) lack of harmony between two or more musical notes; a tension resulting from a combination of two or more unsuitable elements

**distress** (131): (n.) 1. extreme anxiety, sorrow, or pain; 2. troubles caused by lacking money or basic life necessities; (v.) to cause somebody anxiety, sorrow, or pain

**divergent** (29): (adj.) tending to be different or to develop in different directions

**diverse** (36): (adj.) showing a great deal of variety; very different

**divert** (153): (v.) 1. to cause someone or something to change course or turn from one direction to another; 2. to distract someone or his or her attention from something

**divisive** (85): (adj.) tending to cause disagreement or hostility between people

**divulge** (21): (v.) to make private or sensitive information known

**dogged** (137): (adj.) having or showing tenacity and grim persistence

**dogmatic** (174): (adj.) inclined to lay down principles as absolute truth

**domestic** (56): (adj.) 1. of or relating to running a home or family relations; 2. existing or occurring inside a particular country

**domicile** (133): (n.) the country that a person treats as his or her permanent home

**donate** (75): (v.) 1. to give one's money or goods for a cause, especially a charity; 2. to allow the removal of one's blood or organ(s) from one's body for transplant or transfusion

**dormant** (78): (adj.) 1. (of an animal) having normal physical functions suspended as if in a deep sleep; 2. (of a volcano) temporarily inactive; 3. (of a disease) showing no symptoms but liable to recur

**dose** (119): (n.) a quantity of a medicine or drug (or something analogous and unpleasant) recommended to be taken at a particular time; (v.) to administer a quantity of a medicine or drug to someone

**douse** (84): (v.) to pour a liquid over, to drench

**doze** (56): (v.) to sleep lightly

**drawback** (46): (n.) a feature that renders something less acceptable; a disadvantage or problem

**drone** (110): (n.) a low, continuous humming sound; (v.) to make a continuous low humming sound; to speak tediously in a monotonous tone

**dual** (90): (adj.) consisting of two parts, elements, or aspects

**durable** (30): (adj.) able to withstand wear, pressure, or damage

**dutiful** (135): (adj.) conscientiously or obediently fulfilling one's role

**dynamic** (151): (adj.) characterized by constant change, activity, or progress

# E

**eccentric** (142): (adj.) 1. unconventional and slightly strange; 2. off-center (n.) a person with unconventional and slightly strange behavior

**ecstatic** (180): (adj.) feeling overwhelming joy or excitement

**effect** (175): (n.) 1. a change that is the result of another action or cause; 2. the extent to which something succeeds or is operative; 3. an impression produced in the mind of a person; (v.) to cause something to happen or bring about

**effectual** (118): (adj.) (typically of something abstract or inanimate) successful in producing a desired or intended result; effective

**egress** (99): (n.) an exit

**elaborate** (4): (adj.) 1. having many carefully arranged or designed details; detailed in plan or design; 2. lengthy and exaggerated; (v.) to add more detail concerning something already said

**elderly** (169): (adj.) a person who is old or showing signs of aging

**election** (144): (n.) a formal organized process of selecting or being selected, typically for members of a political party

**elocution**(15): (n.) the skill of articulate and expressive speech

**elusive** (1): (adj.) hard to find, catch, or achieve

**embrace** (91): (n.) the act of holding someone closely in one's arms; (v.) 1. to hold someone closely in one's arms; 2. to accept or support a belief, theory, or change willingly and enthusiastically; 3. to include or contain something as a constituent part

**eminent** (69): (adj.) characterizing a person who is famous or respected within a certain field or profession

**empathy** (29): (n.) the ability to understand and share the feelings of another

**emphasis** (54): (n.) special importance, value, or prominence given to something

**encompass** (66): (v.) to surround or have hold within; to include comprehensively

**encounter** (134): (n.) an unexpected or casual meeting with someone or something; (v.) 1. to unexpectedly experience or be faced with something difficult or hostile; 2. to meet

**encumber** (92): (v.) to restrict or burden someone or something in such a way that free action or movement is difficult; to saddle a person with debt or mortgage; to fill or block up (a place)

**endeavor** (96): (n.) an attempt to achieve a goal; an enterprise or undertaking; (v.) to try hard to do or achieve something

**engrave** (28): (v.) to cut or carve a text or design on the surface of a hard object

**enhance** (173): (v.) to intensify, increase, or improve the quality of something

**enigma** (4): (adj.) a mystery

**enlighten** (94): (v.) to give someone greater knowledge and understanding about a subject or situation

**enormous** (76): (adj.) very large in size, quantity, or extent

**ensnare** (63): (v.) to catch in or as in a trap

**entertain** (65): (v.) 1. to provide someone with amusement or enjoyment; 2. to give attention or consideration to an idea, suggestion, or feeling

**enthrall** (93): (v.) to capture the fascinated attention of

**entice** (18): (v.) to attract or tempt by offering pleasure or advantage

**entity** (119): (n.) a thing with a distinct, independent existence

**epoch** (178): (n.) a period of time in one's life or in a historical period marked by notable events; (geology) a long time period that is divided into ages

**equitable** (75): (adj.) fair and impartial

**era** (22): (adj.) a long and distinct period of history with a particular feature or characteristic

**erode** (52): (v.) to gradually wear away (usually of water, wind, or other natural elements)

**erratic** (106): (adj.) uneven in pattern or movement

**erroneous** (94): (adj.) wrong, incorrect

**essential** (16): (adj.) absolutely necessary; extremely important

**ethereal** (180): (adj.) 1. feeling too light or delicate for the world; 2. heavenly or spiritual

**ethical** (11): (adj.) of or relating to moral principles; morally correct

**etiquette** (172): (n.) the customary code of appropriate behavior in society; manners

**euphoria** (124): (n.) a feeling or state of intense happiness or excitement

**evacuate** (116): (v.) 1. to remove someone (or several people) from a place of danger to a safe place; 2. to remove air, water, or other contents from a container

**eventual** (17): (adj.) occurring at the end or as a result of a sequence of events; ultimate; final

**evict** (24): (v.) to expel someone from a property with the assistance of the law

**evoke** (68): (v.) to bring or call to mind; to elicit a response; to invoke a spirit or deity

**exemplary** (22): (adj.) 1. serving as a desirable model; representing the best of its kind; 2. (in terms of punishment) serving as a warning or deterrent

**exhilarate** (90): (v.) to make (someone) feel very happy, animated, or elated

**exist** (78): (v.) 1. to have objective reality or being; 2. to live (under especially adverse conditions)

**exonerate** (29): (v.) to absolve someone from blame for a wrongdoing

**exorbitant** (169): (adj.) a price or amount charged that is unreasonably high

**exotic** (81): (adj.) originating in or characteristic of a foreign country; appealing because of having come from a far away place

**expanse** (10): (n.) an area of something that contains a wide and continuous surface; the distance to which something can stretch

**expel** (35): (v.) to deprive someone membership or involvement in a school or organization; to force someone to leave a place

**expenditure** (72): (n.) the action of spending funds

**express** (73): (adj.) operating at high speed; (n.) a rapid moving vehicle or delivery service; (v.) 1. to convey a thought or feeling in words or by gestures and conduct; 2. to send quickly or at high speed

**expunge** (88): (v.) to erase or remove completely

**exquisite** (149): (adj.) extremely beautiful and delicate; intensely felt; highly sensitive or discriminating

**exterior** (151): (adj.) forming, existing on, or related to the outside of something; (n.) the outer surface or structure of something

**extol** (116): (v.) to praise

**extract** (84): (n.) 1. a short passage taken from a piece of writing, music, or film; 2. a preparation containing the active ingredient of a substance in concentrated form; (v.) to remove or take out, especially by force

**extrapolate** (15): (v.) to extend the application of a method or a conclusion to an unknown trend by assuming that existing trends will continue or that similar methods will be applicable

**extravagant** (100): (adj.) lacking restraint in spending money or resources; exceeding what is reasonable or appropriate

# F

**facile** (114): (adj.) easily achieved or effortless; superficial

**facilitate** (57): (v.) to make an action or process easier

**fallacy** (77): (n.) a mistaken belief, especially one founded on unsound argument

**fallow** (177): (adj.) farmland that is ploughed and harrowed but left uncultivated to restore its fertility for crop production

**falsetto** (83): (adj.) for a male singer to sing notes higher than normal in range

**familial** (59): (adj.) of, relating to, or concerning a family and its members

**famine** (127): (n.) an extreme scarcity of food

**fanatic** (118): (n.) a person filled with excessive single-minded passion, often for an extreme religious or political cause

**fasten** (12): (v.) to close or join securely; to fix in place; to fix one's attention on something

**fate** (33): (n.) the development of events beyond a person's control, regarded as determined by a supernatural power

**fatigue** (152): (n.) extreme tiredness, especially resulting from mental or physical exertion or illness

**favor** (162): (n.) an attitude of approval or liking; 2. an act of kindness beyond what is due or necessary; (v.) to show approval or preference for

**feat** (143): (n.) an action or achievement that requires great courage or skill

**felon** (81): (n.) a person who has been convicted of a felony

**feral** (44): (adj.) (usually of an animal) in a wild state, especially after escaping domesticity or captivity

**ferocious** (96): (adj.) savagely fierce, cruel, or violent

**fiasco** (119): (n.) a complete failure, usually in a ludicrous or humiliating way

**fickle** (91): (adj.) changing one's loyalties, interests, or affection frequently

**fiction** (52): (n.) prose literature in the form of novels that describes imaginary people and events

**fidelity** (122): (n.) faithfulness to a person, cause, or belief as exhibited by continuing loyalty and support; faithfulness to a spouse

**fissure** (144): (n.) a long narrow opening made by cracking or splitting, especially in the earth; (v.) to split or crack something to cause a long narrow opening

**flabbergast** (127): (v.) to greatly surprise someone, to astonish

**flinch** (3): (n.) a fast, nervous movement of the body as an instinctive response to pain, surprise, or fear; (v.) to make a fast, nervous movement of the body as an instinctive response to pain, surprise, or fear

**fling** (127): (n.) a short period of enjoyment or wild behavior; (v.) to throw or hurl forcefully

**flourish** (12): (n.) an elaborate literary or rhetorical expression; (v.) for a person or other living organism to grow in a healthy or vigorous way, usually as the result of a favorable environment

**fluctuate** (138): (v.) to rise and fall irregularly in number or amount

**flux** (137): (n.) 1. the action or process of flowing or flowing out; 2. continuous change

**focal** (150): (adj.) of or relating to the center or main point of interest

**focus** (19): (n.) 1. the center of interest or activity; 2. the state or quality of having or producing clear visual definition; (v). 1. to adapt to the prevailing level of light so as to see clearly; 2. to pay attention to (focus on)

**forage** (166): (v.) to search widely for food or provisions

**forestall** (74): (v.) to prevent an event or action from happening by taking advance action; an act to delay

**forlorn** (103): (adj.) pitifully sad, abandoned, or lonely

**fortify** (50): (v.) to strengthen a place with defensive works so as to protect it from attack; to strengthen or invigorate someone mentally or physically

**fortitude** (166): (n.) courage in pain or adversity

**foster** (62): (v.) to encourage or promote the development of something; to develop a feeling or idea within oneself

**foundation** (38): (n.) 1. the lowest load-bearing part of a building, typically underground; 2. the underlying basis or principle for something; 3. an institution or organization with an endowment

**founder** (175): (n.) a person who establishes a business, organization, club, or institution; (v.) (usually of a ship) to fill with water and sink

**frequent** (167): (adj.) 1. occurring on many occasions, often, or habitual; 2. occurring in short distances apart; (v.) to visit a place often or habitually

**fretful** (130): (adj.) feeling or expressing distress or irritation

**frivolous** (115): (adj.) not having any serious purpose or value

**frock** (124): (n.) a woman's dress

**fruitful** (57): (adj.) producing much fruit, fertile; producing good or helpful results

**furious** (62): (adj.) extremely angry

# G

**gainsay** (114): (v.) to deny or contradict a fact or statement

**galactic** (106): (adj.) of or relating to galaxies, especially the Milky Way

**gale** (51): (n.) a very strong wind

**gape** (32): (v.) to stare with one's mouth open wide, typically in amazement or wonder; to become wide or open

**garrulous** (37): (adj.) excessively talkative in a roundabout way, especially on trivial matters

**generalize** (91): (v.) to make a general or broad statement by inferring from specific cases; to make something more widespread or common

**generate** (17): (v.) to produce; to cause a particular situation or emotion to come about

**generosity** (2): (n.) the quality of being kind, giving, and helpful

**genteel** (83): (adj.) polite, refined, or respectable, often in an affected or ostentatious way

**gesture** (143): (n.) a movement of the body, especially the hand or head, to express an idea or meaning, or to convey one's feelings or intentions; (v.) to move a part of the body, especially the hand or head, to express an idea or meaning, or to convey one's feelings or intentions

**gimmick** (17): (n.) a device or trick aimed at attracting attention, publicity, or business

**glint** (48): (n.) a small flash of light; (of one's eyes) a shine with a particular emotion; (v.) to give out or reflect small flashes of light

**gloss** (95): (n.) a shine or luster on a smooth surface; (v.) to conceal or disguise something by treating it briefly or representing it misleadingly

**glut** (37): (n.) an excessively abundant supply of something

**goad** (35): (v.) to provoke or annoy someone so as to stimulate some action or reaction

**goodwill** (114): (n.) friendly, helpful, or cooperative feelings or attitude

**gouge** (21): (v.) to scoop; to make a groove, hole, or indentation; to cut or force something out roughly or brutally

**gourmand** (122): (n.) one who enjoys eating and who often eats too much

**grant** (110): (n.) a sum of money given by an organization, especially a government, for a particular purpose; (v.) 1. to agree to give or allow (something requested) to; 2. to agree or admit to someone that something is true

**graphic** (99): (adj.) 1. of or related to visual art; 2. giving a vivid picture with explicit detail; (n.) a pictorial item displayed on a screen or stored as data

**gratification** (33): (n.) pleasure, typically when attained from the satisfaction of a desire

**gregarious** (146): (adj.) a person who is fond of company, sociable

**grotto** (164): (n.) a small picturesque cave, especially a fake one in a garden or park

**grovel** (123): (v.) to lie or move abjectly on the ground with one's face downward

**gullible** (160): (adj.) credulous; easily persuaded to believe something

# H

**harrowing** (152): (adj.) acutely distressing

**harsh** (97): (adj.) unpleasantly jarring to the senses or rough; cruel or severe

**hasten** (94): (v.) to be quick to do something; to move hurriedly

**heave** (16): (n.) a push, haul, or throw requiring great effort; (v.) 1. to push, haul, or throw with great effort; 2. to produce a sigh

**heinous** (62): (adj.) a person, wrongful act, or crime that is utterly odious or wicked

**heirloom** (103): (n.) a valuable object that has belonged to a family for several generations

**henchman** (22): (n.) a faithful supporter, especially one inclined to engage in unethical behavior by way of practice

**herculean** (108): (adj.) requiring great strength or effort

**heritage** (10): (n.) valued objects and qualities like cultural traditions, unsullied countryside, and historic buildings that have been passed down over generations

**hesitant** (33): (adj.) tentative, unsure, or slow in acting or speaking

**heterogeneous** (171): (adj.) diverse in content or in character

**hobby** (90): (n.) an activity one regularly does in one's leisure time for pleasure

**hospitable** (66): (adj.) friendly and welcoming to guests; (of an environment) pleasant and favorable for living in

**hovel** (161): (n.) a small and squalid dwelling

**humble** (146): (n.) 1. having or showing a modest or low estimate of one's importance; 2. of low social, administrative, or political rank; (v.) to lower (someone) in dignity or importance

**humidity** (58): (n.) concerning the amount of water vapor in the air

**hygiene** (23): (n.) conditions or practices conducive to maintaining health and preventing disease, especially through cleanliness

**hypocrisy** (42): (n.) the practice of claiming to have certain moral standards or beliefs to which one's behavior does not conform

# I

**ideal** (78): (adj.) satisfying one's conception of what is perfect or most suitable; (n.) a person or thing regarded as perfect; a standard of perfection or principle to be aimed at

**idiom** (127): (n.) a group of words having an established meaning that is not deducible from the words themselves

**idiosyncrasy** (30): (n.) a mode of behavior or way of thought peculiar to an individual; a distinctive characteristic peculiar to a person or thing

**ignoble** (99): (adj.) not honorable in character or in purpose

**illegible** (125): (adj.) not clear enough to be read

**illusion** (164): (n.) a thing that is likely to be wrongly perceived by the senses; a deception; a false idea or belief

**illustrate** (111): (v.) 1. to provide (a book, newspaper, etc.) with pictures; 2. to explain or make something clear by way of charts, pictures, and other visuals; 3. to serve as an example of

**imitate** (166): (v.) to take or follow as a model; to copy someone else's mannerisms; to copy or simulate

**immaculate** (5): (adj.) 1. perfectly neat or clean; 2. free of mistakes

**imminent** (99): (adj.) about to happen

**impede** (82): (v.) to delay or prevent someone or something by preventing him, her, or it

**implore** (164): (v.) to beg someone earnestly to do something

**imply** (27): (v.) to strongly suggest the truth, existence, or logical consequence of something

**impose** (63): (v.) 1. to force something unwelcome or unfamiliar to be accepted or put into place; 2. to take advantage of someone by demanding their attention or commitment

**impress** (1): (v.) 1. to make one feel admiration and respect; 2. to make a mark upon an object by using a stamp or seal; 3. to fix an idea in someone's mind

**impudent** (111): (adj.) not showing due respect for another person

**inadvertent** (32): (adj.) not resulting from or achieved through deliberate planning

**inauspicious** (175): (adj.) unfavorable; unpromising

**incentive** (49): (n.) a thing that motivates or encourages one to do something

**incidental** (151): (adj.) accompanying but not a major part of something

**incision** (121): (n.) a surgical cut made into the skin or flesh

**incite** (147): (v.) to encourage or stir up (violent or unlawful behavior)

**inclination** (108): (n.) 1. a person's natural tendency to act in a particular way; a propensity or disposition; 2. a slope or slant; 3. the angle at which a straight line or plane intersects another

**incoherent** (112): (adj.) expressed in an incomprehensible or confusing way

**incorrigible** (123): (adj.) (of a person or his or her tendencies) unable to be corrected, reformed, or improved

**incredulous** (71): (adj.) a person who is unable or unwilling to believe something

**incur** (98): (v.) to become subject to (something unwelcome or unpleasant) as a result of one's own behavior or actions

**indicate** (173): (v.) 1. to point out or show; to briefly state something; to gesture; to show or register a reading (of a meter or gauge); 2. to suggest or show signs of a necessary course of action

**indict** (161): (v.) to formally accuse or charge with a serious crime

**indignation** (166): (n.) anger or annoyance caused by what is perceived as unfair treatment

**indulgent** (65): (adj.) having or indicating a tendency to be overly generous or lenient with someone

**inevitable** (165): (adj.) certain to occur; unavoidable

**inextricable** (75): (adj.) impossible to disentangle or separate; impossible to escape from

**infuse** (155): (v.) to fill or pervade; to instill a quality in someone or something

**ingenious** (121): (adj.) clever, original, and inventive

**inhabit** (175): (v.) (of a person or animal) to live in a particular place or geographic region

**inhibit** (151): (v.) to hinder, restrain, or prevent an action or process; to make someone self-conscious and unable to act in a natural way

**iniquity** (109): (n.) immoral or grossly unfair behavior

**initiate** (140): (v.) 1. to cause something to begin; 2. to admit someone into a secret society or group

**innate** (177): (adj.) inborn or natural

**innumerable** (106): (adj.) too many to be counted (used often in exaggeration)

**inquisitive** (70): (adj.) curious and asking many questions

**inscribe** (38): (v.) to write or carve words or symbols on something, especially as a permanent record

**insinuate** (71): (v.) to suggest or hint at (something bad or reprehensible) in an unpleasant way

**inspect** (138): (v.) to examine someone or something closely to assess condition and/or shortcomings

**inspire** (157): (v.) to fill someone with the urge or ability to feel or do something

**instance** (65): (n.) an example or single occurrence of something

**instantaneous** (103): (adj.) occurring or done immediately

**instigate** (156): (v.) to bring about or initiate an action or event; to provoke

**insurgent** (42): (adj.) rising in active revolt; (n.) a rebel or revolutionary

**intellectual** (91): (adj.) of or relating to use of mental faculties; possessing highly developed mental faculties; (n.) a person with highly developed mental faculties

**intercept** (132): (n.) an act or instance of obstructing someone or something so as to prevent it from continuing to a destination; (v.) to obstruct someone or something so as to prevent it from continuing to a destination

**intersect** (31): (v.) to divide something by passing or lying across it

**intricate** (42): (adj.) very complicated or detailed

**intriguing** (9): (adj.) arousing curiosity or interest; fascinating

**invade** (47): (v.) for an armed forces to enter a region and occupy it; to enter an area in large numbers; for a disease to spread into an organism or body part; to encroach or intrude on

**invariable** (13): (adj.) unchanging

**invincible** (5): (adj.) too powerful to be overcome or defeated

**irrational** (142): (adj.) not logical or reasonable

# J

**jeer** (49): (n.) a rude, mocking remark; (v.) to make rude and mocking comments, typically in a rude manner

**jeopardy** (56): (n.) danger of loss, harm, or failure

**jovial** (86): (adj.) cheerful and friendly

**joyous** (113): (adj.) full of happiness and excitement

**jubilant** (144): (adj.) feeling or expressing great happiness

**jubilee** (178) : (n.) a special anniversary of an event (especially 25 years, 50 years, etc.)

**judge** (13): (n.) an individual with the authority to decide cases in courts of law; an individual who decides the results of competition or infractions of rules; (v.) 1. to form an opinion or conclusion about; 2. to decide a case in court; 3. to decide the results of a competition

**judicious** (30): (adj.) having done or showing good judgment or sense

**juncture** (104): (n.) a particular point in events or time; a place where things join

# K

**kiln** (101): (n.) a furnace or oven for burning, baking, or drying, especially one for firing pottery

**kindle** (159): (v.) to light or set on fire; to arouse or inspire

**kinetic** (178): (adj.) of, concerning, or relating to motion

**laceration** (123): (n.) a deep cut in the skin or flesh

# L

**lament** (15): (n.) 1. a passionate expression of grief or sorrow; 2. a song or poem expressing sorrow; 3. an expression of disappointment; (v.) to mourn a person's death

**languid** (3): (adj.) 1. concerning a person, manner, or gesture showing a lack of exertion or effort; lacking energy; 2. a time period that's peaceful or pleasantly lazy

**laudable** (157): (adj.) praiseworthy; commendable

**lavish** (5): (adj.) extremely rich, luxurious, or elaborate; characterizing a person who is very generous or extravagant; given to profusion; (v.) to heap generous quantities upon

**lax** (9): (adj.) not strict, severe, or careful; loose; relaxed

**legitimate** (60): (adj.) conforming to the law or rules; (v.) to justify or make lawful

**lenient** (35): (adj.) (of punishment or a person in authority) tending to be permissive, merciful or tolerant

**lesion** (176): (n.) part of tissue or an organ that has suffered a cut, wound, ulcer, or abscess

**lethargic** (34): (adj.) sluggish, apathetic

**levity** (126): (n.) humor or frivolity; often treating a serious matter in a manner lacking due respect

**lewd** (7): (adj.) offensive and crude in a sexual way

**lexicon** (112): (n.) the vocabulary of a person, language, or branch of knowledge

**liberate** (168): (v.) to set someone free from a situation (esp. slavery or imprisonment); to free one from a situation that limits free thought or expression or has rigid social conventions; to free from enemy occupation

**liberty** (21): (n.) 1. the state of being free within society; the state of not being incarcerated or enslaved; 2. the power to act as one pleases

**limber** (32): (adj.) lithe; supple

**linchpin** (94): (n.) a person or thing vital to an enterprise or organization

**lithe** (95): (adj.) (especially of a person's body) thin, supple, graceful

**lore** (107): (n.) a body of traditions and knowledge on a subject or held by a particular group, typically transmitted by word of mouth

**lull** (39): (n.) a temporary interval of quiet or lack of activity; (v.) to calm or send to sleep typically with soothing sounds or movements

**luminous** (66): (adj.) full of light; shedding light; bright or shining, especially in the dark

**lunge** (157): (n.) a sudden forward thrust of the body typically to attack someone or to seize something; (v.) to make a sudden forward thrust with a part of the body or a weapon

# M

**magnetic** (154): (adj.) 1. capable of being attracted by or acquiring the properties of a magnet; 2. very attractive or alluring

**magnitude** (149): (n.) 1. the size or extent of something; 2. size

**malevolent** (126): (adj.) having a desire to harm or do evil to others

**malicious** (80): (adj.) characterized by an intention to do harm

**malign** (50): (adj.) evil in nature or effect, malevolent; (v.) to speak about another in a spitefully cruel manner

**mandatory** (145): (adj.) required by law or rules; compulsory

**maneuver** (34): (n.) a movement or series of moves that requires skill and care; 2. a carefully planned scheme or action; (v.) 1. to move skillfully or carefully; 2. to carefully guide or manipulate something or someone to achieve an end

**manifold** (48): (adj.) many and various

**manipulate** (94): (v.) 1. to handle or control (a tool, mechanism, etc.) in a skillful manner; to edit, alter, or move text or data on a computer; 2. to control or influence a person or situation cleverly, unscrupulously, or unfairly; to alter data or present statistics so as to mislead

**manufacture** (40): (n.) the making of articles on a large scale using machinery; (v.) 1. to make something on a large scale using machinery; 2. to invent or fabricate evidence or a story

**mar** (100): (v.) to impair the appearance, to disfigure; to impair the quality of

**margin** (113): (n.) 1. the edge or border of something; 2. the amount by which a thing is won or falls short

**marvel** (141): (n.) an astonishing or wonderful person or thing; (v.) to be filled with wonder or astonishment

**massive** (70): (adj.) exceptionally large, heavy, solid, or important

**matinee** (30): (n.) a daytime theater performance or movie showing

**mature** (50): (adj.) fully developed physically; full-grown; (v.) to become physically or emotionally developed

**mayhem** (20): (adj.) damaging or violent disorder; chaos

**meager** (42): (adj.) lacking in quantity or quality

**medley** (25): (n.) a varied mixture of people or things; a mixture

**meek** (43): (adj.) quiet, gentle, submissive; easily imposed upon

**melancholy** (2): (adj.) having or feeling sad and pensive; (n.) a feeling of sadness, typically with no apparent cause

**melodramatic** (24): (adj.) overly emotional or dramatic

**memento** (125): (n.) an object kept as a reminder or souvenir of a person or event

**mendicant** (96): (adj.) given to begging; (n.) a beggar

**menial** (122): (adj.) (of work) not requiring much skill and of little prestige

**mercy** (47): (n.) compassion or forgiveness shown toward someone whom it is within one's power to punish or harm

**merge** (87): (v.) to combine or cause to combine into a single entity

**merger** (108): (n.) a combination of two things (usually companies) into one

**merit** (87): (n.) the quality of being good or worthy; (v.) to deserve or be worthy of (typically a reward, punishment, or attention)

**mettle** (1): (n.) one's ability to manage a difficult situation in an enthusiastic and spirited way

**migrate** (125): (v.) to move from one region or habitat to another (often seasonally); to move from one country to another; to move from one part of something to another

**mimic** (28): (v.) to imitate someone's actions or words, typically with an attempt to ridicule

**miscellaneous** (144): (adj.) (of items or people) of various types or from different sources

**mischief** (69): (n.) playful behavior often involved in troublemaking and usually exhibited by children; playfulness intended to tease, mock, and create trouble; harm or trouble caused by something

**miserable** (86): (adj.) 1. concerning one who is or a situation that is extremely unhappy or uncomfortable; 2. pitiably small or inadequate

**mitigate** (175): (v.) to make less painful, serious, or severe

**modicum** (45): (n.) a small quantity of a particular thing, especially one that is valuable

**monarch** (171): (n.) a sovereign head of state such as a king, queen, or emperor

**mores** (113): (n.) the fundamental customs and conventions of a community

**mortgage** (4): (n.) the charging of property (usually a home) by a debtor to a creditor as security for a debt; (v.) to convey property to a creditor as security on a loan

**motivate** (153): (v.) 1. to provide someone with an objective for doing something; 2. to stimulate one's interest in doing something

**mundane** (149): (adj.) lacking excitement or interest; dull

**munificent** (84): (adj.) (of a gift or sum of money) greater or more generous than is necessary

**murky** (50): (adj.) dark and gloomy, usually because of thick mist

**muster** (140): (v.) to summon up a feeling, attitude, or response

**mute** (141): (adj.) refraining from speech or temporarily speechless; (n.) a person without the power of speech; (v.) to deaden, muffle, or soften the sound of

# N

**narrate** (54): (v.) to give a spoken or written account of something

**nebula** (173): (n.) 1. a cloud of gas in outer space; 2. any bright spot in the night sky

**negative** (118): (adj.) 1. consisting in or characterized by the absence rather than the presence of distinguishing features; 2. not desirable or optimistic; 3. characterizing a number less than zero

**negligent** (76): (adj.) failing to take proper care in doing something

**negotiation** (32): (n.) discussion aimed at reaching an agreement

**neophyte** (29): (adj.) a person who is new to a subject, skill, or belief

**neutral** (168): (adj.) 1. not helping or supporting either side in a conflict; 2. having no strongly marked positive or biased characteristics; 3. (physics) neither positively nor negatively charged; 4. (chemistry) neither acid nor alkaline

**newfangled** (115): (adj.) different from what one is used to; objectionably new

**noisome** (92): (adj.) having an extremely offensive smell; disagreeable; unpleasant

**nomad** (124): (n.) a person or a member of a people who travel from place to place

**nonessential** (53): (adj.) not absolutely necessary

**notice** (102): (n.) 1. attention, observation; 2. notification or warning of something, especially to allow preparations to be made; 3. a displayed sheet giving news or information; (v.) to become aware of

**notorious** (20): (adj.) famous or well-known, especially for a bad deed or quality

**novice** (155): (n.) a person who is new or inexperienced in a field or situation

**noxious** (102): (adj.) harmful, poisonous, or very unpleasant

**nucleus** (136): (n.) the central and most important part of an object, group, or movement, forming a basis for its development and growth

**null** (80): (adj.) 1. having no legal or binding force; invalid; 2. having or associated with the value zero

**nutritious** (74): (adj.) nourishing and efficient as food

# O

**oasis** (117): (n.) a fertile spot in a desert where water is found

**oath** (61): (n.) a solemn promise, often invoking a divine witness, regarding one's future behavior or action

**obdurate** (3): (adj.) stubbornly refusing to change one's opinion or course of action

**obese** (39): (adj.) grossly fat or overweight

**objectionable** (116): (adj.) arousing distaste or opposition; unpleasant or offensive

**objective** (26): (adj.) not influenced by personal feelings; (n.) a thing aimed at or sought; a goal

**obligate** (160): (v.) to require, especially legally or morally

**oblige** (137): (v.) to make someone morally or legally bound to an action or course of action

**obtuse** (180): (adj.) 1. annoyingly insensitive or slow to understand; 2. an angle whose measure is greater than 90 degrees and less than 180 degrees

**obvious** (5): (adj.) easily perceived or understood; easily apparent; self-evident; blatant

**occupy** (1): (v.) 1. to reside or have one's business in; to be situated in; to fill or take up; to hold (a job); 2. (military) to enter, take control of, and remain in a place

**odious** (54): (adj.) extremely unpleasant; repulsive

**official** (23): (adj.) relating to an authority or body and its duties, actions, or responsibilities; (n.) a person holding public office and having official duties

**olfactory** (79): (adj.) of or relating to the sense of smell

**ominous** (130): (adj.) giving the impression that something bad or unpleasant is about to happen

**omit** (64): (v.) to leave out or exclude, either intentionally or deliberately

**onus** (72): (n.) used to refer to something that is one's duty or responsibility

**operate** (115): (v.) 1. to control the functioning of a machine, process, or system; 2. to manage and run a business; 3. to perform a surgical procedure

**opinion** (113): (n.) a view or judgment formed about something, not necessarily based on fact or knowledge; a formal statement by an expert rendering advice or judgment on a matter

**optimal** (92): (adj.) best or most favorable

**opulent** (27): (adj.) ostentatiously rich and luxurious; extremely lavish

**oration** (111): (n.) a formal speech, ordinarily one that is given on a ceremonial occasion

**ordeal** (28): (n.) a painful or horrific experience, often one that is protracted

**ostentatious** (168): (adj.) characterized by pretentious display meant to attract attention

**ostracize** (161): (v.) to exclude someone from a group or society

# P

**pacifist** (139): (n.) one who believes war and violence are unjustifiable

**palatable** (87): (adj.) 1. food or drink that is pleasant to taste; 2. an action or proposal that is acceptable or satisfactory

**paltry** (112): (adj.) a small or meager amount of something

**panorama** (171): (n.) 1. an unbroken view of a whole region surrounding an observer; 2. a complete survey or presentation of a sequence of events or a subject

**paragon** (3): (n.) a person or thing regarded as the perfect example of something

**pariah** (63): (n.) an outcast

**pathetic** (103): (adj.) arousing pity, especially through vulnerability or sadness; miserable; inadequate

**pathology** (180): (n.) the science of the causes and effects of disease

**patron** (113): (n.) 1. a person who gives financial support to another individual, a cause, an organization, or an activity; 2. a customer (typically a regular one)

**peculiar** (32): (adj.) 1. strange or odd; unusual; 2. belonging exclusively to

**penchant** (58): (n.) a strong and habitual liking for something or tendency to do something

**perceptive** (169): (adj.) exhibiting sensitive insight

**pernicious** (33): (adj.) having a harmful effect, especially in a harmful or subtle way

**perseverance** (31): (n.) steadfastness in doing something despite difficulty or delay in achieving success

**personable** (164): (adj.) (of a person) having a pleasant manner or appearance

**pester** (63): (v.) to trouble or annoy someone with frequent interruptions or requests

**phobia** (74): (n.) an extreme or irrational fear of or aversion to something

**physiognomy** (150): (n.) a person's facial features or expression, especially when regarded as indicative of character or ethnic origin; the art of judging character from facial characteristics

**pigment** (109): (n.) the natural coloring of plant or animal tissue; a substance used for coloring or painting, especially a dry powder that, when mixed with water or oil, forms a paint or ink

**pithy** (2): (adj.) brief and forceful in expression

**pittance** (89): (n.) a very small or inadequate amount of money paid to someone as an allowance or wage

**placid** (52): (adj.) a person or animal not easily upset or excited; (of a place or stretch of water) calm and peaceful, with little movement or activity

**plausible** (51): (adj.) an argument or statement that seems reasonable or logical

**plead** (176): (v.) 1. to present an emotional appeal or to beg; 2. to present and argue for a particular position in a public context, especially a court

**pledge** (8): (n.) 1. a solemn promise or understanding; 2. a promise of a donation to a charity; (v.) 1. to commit by solemn promise; 2. to formally declare or promise that something will be the case

**plentiful** (168): (adj.) existing in great quantity; abundant

**pliable** (44): (adj.) 1. easily bent; flexible; 2. easily influenced

**plight** (27): (n.) a difficult, dangerous, or unfortunate situation

**poach** (12): (v.) 1. to illegally hunt or catch; 2. to acquire in a secretive way

**poised** (90): (adj.) having a composed and self-assured manner

**policy** (129): (n.) a course or principle of action adopted or proposed by a government, party, business, or individual

**polish** (162): (n.) a substance that gives an object a smooth and shiny surface when the latter is rubbed; (v.) to make the surface of something smooth and shiny by rubbing it

**pompous** (121): (adj.) affectedly and irritatingly self-important or grand

**ponder** (170): (v.) to think carefully about something before making a decision

**populate** (76): (v.) to fill with people; to form the population of a particular town, area, or country

**portentous** (75): (adj.) ominously significant or important; momentous

**portly** (130): (adj.) stout or fat (usually in reference to a man)

**pose** (103): (n.) 1. a way of standing or sitting, usually adopted in order to be photographed, drawn, or painted; 2. a particular way of behavior adopted in order to give others a false impression or to impress others; (v.) 1. to present or constitute (a problem, danger, or difficulty); 2. to assume a particular attitude in order to be photographed, drawn, or painted; 3. to behave affectedly in order to impress others

**potent** (19): (adj.) having great power, influence, or effect

**pragmatic** (161): (adj.) practical; sensible; realistic

**praise** (95): (n.) the expression of approval or admiration of someone or something; (v.) to express warm approval of

**precarious** (87): (adj.) not securely held in position; dependent on chance, uncertain

**precocious** (8): (adj.) (of a child) having developed certain skills or abilities at an earlier age than usual; indicative of early development

**predate** (46): (v.) to exist or occur at a date earlier than something

**predecessor** (104): (n.) a person who held a job or office before another; a thing that has been followed or replaced by another

**predicament** (102): (n.) a difficult, unpleasant, or embarrassing situation

**prediction** (83): (n.) a forecast or estimation of future events

**premonition** (7): (n.) a strong feeling that something (typically unpleasant) is about to happen

**preponderance** (68): (n.) the fact or quality of being great in number, quantity, extent, or importance

**preposterous** (71): (adj.) absurd or ridiculous; contrary to common sense

**presage** (40): (n.) a sign or warning that something (typically bad) will happen; an omen or portent; (v.) (of an event) to be a sign that something (typically bad) will happen

**prestidigitation** (76): (n.) slight of hand; legerdemain

**presumptuous** (62): (adj.) (concerning a person and his or her behavior) failing to observe the limits of what is deemed appropriate

**pretentious** (66): (adj.) attempting to impress by assuming greater importance, talent, culture, or credibility than one actually possesses

**prevalent** (130): (adj.) widespread over a particular area or at a particular time

**prevaricate** (110): (v.) to speak or act in an evasive way

**prey** (139): (n.) 1. an animal that is hunted or killed by another for food; 2. a person easily injured or taken advantage of; (v.) 1. to hunt and kill for food; 2. to take advantage of

**priceless** (110): (adj.) so precious that its value cannot be determined

**primitive** (85): (adj.) 1. concerning the character of an early stage in the evolutionary or historical development of something; 2. not developed or derived from anything else

**prior** (129): (adj.) existing or occurring before in time, order, or importance

**process** (69): (n.) series of actions or steps taken in order to achieve a particular end; (v.) to perform a series of mechanical or chemical operations on something in order to change or preserve it

**procrastinate** (86): (v.) to delay or postpone action; to put off doing something

**procure** (13): (v.) to obtain something, usually with effort

**proficient** (55): (adj.) competent or skilled in doing or using something

**profound** (22): (adj.) 1. (of a state, quality, or emotion) very great or intense; 2. (concerning a statement or person) having or showing great knowledge or insight

**progressive** (67): (adj.) 1. developing in stages; proceeding step by step; 2. favoring or implementing social reform or new, liberal ideas

**prolific** (177): (adj.) 1. a plant animal or person producing much fruit, foliage, or offspring; 2. an author, artist, or composer who produces a great deal; 3. present in large numbers or quantities

**prologue** (167): (n.) an introductory section of a literary work or musical piece

**prolong** (138): (v.) to extend the duration of

**propaganda** (77): (n.) information that is typically biased or misleading that is used to promote or publicize a particular political cause or point of view

**prose** (85): (n.) written or spoken language in its typical form, without metrical structure

**prosperous** (136): (adj.) flourishing financially; successful in material terms

**protrude** (129): (v.) to extend beyond or above a surface

**provocative** (81): (adj.) deliberately evoking annoyance, anger, or another strong reaction; deliberately attempting to arouse sexual desire

**prudish** (67): (adj.) having the tendency to be easily shocked by matters related to sex or nudity

**pugnacious** (43): (adj.) eager to argue, quarrel, or fight

**pungent** (137): (adj.) having a sharply strong smell or taste

**pursuit** (122): (n.) the act of following or chasing someone or something

**putrid** (60): (adj.) characteristic of rotting matter and having a foul smell

# Q

**quaint** (156): (adj.) attractively unusual or old-fashioned, often resembling small town or rustic life

**qualm** (31): (n.) an uneasy feeling of doubt, worry, or fear, especially about one's own conduct; a misgiving

**quarantine** (44): (n.) a state, period, or place of isolation in which people or animals that have arrived from elsewhere or been exposed to infectious or contagious diseases have been placed; (v.) to impose isolation on a person or animal (typically one carrying a disease)

**quell** (37): (v.) to put an end to rebellion or disorder, usually by force

**quench** (148): (v.) to satisfy one's thirst by drinking; to satisfy a desire

# R

**rancid** (158): (adj.) (of foods) smelling or tasting unpleasant as a result of being old or stale

**random** (45): (adj.) made, done, or chosen without method or conscious thought

**rankle** (161): (v.) to cause persistent irritation, annoyance, or resentment

**ransack** (80): (v.) to move hurriedly through a place stealing things and causing damage

**ratify** (40): (v.) to sign or give formal consent to a law, agreement, or treaty to render it valid

**rational** (26): (adj.) based on accordance with reason or logic

**ravenous** (79): (adj.) extremely hungry

**raze** (98): (v.) to completely destroy (a building, town, or other site)

**realize** (36): (v.) 1. to become fully aware of something as fact; 2. to cause something desired or anticipated to happen; 3. to give actual or physical form to an idea or plan; 4. to make money or a profit from a transaction

**rebuff** (126): (v.) to reject someone or something in an abrupt or ungracious manner

**reception** (101): (n.) 1. the action or process of receiving something sent, given, or inflicted; 2. a formal social occasion held to welcome someone or to celebrate a particular event; 3. the area in a hotel, office, or establishment where guests and visitors are greeted and dealt with

**recognize** (112): (v.) 1. to identify (someone or something) from having a previous encounter; 2. to acknowledge the existence, validity, or legality of

**rectify** (156): (v.) to set something right; to correct

**redress** (31): (n.) a remedy or compensation for a wrong or grievance; (v.) to remedy or set right an undesirable situation

**reduce** (37): (v.) to make or become smaller in size, amount, or degree

**redundant** (174): (adj.) 1. superfluous; no longer needed to be useful or functioning; 2. words or data that can be omitted without loss of meaning

**reel** (6): (n.) a cylinder upon which thread, film, wire, or other materials can be wound; (v.) to feel disoriented, bewildered, or off-kilter from a setback

**reform** (60): (n.) the action of making changes in something (typically a social, political, or economic institution or practice) in order to improve it (v.) to make changes in something (typically a social, political, or economic institution or practice) in order to improve it

**refrain** (82): (v.) to stop oneself from doing something

**rejuvenate** (146): (v.) to make someone or something feel fresher or younger

**relinquish** (18): (v.) to voluntarily give up

**relish** (98): (v.) to enjoy greatly

**reminiscence** (20): (n.) a story or recollection of past events

**remiss** (152) : (adj.) lacking care or attention to duty; negligent

**render** (170): (v.) 1. to provide or give a service or help; 2. to cause to become or make; 3. to represent or depict artistically

**rendezvous** (125): (n.) a meeting at a specific time and place (typically between two people)

**renovate** (10): (v.) to restore something old into a good state

**repetitive** (174): (adj.) characterized by doing something over and over again or something happening over and over again often in a tiresome way

**replica** (67): (n.) an exact copy or model of something, often on a smaller scale

**repose** (7): (n.) a state of rest, sleep, or tranquility, composure; (v.) to be lying, sitting, or at rest in a particular place

**repress** (105): (v.) to subdue someone or something by force; to restrain, prevent, or inhibit

**repudiate** (117): (v.) to refuse to accept or be associated with; to deny the truth or validity of

**repugnant** (64): (adj.) extremely distasteful; unacceptable

**repulse** (21): (v.) 1. to drive back an attack or an enemy by force; 2. to cause someone to feel intense distaste and aversion

**request** (46): (n.) an act of asking politely or formally for something; (v.) to ask politely or formally for something

**requisition** (77): (n.) an official order laying claim to the use of property or materials; (v.) to demand the use or supply of, especially by official order and for military or public use

**rescind** (16): (v.) to revoke, cancel, or appeal (a law, order, or judgment)

**residual** (154): (adj.) remaining after the greater part is gone; (n.) the remaining amount after other things have been subtracted or allowed for

**restitution** (132): (n.) 1. the act of returning something lost or stolen to its proper owner; 2. recompense for loss or injury; 3. the restoration of something to its original state

**resuscitate** (96): (v.) to revive someone from unconsciousness or apparent death; to make an idea or enterprise vigorous again

**retaliation** (25): (n.) the action of returning an attack; a counterattack

**retort** (133): (n.) a sharp, angry, or wittily incisive response to a remark; (v.) to respond to a remark or accusation in a witty or incisive manner

**retract** (107): (v.) to draw or be drawn back in; withdraw

**retribution** (163): (n.) punishment inflicted on someone as vengeance for a wrong or criminal act

**revel** (158): (v.) to enjoy oneself in a noisy and lively way; to delight in

**revelation** (23): (n.) a surprising and previously unknown fact, typically made or revealed in a dramatic way

**ridicule** (19): (n.) the subjection of someone or something to contemptuous or dismissive language or behavior; (v.) to subject someone or something to contemptuous and dismissive language or behavior

**rife** (148): (adj.) (especially of something undesirable or harmful) of common occurrence; widespread

**robust** (44): (adj.) strong and healthy; vigorous

319

**rotund** (15): (adj.) plump; round or spherical

**routine** (47): (adj.) performed as part of regular procedure; (n.) a sequence of actions regularly followed

**ruddy** (93): (adj.) having a healthy red or reddish color; (v.) to make reddish in color

**rudimentary** (39): (adj.) involving or limited to basic principles

**rue** (156): (n.) repentance, regret, compassion, or pity; (v.) to bitterly regret

**ruffle** (128): (v.) to disturb the smoothness or tranquility of; to disorder or disarrange
**ruminate** (9): (v.) to think deeply about something

**rupture** (120): (v.) (usually of a pipe, vessel, or bodily organ) to break or burst suddenly

# S

**sabbatical** (142): (n.) a period of paid leave granted for study or travel

**sacred** (68): (adj.) 1. religious rather than secular; 2. something connected with God or the gods and thus worthy of veneration; 3. regarded with great reverence and respect

**sage** (73): (adj.) wise; (n.) a profoundly wise (and often old) person

**salutation** (48): (n.) a gesture or utterance made as a greeting or acknowledgement of another's arrival or departure

**sanction** (167): (n.) 1. a threatened penalty for disobeying a law or rule; 2. official approval or permission for an action; (v.) 1. to give official approval or permission for an action; 2. to impose a penalty on

**sanitary** (67): (adj.) of or relating to conditions affecting health or hygiene

**sate** (136): (v.) to fully satisfy a desire or appetite

**savor** (7): (v.) to taste, drink, or enjoy something thoroughly and completely

**scalpel** (114): (n.) a surgical knife

**scanty** (66): (adj.) small or insufficient in quantity or amount

**scarce** (95): (adj.) (of food, money, or another resource) insufficient for the demand; occurring in small numbers or quantities

**scathing** (78): (adj.) severely critical or scornful

**schism** (179): (n.) a split or division between strongly opposed parties or groups within a party caused by differences of opinion or belief

**scour** (121): (n.) the action of cleaning or brightening the surface of something by rubbing it hard, typically with an abrasive or a detergent; (v.) to clean or brighten the surface of something by rubbing it hard, typically with an abrasive or a detergent; 2. to subject a place or text to a thorough search in order to try to locate something

**scourge** (119): (n.) a person or thing that causes great trouble or suffering

**seclude** (90): (v.) to keep (someone) away from other people

**sedate** (12): (v.) calm, dignified, and unhurried; quiet and dull

**seer** (71): (n.) a person who is able to see what the future holds

**sentry** (71): (n.) a soldier stationed to keep guard over a place

**sequential** (150): (adj.) forming or following in a logical order

**settle** (38): (v.) 1. to resolve or reach an agreement an argument or problem; 2. to adopt a more steady and secure lifestyle, usually with a job and a home; 3. to sit or come to rest in a comfortable position

**severe** (139): (adj.) very great or intense; very strict or harsh

**shirk** (109): (v.) to avoid or neglect a duty or responsibility

**shrewd** (121): (adj.) having or showing sharp powers of judgment; astute

**shun** (80): (v.) to persistently avoid, ignore, or reject someone or something through antipathy or caution

**simulate** (131): (v.) to imitate the appearance or character of

**sluggard** (18): (n.) a lazy person

**smite** (72): (n.) a heavy blow with a weapon or from the hand; (v.) 1. to strike with a firm blow; 2. to affect severely

**solid** (116): (adj.) 1. firm and stable in shape, not liquid or fluid; 2. not hollow; 3. dependable, reliable; (n.) a substance that is firm and stable in shape and not a liquid or fluid

**somber** (61): (adj.) dark or dull in color and tone; gloomy

**somnolent** (77): (adj.) sleepy or drowsy

**soothsayer** (26): (n.) a person supposedly able to see the future

**souvenir** (43): (adj.) a thing kept as a reminder of a person, place, or event

**sovereign** (63): (adj.) possessing supreme or ultimate power; (n.) a supreme ruler, especially a monarch

**specify** (174): (v.) to identify or state a fact clearly and definitely

**specter** (23): (n.) a ghost

**speculate** (89): (v.) to form a theory about something without having firm evidence

**splendid** (117): (adj.) magnificent; very impressive

**spontaneous** (146): (adj.) performed by impulse and without any planning or premeditation

**squalid** (169): (adj.) 1. a place that is filthy and unpleasant, usually because of neglect or poverty; 2. exhibiting a lack of moral standards

**stalemate** (151): (n.) a situation where further action or progress by opposing parties seems impossible; a draw

**stamina** (58): (n.) the ability to sustain prolonged physical or mental effort

**stampede** (47): (n.) a sudden panicked rush of a number of horses, cattle, or other animals; (v.) (of horses, cattle, or other animals) to rush wildly in a sudden mass panic

**stance** (22): (n.) 1. the attitude of a person or organization toward something; 2. the way in which someone stands; posture

**stanza** (176): (n.) a group of lines forming the basic metrical unit of a poem

**stature** (34): (n.) 1. a person's natural height; 2.importance or reputation gained by ability or achievement

**statute** (72): (n.) a written law passed by a legislative body; a rule of an organization or institution

**stealthy** (20): (adj.) behavior done in a surreptitious manner so as to not be seen or heard

**stern** (41): (adj.) describing a person who is serious and unrelenting, especially in matters of assertion of authority and exertion of discipline; strict and severe; (n.) the rearmost part of a ship or boat

**stifle** (81): (v.) to suffocate; to stop one from acting on an emotion; to restrain or prevent

**stolid** (69): (adj.) characterizing one who is calm and showing little emotion

**strategy** (167): (n.) a plan of action or policy designed with a specific aim

**strenuous** (137): (adj.) requiring or using great exertion

**strive** (120): (v.) to make great efforts to achieve or obtain something

**stupefy** (68): (v.) to astonish and shock, often to the point of being unable to think or act properly

**sturdy** (16): (adj.) strong and solidly built; showing resistance and determination

**subdue** (61): (v.) to overcome, calm, or bring under control (a feeling or person)

**submerge** (177): (v.) 1. to place under water or some other liquid; 2. to completely cover or obscure

**submissive** (18): (adj.) ready to conform to the commands or will of others

**subsidy** (126): (n.) a sum of money granted by the government or a public body to assist an industry or business so that the price of a commodity will remain affordable

**subsist** (13): (v.) to maintain or support oneself, generally at a minimal level

**succumb** (132): (v.) to fail to resist (pressure, temptation, or some other force)

**suffice** (104): (v.) to be enough or adequate; to meet the needs of

**summit** (100): (n.) 1. the highest point of a hill or mountain; 2. a meeting between heads of government

**superficial** (41): (adj.) existing or occurring on the surface; not thorough, deep, or complete; shallow

**supreme** (152): (n.) superior to all others; strongest, most important, or most powerful; very great or intense

**surly** (158): (adj.) bad-tempered and unfriendly

**surrogate** (173): (n.) a substitute, especially another person deputizing for another in a specific role or office

**suspend** (149): (v.) 1. to temporarily prevent from continuing to be in force or in effect; to defer or delay an action or judgment; 2. to hang something from somewhere

**swagger** (163): (n.) a confident, arrogant, or aggressive walk; (v.) to walk in a confident, arrogant, or aggressive way

**swarthy** (88): (adj.) dark-skinned

**swivel** (28): (n.) a coupling between two parts that enables one to revolve about the other; (v.) to turn about a point or axis on a coupling between two parts that enables one to revolve about the other

**symbol** (14): (n.) a thing that represents or stands for something else, especially a material object that stands for something else

**synopsis** (144): (n.) a brief summary or general survey of something

# T

**tacit** (104): (adj.) understood or implied without being stated

**taciturn** (48): (adj.) a person who is reserved and uncommunicative in speech; saying little

**tact** (53): (n.) sensitivity in dealing with others or with difficult issues

**tailor** (70): (n.) a person whose occupation is to adjust clothing (suits, pants, jackets) to fit individual customers; (v.) 1. to make clothes fit individual customers; 2. to make or adapt for a particular purpose or person

**tamper** (89): (v.) to interfere with something in order to cause damage or make unauthorized alterations

**tangible** (25): (adj.) 1. perceptible by touch; 2. clear and definite, real

**tardy** (61): (adj.) delaying or delayed beyond the expected time; late

**tedious** (10): (adj.) extremely long, slow, or dull; tiresome; monotonous

**telepathic** (6): (adj.) capable of transmitting thoughts to people without knowing their thoughts; psychic

**temperance** (170): (adj.) moderation or self-restraint, especially from drinking

**tempt** (15): (v.) to entice; to allure; to try to entice one to do something that he or she finds attractive but that he or she also knows is wrong

**tenacious** (84): (adj.) tending to keep a firm hold of something; not readily relinquishing a position, principle, or course of action

**tentative** (82): (adj.) not certain or fixed; provisional

**terminate** (38): (v.) to bring to an end

**terrestrial** (53): (adj.) relating to the land or the Earth

**texture** (12): (n.) the feel, quality, or appearance of a substance or surface; the quality created by a combination of elements in a musical or literary work

**thaw** (162): (v.) (usually of ice or snow) to become liquid or soft as a result of warming

**theoretical** (97): (adj.) concerned with or involving the abstract ideas of a field or study rather than its practical application

**thorough** (52): (adj.) complete with regard to every detail

**thrive** (159): (v.) to flourish; to grow vigorously

**thwart** (155): (v.) to prevent someone from accomplishing something; to stymie

**timid** (148): (adj.) showing a lack of courage or confidence; frightened

**timorous** (147): (adj.) showing or suffering from nervousness, fear, or lack of confidence

**token** (7): (n.) an object serving as a visible or tangible representation of a fact; a characteristic or distinctive sign or mark of something

**tolerate** (19): (v.) to allow the existence, practice, or occurrence of something; to be able to withstand something, to endure or accept

**tome** (13): (n.) a book, particularly one that is large, heavy, and scholarly

**torpid** (180): (adj.) mentally or physically exhaustive; lethargic

**tortuous** (171): (adj.) twisting or winding

**trade** (131): (n.) 1. the action of buying and selling goods and services; 2. a job typically requiring manual skills and specialization; (v.) 1. to buy and sell goods and services; 2. to exchange something for something else, typically as a commercial transaction

**tradition** (79): (n.) the transmission of customs and beliefs from one generation to the next

**tranquility** (176): (adj.) calmness; serenity; peacefulness

**transact** (146): (v.) to conduct or carry out (business)

**transparent** (147): (adj.) 1. allowing light to pass through so that objects are easily seen; 2. easy to perceive or detect; having thoughts or feelings that are easy to detect

**transpire** (79): (v.) to occur or happen

**traumatic** (118): (adj.) emotionally disturbing or distressing

**trek** (135): (n.) a long arduous journey, especially one made on foot

**trepidation** (39): (n.) a feeling of fear or agitation about something that may happen

**trite** (6): (adj.) concerning a remark, opinion, or idea that has lost its import and freshness due to overuse

**triumph** (147): (v.) a great victory or achievement

**trivial** (58): (adj.) of little value or importance; (of a person) concerned only with trifling or unimportant things

**truce** (40): (n.) an agreement between enemies or opponents to stop fighting or arguing for a certain time

**tumult** (107): (n.) a loud confused noise, especially one caused by a mass of people; confusion or disorder

**turbulent** (41): (adj.) characterized by conflict, disorder, or confusion; liquid that moves violently and unsteadily

**typical** (5): (adj.) characteristic of a particular person, thing, group, era, or genre

**tyrannical** (18): (adj.) exercising power in an arbitrary or cruel way

# U

**uncanny** (41): (adj.) strange or mysterious in an unsettling way

**unconditional** (164): (adj.) not subject to any stipulations or limitations

**underlying** (145): (adj.) to be the cause or basis of

**undermine** (135): (v.) to damage or weaken something (often an intellectual argument)

**unilateral** (117): (adj.) 1. (of an action or decision) performed by or affecting only one person, group, or country involved in a particular situation, without the agreement of another or the others; 2. relating to, occurring on, or affecting only one side of an organ or structure, or of the body

**universal** (141): (adj.) of or done by all people

**unprecedented** (8): (adj.) never done or known before

**unruly** (142): (adj.) disorderly, disruptive, and not amenable to discipline or control

**unswerving** (78): (adj.) steady or constant; unchanging or unwavering

**untainted** (73): (adj.) not contaminated or polluted

**upbraid** (41): (v.) to scold; to find fault with someone

**uphold** (31): (v.) to confirm or support something that has happened; to maintain a custom or practice

**urge** (2): (n.) a strong desire or impulse; (v.) to try to persuade; to recommend strongly; to encourage (an animal or person) to move rapidly or in a certain direction

**usurp** (122): (v.) to take a position of power or importance illegally or by force

# V

**vague** (101): (adj.) of uncertain, indefinite, or unclear character or meaning

**valor** (178): (n.) courage in the face of danger

**vandalize** (49): (v.) to deliberately destroy or damage public or private property

**vanquish** (179): (v.) to defeat thoroughly

**variance** (101): (n.) the fact or quality of being different, divergent, or inconsistent

**variety** (70): (n.) the quality of being different or diverse; the absence of sameness; lacking homogeneity

**vehement** (36): (adj.) showing strong feeling, especially forceful, passionate, or intense

**vent** (26): (v.) to give free expression to a strong emotion

**verify** (149): (v.) to ensure that something is true, accurate, or justified

**versatile** (156): (adj.) able to adapt to many different functions or activities

**veto** (23): (v.) a constitutional right to reject a decision or a proposal by a law-making body

**vex** (148): (v.) to make one feel annoyed, frustrated, or worried, especially with trivial matters

**vim** (155) : (n.) energy; enthusiasm

**virtuous** (36) : (adj.) exhibiting high moral standards

**vogue** (120): (adj.) popular; fashionable; (n.) the prevailing fashion or style at a particular time

**void** (38): (adj.) 1. not valid or legally binding; 2. completely empty; (n.) a completely empty space; (v.) to declare that something is not valid or legally binding

**voluminous** (140): (adj.) occupying much space

**vouch** (106): (v.) to assert or confirm from one's experience that something is true or accurately as described

**vulnerable** (143): (adj.) susceptible to physical or emotional harm

# W

**wan** (120): (adj.) (of skin) pale and weak, giving the impression of illness or exhaustion

**wane** (14): (v.) to decrease in vigor or power; to recede; to ebb

**warp** (96): (v.) to bend or cause to become bent out of shape, typically because of dampness

**warrant** (120): (n.) a document issued by a legal or government official authorizing the police or some other body to make an arrest, search premises, or execute some other action to carry out justice; (v.) to justify or necessitate a course of action

**wary** (134): (adj.) feeling or showing caution about possible dangers or problems

**wax** (92): (v.) to become larger or stronger

**wayward** (160): (adj.) difficult to predict or control because of unusual or perverse behavior

**wealth** (158): (n.) an abundance of valuable possessions or money; plentiful supplies of a particular resource

**weather** (95): (n.) the state of the atmosphere at a place and time as regards heat, precipitation, humidity, etc.; (v.) 1. to wear away and change the texture of something by long exposure to the atmosphere; 2. to come safely through a storm or turbulent situation

**welcome** (153): (adj.) (of a guest or new arrival) gladly received; (n.) an instance or manner of greeting someone; (v.) 1. to greet someone arriving in a glad or friendly way; 2. to react with pleasure or approval to an event or development

**whet** (4): (v.) 1. to acutely arouse someone's interest in something; 2. to sharpen the blade of an object (usually a knife)

**willing** (24): (adj.) ready, eager, or prepared to do something

**wince** (159): (n.) a slight grimace or recoiling caused by pain or distress; (v.) to grimace, shake, or recoil as the result of pain or distress

**wither** (65): (v.) (of a plant) to become dry and shriveled; (of a person) to become shrunken or wrinkled from age or disease; to cease to flourish

**withstand** (11): (v.) to remain undisturbed or unaffected by something, to resist; to offer strong resistance or opposition to

**wound** (27): (n.) an injury to living tissue caused by a cut, blow, or other impact; (v.) to inflict an injury on someone

**wreak** (27): (v.) to inflict a large amount of harm or damage

# Y

**yearn** (57): (v.) to have an intense feeling of longing for something or someone, especially if one is separated from it

**yield** (105): (n.) the full amount of an agricultural or industrial product; (v.) 1. to produce or provide; to generate; 2. to give way to arguments, demands, pressure, or traffic

# Z

**zany** (11): (adj.) amusingly unconventional and idiosyncratic

**zenith** (65): (n.) the highest point reached
by a celestial or other object

44314553R00186

Made in the USA
Lexington, KY
09 July 2019